Charter Schools
Lessons in School Reform

TOPICS IN EDUCATIONAL LEADERSHIP

Larry W. Hughes, Series Editor

Charter Schools
Lessons in School Reform

LIANE BROUILLETTE
University of California, Irvine

2002

LAWRENCE ERLBAUM ASSOCIATES, PUBLISHERS
Mahwah, New Jersey   London

Lawrence Erlbaum Associates, Inc., Publishers
10 Industrial Avenue
Mahwah, New Jersey 07430

Cover design by Kathryn Houghtaling Lacey

Library of Congress Cataloging-in-Publication Data

Charter schools : lessons in school reform / edited by Liane Brouillette.
    p. cm.
  Includes bibliographical references and indexes.
  ISBN 0-8058-3724-8 (cloth : alk. paper)
    1.   Charter schools—United States. 2. Education change—United States. I. Brouillette,
Liane, 1947-

LB2806.36 .C54 2002
371.01—dc

                                                2001051292

Books published by Lawrence Erlbaum Associates are printed on acid-free paper,
and their bindings are chosen for strength and durability.

Printed in the United States of America
10 9 8 7 6 5 4 3 2 1

Contents

    A CASE STUDY OF A SCHOOL–UNIVERSITY
    COLLABORATION
    Catharine T. Perry

        Conceptual Framework *78*
        Bureaucratic and Social Context *79*
        Research Methodology *81*
        Beginning an Experiment in Innovation *81*
        The Honeymoon Period *83*
        The Vision Meets the Students *87*
        Crisis: The Leader Leaves *90*
        Aftermath and Regrouping *93*
        Conclusions *94*
        Implications *95*
        References *97*

5. BEATING THE ODDS IN THE INNER CITY: WESLEY   99
    ELEMENTARY BECOMES A CHARTER SCHOOL

        Research Purpose and Methods *100*
        The Influence of Social Change *100*
        Wesley Elementary and the "Phonics Wars" *107*
        Taking Off Our Cultural Blinders *111*
        Beyond the Ideal of "One Best System" *117*
        Charter School Status *125*
        Social Justice Seen From Differing
            Perspectives *133*
        Following in the Footsteps of Houston's
            Most Famous Principal *139*
        Epilogue *139*
        References *140*

Foreword

Seymour Sarason

Few things are more satisfying to an author than when somebody takes his ideas seriously and tests them by careful observation and recording. When I learned that Dr. Brouillette was doing just that, I was both delighted and a mite anxious. However much I would like it to be true, I knew I had no corner on the truth; I had not said the last word on the problematics in the creation of a new setting. What if Dr. Brouillette concluded that my conceptualization was very incomplete or egregiously wrong in some of its detail? So, when I read her manuscript I was relieved that in the main she found my argument to be helpful and valid. So much about *my* relief and satisfaction!

My enthusiasm for this book goes beyond the status of my ideas. For one thing, the reader is treated to what careful observation and recording entails. It is not easy. Relatively speaking, a charter school is small but it nevertheless is socially and psychologically a very complex affair; it is to Dr. Brouillette's credit that her ethnographies demonstrate that complexity. Like the best of the ethnographies in anthropology, the reader gets the feeling of "having been there," even though the story is like a very large mural whose details initially strike you as many and diverse but very quickly reveal an organizing focus or center.

The reader who is unfamiliar with charter schools or their literature would do well to read this book as a basis for judging what else you decide to read. Dr. Brouillette does an analysis that permits her to point out that it is "a difference that makes a difference" whether a charter school was created primarily by parents, or by educators, or by some other group.

Another important contribution is the very interesting way Dr. Brouillette embeds charter schools in the history of education, going back a long time. This is not in her hands dry history, a token gesture to the scholarly standards, but done with broad brush strokes that I found instructive and stimulating. The author is a thinker, a cautious but creative one who has made a seminal contribution to how we should understand what too few charter school advocates understand and say: Conceptually, in terms of action, methodology, process, and outcomes, charter schools had best be seen as in their infancy. It is to her credit that she does this in a fair, balanced, nonpartisan way. The reader may even wonder if she is for or against charter schools.

Whatever her personal opinion, it did not influence what she observed and reported. Although her book will not be a source of satisfaction to charter school advocates, what should be encouraging to them is that she underlined those factors that, if taken seriously, will make a difference in outcomes. For that to happen, however, will require that policymakers be less enamored of policy and become more knowledgeable about the obstacles that confront those who seek to create a new setting like a charter school. Virtuous intent plus idealism are necessary, but by no means sufficient, for the achievement of desired goals. Between virtuous intent and desired goals are conceptual, practical, personal, and institutional potholes that are, to indulge in understatement, trying indeed.

Sloppy thinking is not conducive to clear writing. Clear thinking is no guarantor of clear writing. Dr. Brouillette is a clear thinker whose writing style is clear.

Preface

Despite the exponential growth of the charter school movement since the 1990s, much of the public remains confused as to exactly what a charter school is. In part, this is because the media have tended to portray educational policy debates as two-sided contests between those who wish to "privatize" public education and those who wish to impose tighter government control over what goes on in the classroom. When other alternatives are mentioned, these options tend to be characterized as mere intermediate steps "on the road to" either increased reliance on markets or more stringent government mandates. Yet the nature of the charter school movement cannot be adequately understood without looking beyond this polarity, to the different relationship families once had with public schools.

For the first century of United States history, collaboration between families and schools was unavoidable. Grass-roots support for education was pivotal; without it there would be no school. The bureaucratization of schooling during the last century has, however, dramatically reduced the voice that public school students and their families have in decisions that profoundly affect their lives. Inevitably this has given rise to tensions. Ours is, after all, a society that deeply believes that citizens ought shape the government (not the other way around). As school governance has become more top-down and hierarchical, there has been a sea change in popular attitudes toward the public school. Community members have come to see themselves less as the partners of school officials than as spectators and critics; student attitudes have shown an increasing resemblance to those long associated with military draftees.

Various restructuring efforts have been introduced in recent decades with the aim of increasing parent participation in school decision making. School choice programs have given students more options as to the kind of school they attend. Yet most reforms have had limited effects. In *A Geology of School Reform: The Successive Restructurings of a School District,* I looked at the waves of reform that swept through one suburban school district between the early 1950s and the early 1990s. The most recent of these reforms was site-based decision making. As the 1990s began, site-based reforms appeared to hold great promise as a way to make schools more responsive to community needs. Shared decision making was central to the effectiveness of these reforms. However, reaching a consensus required the collaboration of the school's major stakeholder groups. In those schools and school districts that were most in need of reform, the trust and good will needed to make this process work were often hard to come by.

After *A Geology of School Reform* was published, colleagues posed questions that turned out to be prophetic: What happens when a school or a district only goes through the motions of shared decision making, trying to placate disgruntled parents, but giving them no real voice? What do you do when the core beliefs of the stakeholders involved are too different to be bridged by any practical negotiated settlement? How do you avoid ending up with an ill-fitting compromise that gives everyone a little of what they want but, in the end, accomplishes no one's goals? How can meaningful reform be introduced where the political culture of a school district makes change from within well nigh impossible? How does shared decision making help the parent whose child has special needs that cannot be well served by the neighborhood school?

Charter schools represent a markedly different approach. Instead of attempting to develop consensus among the disparate stakeholders at a neighborhood school, charter schools begin with a specific vision, laid out in the charter application. Both staff and students are "volunteers" who have chosen to be there and thus have an investment in the school's success. Operating under its own charter, the school is freed from many of the restrictions that limit the freedom of teachers and administrators at other public schools. These advantages have allowed charter schools to avoid problems that had plagued attempts to implement shared decision making at existing school sites. The charter school movement grew quickly. In 1990 there were no charter schools in the United States. In the year 2000, there were more than 2000 charter schools; 36 states and the District of Columbia now allow citizens to start charter schools.

This book takes the reader inside the charter school movement, answering such questions as: What is it like to create a charter school? What motivates the people who initiate such schools? What lessons can be learned from the experiences of those who have founded charter schools? Seven schools in three states are examined. Readers might ask, "What can be learned from so small a sample?" However, a number of excellent large-scale studies have already been done. What has been lacking is the in-depth examination of specific cases in an effort to learn from early successes and failures. Among the questions that remain unanswered are: How do the organizational dynamics of teacher-initiated, parent-initiated, and institutionally sponsored schools differ? How might the varying state regulations and political environments surrounding charter schools affect these schools' chances of success?

Seymour Sarason's work on the creation of settings is used as the basis for examining the experiences of charter school founders, making it possible to draw on a broader knowledge base than that provided by the seven schools included in this study. Use of Sarason's conceptual framework made it possible to differentiate generic start-up problems from challenges specific to charter schools; it also assisted in identifying the diverse factors—ranging from leadership to external relations to the capacity for internal renewal—that were likely to have a significant long-range impact on the success of a new setting. In addition, this study suggested that Sarason's framework could have great practical value for those initiating new charter schools, enabling them to anticipate (and make plans to deal with) the problems likely to be encountered in opening any new school.

In closing, I would like to express my heartfelt appreciation to all who have assisted in putting this book together: to contributors Susan Korach, Catharine Perry, and Barbara Korth for their excellent fieldwork; to Seymour Sarason for taking the time to examine each chapter and make insightful suggestions; to Joe Nathan for sharing his broad knowledge of the charter school movement. To those schools that allowed us to share in their experiences, learning from their triumphs and their struggles, I would like to extend my deepest gratitude. I hope that, on reading this book, members of these schools communities will see an accurate reflection of the exhilaration and challenges they experienced in creating a new school.

—Liane Brouillette

Chapter 1

Charter Schools:
Redefining a Social Contract?

> *The great irony in American education is that in a society prizing diversity, in a society in which local control of education is a kind of icon, the nation's 100,000-odd schools are not diverse but identical. It is not too far from the truth to say that if you have seen one elementary school in America, you have seen them all; one middle school is pretty much a reflection of another; the major distinction communities seek in their secondary schools is a winning football team.* (Notes from the Front Lines, *quoted in MA Charter School Handbook; Charter School Resource Center, 1997, p. 1*)

Since the original charter school legislation was passed in 1991, enormous interest has been generated by the possibilities inherent in this network of more autonomous public schools. According to the U.S. Department of Education's *Fourth Year Report of the National Study of Charter Schools* (2000), 36 states and the District of Columbia have enacted charter school legislation. Thirty states already had charter schools in operation as of September 1999; yet a survey done by the Public Agenda Foundation that same year found that most people had only the vaguest notion of what the term *charter school* meant. This book takes the reader inside the fast-growing charter school movement, focusing on the unique manner in which charter schools draw on the resources of civil society in order to further the cause of educational reform.

Broadly speaking, charter schools represent the resurgence of a "do-it-yourself" attitude toward public education that had not been much in evidence in the United States through much of the 20th century. The days when groups of local citizens would get together to organize a public school, find a building, hire the teachers, had all but faded from memory. For over a century, whenever significant educational reforms have been introduced, the changes tended to be in the direction of trying to make school districts more "efficient." Most often, this meant reorganizing school districts so that they could be run in a top-down manner, more like corporations. Thus, the "principal teacher" of an earlier era became the present-day "principal," no longer a leader among equals but an administrator whose job it is to organize and evaluate the work of others.

Most educational debates in recent years have tended to focus either on proposals for increased academic standards, based on stricter state requirements, or on introducing market mechanisms into the way that public schools are financed. Therefore it can be easy to forget that there are other alternatives. Yet for most of the nation's history it was assumed that, just as the parent–child relationship exists in a realm that cannot readily be assigned to either the market economy or the political arena, the relationship between a community and its school was not primarily either economic or political. What was taught in schools in different communities varied considerably, depending on local culture, preferences, and needs. Charter schools take a similarly localized approach, serving families brought together by choice.

Most charter school supporters share a perception that, amid the current push for educational standardization, something of value has been lost. This book takes the reader inside the charter school movement, describing the experiences of charter school founders, along with the historical influences and policy issues that have shaped specific charter schools. The core of the book is formed by seven case studies: six charter schools and one district-sponsored alternative school. Schools profiled were chosen to represent the diversity—inner city and suburban, back-to-basics and child-centered—of the charter school movement, thus highlighting the variation that exists, both from school to school and from state to state. Elementary, middle, and high schools were included. Among those represented are teacher- and parent-initiated schools, as well as schools set up in partnership with outside institutions.

A case study of a noncharter alternative school (founded through a collaborative effort between an elite private university and a large urban school district) was included to provide an opportunity to explore similarities and contrasts between the charters and an innovative school that enjoyed advantages that most charter schools lack. Of the schools in this study, the noncharter alternative school was, by far, the best financed, benefiting also from an extensive planning effort that brought in nationally recognized experts as consultants. Thus, this noncharter school serves as a useful reminder that school reform in the 1990s has not been limited to the charter school movement, while also highlighting how differences in governance structure may influence the development of innovative schools.

Among the charter schools we examine, some have received considerable help from their local school district; other schools were created only after heated public debate and remain on uneasy terms with the local school district. Some schools were parent initiated; others were initiated by groups of teachers; still others had institutional sponsors. Moreover, each of the three states we look at handles charter schools differently. In Massachusetts, there is a central agency within the state's Department of Education that oversees charter schools; charter recipients are selected, by the state, through a Request for Proposal process. In contrast, Colorado makes the local school district the chartering agency (although groups appealing for a charter can appeal to the Colorado Board of Education, which can direct a school board to approve a charter). Texas allows both school districts and the state to act as chartering agencies.

WHAT ARE CHARTER SCHOOLS?

Charter schools are publicly sponsored, autonomous schools that are substantially free of direct government control, but are held accountable for achieving certain levels of student performance and other specified outcomes (Cookson, 1995). The first such schools were created in Minnesota, where a provision was passed in 1991 that allowed licensed teachers to create innovative schools, essentially on contract to a public school board. These schools could be either existing, but redesigned, schools or new schools. The idea had been suggested by Albert Shanker, president of the American Federation of Teachers, in a 1988 speech to the National Press Club, where he commented:

> I hear this all over the country. Somebody says, "Oh, Mr. Shanker, we tried something like that 15 years ago. We worked around the clock, and we worked weekends. . . . I never worked so hard in my life. And then a new school board was elected or a new principal or superintendent came in and said, 'That's not my thing.' " And that's the end of the school or program. You'll never get people to make that kind of commitment if our educational world is just filled with people who went through the disappointment of having been engaged and involved and committed to building something only to have it cut out from under them. (Nathan, 1996a, p. 63)

Public school choice already had a strong base in Minnesota; Minneapolis and St. Paul had offered alternative schools and magnet schools since the 1970s (Nathan, 1996b). Prior to passage of the first charter school legislation in 1991, Minnesota Governor Rudy Perpich, a Democrat, had introduced proposals for several other public school choice programs. State residents had learned that thoughtful competition could stimulate improvements. As Joe Nathan (1996b) pointed out:

> In 1985, only 33% of Minnesotans favored cross-district public school choice, while 60% opposed it. By 1992, polls by major education groups found that 76% of the state's residents supported the idea, while only 21% opposed it. Support grew because 1) thousands of students who had dropped out used these laws to return to school; 2) the number of advanced courses in high schools more than doubled, as schools responded to the competition provided by the postsecondary options law; 3) public school choice brought families back into public education; and 4) choice allowed educators to create new, distinctive schools. (p. 19)

Minnesota State Senator Ember Reichgott Junge, a Democrat, and several local activists heard Shankar's call for a new kind of public school and refined the idea to fit Minnesota. The charter school bill that finally was passed was far weaker than supporters had hoped. However, a door had been opened, allowing for the establishment of a new kind of public school. Within 5 years, 25 states had adopted charter school legislation, although the details varied widely.

CHARACTERISTICS OF CHARTER SCHOOLS

Charter school founders typically seek to implement an alternative vision of schooling, one they believe requires the creation of a school with greater autonomy than is traditionally allowed in the public school system. Unlike magnet or alternative schools, charter schools exist outside the normal school district hierarchy. They operate under a written contract, or charter, from a state or local government agency. In most states, administration of charter schools is limited to nonprofit organizations (although some states do allow profit-making organizations to operate charter schools). Although regulations governing charter schools vary greatly from state to state, charter school advocate Joe Nathan (1996b) pointed out that, broadly speaking, charter school laws share the following elements:

- The state authorizes more than one organization to start and operate a public school in a community. The state thus withdraws what Ted Kolderie called the "exclusive franchise" that has historically been given to public school districts (Kolderie, 1990). Elimination of this exclusive franchise "removes from the district its ability to take its students for granted." Organizers of charter schools may approach either a local board or some other public body to be their sponsor.

- The newly organized (or converted) schools would be public schools. They would not charge tuition and would be open to all kinds of students, without admission tests.

- The schools would be responsible for improved student achievement. Each school would negotiate a 3- to 5-year contract (or "charter") with the sponsoring agency, specifying (a) areas in which students would learn more and (b) how that learning would be measured. Schools that failed to achieve their contracted improvements would be closed by the sponsoring organization.

- In return for this accountability for improved results, the state would grant an up-front waiver of virtually all rules and regulations governing public schools. Aside from health, safety, and other specified regulations, charter schools would be exempt from state regulations about how to operate.

- The charter school would be a school of choice. No one would be assigned to work in or to attend the school who had not chosen to do so.

- The school would be a discrete entity. The school would be a legal entity, with its own elected board. Teachers could organize and bargain collectively. However, this bargaining unit would be separate from, and not bound by, the contracts negotiated by any district bargaining unit.

- The full per-pupil allocation would move with the student. The amount would be roughly equal to the average state per-pupil allocation or the average allocation from the district from which the student comes. If the state provides extra funds for students with disabilities or for students from low-income families, these funds would also follow the student.

- Participating teachers would be protected and given new opportunities. The state would permit teachers to take a leave from their public school systems and retain their seniority. Teachers could stay in local or state retirement systems.

THE DEBATE OVER CHARTER SCHOOLS

Since 1991, charter schools have received support from Democrats and Republicans, teacher organizations, business groups, and parent associations. Reasons for this support vary. Three underlying belief systems have been seen as motivating charter school supporters—anti-bureaucracy, market-based education, and teacher professionalism (Garn, 1999). The *anti-*

bureaucracy view holds that, by legislating an ever-growing number of "best practice" methods and penalizing deviation, various government agencies have created a top-down educational system that chokes out innovations. Educators, parents, and community activists who start charter schools argue that, freed from such restrictions, they can more effectively serve the real needs of the students they serve. How much freedom from local and state regulations charter schools are granted varies from state to state, but in states with strong charter school laws, charters enjoy significantly more freedom in regard to choosing faculty, curriculum, and methods of self-governance than do regular neighborhood schools in the same districts.

Those who hold a *market-based* view contend that district schools continue to go on as they always have, regardless of educational outcomes, because they have a monopoly on public school students. Charter schools, which do not have a captive population, are forced to compete for the allegiance of parents and students. Having to compete with charters forces other public schools to adapt, in order to retain their students. Those with market-based views believe that, by injecting competition into the public school environment, the quality of education is improved. Another group of charter school supporters are motivated by a belief in *teacher professionalism*. For these proponents, charter schools are about valuing the expertise of teachers and giving them control over decisions that affect learning in the classroom. They see charter schools as collaborative enterprises, where teachers and parents work together for the good of the child.

Wells, Grutzik, Carnochan, Slayton, and Vasudeva (1999) pointed out that bipartisan support for charter schools often masks opposing viewpoints regarding the purpose of initiating autonomous schools. Based on interviews with more than 50 policymakers in six states, they identified three conflicting themes that emerged from policymakers' explanations of their support for charter schools. The first theme was voiced by policymakers who saw charter schools as the beginning of a move toward vouchers. The second theme was articulated by policymakers who saw charter school reform as a "last chance" to save the existing public school system. A third theme arose in interviews with policymakers who saw charter schools as one of many (but not necessarily the central) reforms that could strengthen the public schools. According to Wells et al., passage of charter school legislation has been the result of a fragile bargain between political adversaries who sought different ends.

This book suggests another possibility, that educational institutions are, by their very nature, ill suited to respond well either to the coercive power of the state or to the commodification of services typical of the market economy. Schools, at their best, offer an environment where the human spirit can freely unfold, allowing individuals to develop mental capacities and practical skills they will later need to participate fully in economic and political life. No one can predict, in advance, what the needs (or choices) of any individual student will be. Therefore it is inappropriate to mandate that all public school students should have access to only a single, predetermined curriculum. Charter schools represent an important step toward providing a wider range of choice to the families of students who have not been successful in their present public school.

CHARTER SCHOOL DEBATE AS A REFLECTION OF BROADER ISSUES

The eddies of rhetoric that have swirled around the charter school issue are described by Wayson (1999), who noted the polemical tone of much of the debate:

> Each side of the issue uses "red flag" phrases to rally support or opposition. For example, teachers' groups speak of the rights of employees as though they did not know that defining teachers' responsibilities as hours spent rather than results achieved is guaranteed to lower achievement. . . . Licensed teachers are equated with quality instruction as though no one knows the deficiencies of present-day licensure. Proponents of choice unashamedly laud "privatization," "free-market competition," and "entrepreneurialism" as though they know nothing about the failures of private operations in the early 1970s or, more recently, in Baltimore. (pp. 447–448)

How is it that this network of more autonomous public schools has excited such passionate support—and opposition? There is a widespread perception that U.S. public education may be at a crossroads. Criticism has come from many quarters.

The achievement levels of U.S. students do not compare well to those of other countries. For example, in the 1st grade the math skills of American and Asian children are similar. Yet by 5th grade the gap in achievement has expanded to where there is virtually no overlap in the scores of American children and their peers in Japan, China, and Taiwan (Stevenson, Lee, & Stigler, 1986). At 11th grade, only 14.5% of Chinese and 8.0% of Japanese students attain scores below the *average* American score (Stevenson, Chen, & Lee, 1993). Results from TIMSS, the Third International Mathematics and Science Study, revealed that U.S. 4th graders scored among the best in the world in math and science, but U.S. 8th grade scores were mediocre, and U.S. 12th grade scores were among the lowest. The decline in the relative standing of the U.S. students, as they progressed from elementary school through high school, was startling and disturbing to many educators, parents, and policymakers.

Ever since the report *A Nation at Risk* was published by the National Commission on Excellence in Education in 1983, there have been worries that a "rising tide of mediocrity" was threatening the nation's longtime preeminence in commerce, science and technology. The report argued that "If an unfriendly foreign power had attempted to impose on America the mediocre educational performance that exists today, we might well have viewed it as an act of war." Implicitly, such a critique defined the national well-being primarily in terms of economic position in the world's markets. As a consequence of framing the school reform dialogue in this manner, certain conclusions were drawn. Those nations where scores on international tests were highest had a planned curriculum, driven by standardized tests. Soon pressure was brought to bear to make greater use of standardized testing in the United States. State legislatures moved to tighten graduation requirements and mandate high-stakes tests, which would be used to judge the effectiveness of public schools.

Feeling beleaguered, teachers' groups asked: Were school personnel expected to take the blame for decades of social change? Teachers already had to tend to an ever-growing list of nonteaching duties arising from a host of state- and district-mandated programs, many having little to do with the central tasks of teaching and learning. In high-crime areas, teachers also had to be on guard against intrusion, robbery, assault, and vandalism. As one urban principal pointed out:

> Most people agree that the central goal of the public schools is to teach students to read, write, and compute. Urban schools today simply have too many other things to accomplish under too many unfavorable conditions. The urban school is no longer merely an academic institution: it is also a social and welfare institution. Among the necessary services it provides are recreation, cultural growth, emotional development, basic health care, food service, voter registration, draft registration, driver education, sex education, employment service, immunization, and the collection of census data. (Crosby, 1999, p. 300)

Most often, the added responsibilities had come without sufficient funding or essential personnel. All this added responsibility, without the means to carry it out, had drained time and energy while increasing feelings of futility among public school personnel. Teachers and administrators felt alone, on the front lines, struggling to deal with problems that others ignored. Given the hardships under which they often worked, demands for school reform, made by outsiders, could easily be interpreted as attacks. Similarly, talk about encouraging competition among schools could seem a cynical joke to educators who felt that existing bureaucratic regulations put them at a distinct disadvantage.

The Need for Alternatives

The charter school supporters interviewed for this book tended to talk less about competition among schools than about the rights of children. They pointed out that the American form of government assumes that any governmental institution derives its powers from the consent of the governed. This social contract lies at the root of the charter school debate. What happens when the interests of a child are not well served by the schools that the child is legally required to attend? Charter school supporters point to the fact that two students sitting next to one another in class might be inhabiting vastly different social and emotional worlds. To insist upon a one-size-fits-all formula for public schools thus means that some children are given tremendous advantages over others—from the moment that they enter kindergarten. Such favoritism triggers profound questions about social justice. How can we justify requiring children to attend schools that systematically advantage some over others? Why should children who are not succeeding in their present schools not be given the chance to search out a school that better fits their needs?

This book has its roots in just such questions. As part of a study of a high school equivalency program that enrolled many inner-city youth (Brouillette, 1999), I interviewed many former high school dropouts. They described the stark choices that confront many urban youth. Recalling their high school experiences, former gang members described the difficulty of concentrating on math, knowing that someone sitting behind them had a knife—and a grudge of some sort. Young people with no gang involvement spoke of picking their way through neighborhoods crisscrossed by the territories of rival gangs. By the time they arrived at school, their ability to concentrate had been shattered by tensions not unlike those experienced by soldiers on the battlefield.

What these students valued about the high school equivalency program in which they were enrolled at the time of the study was the opportunity it gave them to escape an environment permeated by fear. Many found that, for the first time since elementary school, they felt free to focus their full attention on what they were learning. Yet, even in the inner city, not all students experienced this same level of stress. Most of the former dropouts interviewed had attended large urban high schools with many different "tracks." Some of the higher "tracks" offered excellent educational programs, of which the gang-involved students who ended up dropping out had not taken advantage. Yet the existence of such academic programs, seemingly within their reach, did not make the problems encountered the students who dropped out any less real.

Even in schools where outstanding teachers—and widely respected academic programs—were available, there were students whose most pressing need was to separate themselves from the toxic peer culture with which they had become entangled. There were students who needed a smaller, more controlled learning environment that would allow them to step outside their accustomed "tough guy" facade and be seen, by the student sitting next to them, to be putting real effort into their schoolwork. Given these facts, the most pressing question was not "What is wrong with these high schools?" but "Why had these young people not been offered viable alternatives that would allow them to start anew without dropping out of school?"

The Need for Detailed Studies of Charter Schools

Although charter schools are too new for it to be possible to assess their long-term impact on educational outcomes, the early evidence would seem to confirm neither the greatest hopes of charter school proponents nor the greatest fears of opponents. There is evidence that these schools are serving as a laboratory for educational innovation, but no dramatic educational strategies have yet emerged (Geske, Davis, & Hingle, 1997). Charter schools enroll similar proportions of low-income students and have a racial composition roughly similar to statewide averages (Office of Educational Research and Improvement, 1999), although charter schools in some states (Connecticut, Massachusetts, Michigan, Minnesota, North Carolina, and Texas) serve significantly higher percentages of minority or economically disadvantaged students.

Wells et al. (1998) conducted 17 case studies in 10 school districts in California (a state that initially enacted a weak charter school law, but also the state that had the most students enrolled in charter schools), comparing claims made by charter school advocates with the experiences reported by educators, parents, and students. They found claims that greater autonomy led to greater satisfaction and decision-making capacity were supported, in part, by their data. Yet the degree of autonomy charters enjoyed varied greatly across schools and districts. Many charter schools had relied heavily on the support and services available to them through local districts or other entities. Unsure how to hold charter schools accountable for academic performance, school districts had been more likely to hold them fiscally accountable. In addition, charter schools often depended heavily on strong, well-connected leaders and on supplemental private resources.

Becker, Nakagawa, and Corwin (1996) analyzed survey data from California's charter schools and comparison schools in the same communities. They also examined parent contracts in use at the charter schools. Becker et al. found that, in order to build parent participation, some California charter schools were experimenting with having parents sign agreements or "contracts" promising a certain amount or type of involvement. Their study reported that charter schools did have greater levels of parent involvement, but that this involvement may have been due to selectivity in the kinds of families participating in charter schools. The parent contracts might have had the effect of restricting enrollment to children whose parents demonstrated the desired willingness to meet school expectations.

Finn, Manno, Bierlein, and Vanourek (1997) visited 60 schools in 14 states and interviewed more than 1,300 individuals about the startup difficulties that charter schools face. They identified six major categories of startup problems:

Governance: mostly internal difficulties having to do with tensions and turmoil within and among governing boards, principals, parents, teaching staff, and other major school constituencies.

Funding: mostly external fiscal woes, centering on lack of money but sometimes involving cash flow, budgeting, and the like.

Students: trouble attracting (and sometimes retaining) enough students of the sort the school intended to serve and/or the arrival of many who pose challenges that the school was not expecting.

Staffing: difficulty engaging enough teachers and other staff members who are suited to, and prepared for, the school's program.

Instruction: includes problems with curriculum, materials, pedagogy, assessment, and other issues pertaining to educational content and its delivery.

Facilities: difficulty obtaining a suitable building or other site for the school program.

Schools that had reached their second or greater year of operation in 1996–1997 were found by Finn et al. to experience fewer or less severe problems than during their startup year. In several important categories (governance, students, instruction), it appeared that the longer these schools were in operation, the more likely they were to have eased or solved their startup problems. Yet, as is common with new schools, many charter schools continued to face significant problems in their second or third (or more) year of operation. Governance remained a concern in a third of the "veteran" schools; money was a problem for two-thirds; students for more than a third; staffing for one in seven; and instruction for three-fifths of these schools. Facilities were fully satisfactory for barely one school in four.

From such studies, an understanding of the common problems faced by charter schools—as well as the tactics charter schools have used to address these dilemmas—has begun to emerge. However, there has as yet been little detailed research on the complex process of starting a charter school, the motivations of charter school stakeholders, or the impact that the charter school experience has had on the students and families involved. The case studies that form the core of this book reveal what it has been like to be in on the "ground floor" of the charter school movement. The charter schools described here were among the first to be initiated in their respective states. Often the founders of these schools received no remuneration for their efforts. Why did they do it? What was it like? Did things turn out as they had hoped? If not, why not?

UNDERSTANDING THE CREATION OF SETTINGS

In chapter 2 we discuss, at some length, the characteristics of bureaucratic institutions such as school districts and the extensive research now available on the process of organizational change. Yet for most of the schools that will be discussed in this book, the problem was not that of changing an existing setting. The founders of these schools faced the differing—but still daunting—challenge of creating a new organization "from scratch." Because charter schools are so often built "from the ground up," they face challenges—such as finding an adequate building or buying textbooks and furniture—that staff members in more traditional schools do not usually have to deal with in such a hands-on way. All too often, charter schools run into major snags because no one checked to see how long it would take to get textbooks delivered—or because no one realized that the building the school had intended to lease would have to be extensively remodeled so as to conform to fire and safety codes that apply to schools.

So as to gain a better understanding the dilemmas faced by the teachers, administrators, and parents who initiate charter schools, we make use of Seymour Sarason's work on the creation of settings (1988). A setting can be said to be created when two or more people get together, for a sustained period of time, to achieve agreed-on goals. When human beings come together to pursue a common purpose, interpersonal issues tend to arise. This is true whether the new setting created is a medical clinic, a social service organization, or a school.

Sarason argued that all new settings face predictable hurdles. *External* problems center on the fact that a new setting exists within a larger social context, where competition for resources and prestige can render relations with existing settings extremely problematic. *Internal* challenges center on (a) determining how lines of authority and communication will be established, and (b) the impact that new people entering the setting have on the original vision/idea. Sarason also outlined the stages that often can be observed in the growth of a new setting: Initiation/Planning, Honeymoon, Implementation, Crisis, and Aftermath. A more complete description of Sarason's framework is given later. First, however, a few words of introduction may help to set the stage.

The Organization as a Work of Art

Creating settings consistent with their purposes and sustaining them for more than brief periods of time is one of the great problems facing any society. Sarason noted that the first chapter of Burckhardt's (1995) classic *The Civilization of the Renaissance in Italy* was entitled "The State as a Work of Art." Burckhardt described the appearance, in the early Renaissance, of a new political spirit that saw the state "as the outcome of reflection and calculation, the state as a work of art." There was a new awareness of the problem presented by "the deliberate adaptation of means to ends." A new self-consciousness became manifest in how records were kept, how changes were described, how discussions were recorded. The Florentine spirit, at once keenly critical and artistically creative, was incessantly transforming the social and political conditions of the state—and as incessantly describing and judging the change. In a sense, our inquiry into the creation of charter schools is an extension of that same impulse.

Any new setting has a "prehistory," local and national, that must be dealt with. Many different individuals and groups have a role in its birth. Resources are always limited (and usually overestimated, in part because of a sense of mission and boundless enthusiasm). Conflict within the setting (and between settings) is a fact of social life. Such conflicts are often exacerbated by conflicts between ideas. In the euphoria of creating something new, these causes of potential difficulty are too often ignored. Sarason argues that verbal agreement about values is no substitute for forging an organizational "constitution" that anticipates and helps deal with human differences—as well as future needs for change. Also, there is a need to build into the organization mechanisms for nourishing the morale and personal growth of participants, once the initial burst of enthusiasm ebbs away. The danger is that, if the usual bureaucratic organization of the work environment is simply replicated—out of habit or because that is what people are used to—the weight of bureaucratic routine will tend to extinguish curiosity and the sense of challenge, sapping away energy and causing the new setting to look more and more like those that have gone before.

What the leader of a new setting needs to possess—to literally feel that he or she "owns"—is a theory that lays out the variables the leader will be dealing with. By "theory," Sarason meant a set of ideas akin to what is in the head of a psychoanalyst as he or she approaches patients. The psychoanalyst has a conception of what a human being is, how human beings develop, the obstacles humans encounter, a knowledge of the criteria of abnormality, and so forth. Theory, understood in this sense, is not only a conception about people in general (and patients in particular), but it is also a conception about therapists and how their actions must reflect an awareness of the human qualities they have in common with patients. Theory therefore functions both as a guide and as a form of control; it tells the therapist what to look for and sensitizes him or her to possible pitfalls.

Before the Beginning: Confronting History

New settings are not viewed by their founders as a mere duplication of what already exists, but as an improvement. In one or another way, the new setting is expected to meet a need not now being met by existing settings. The creation of settings (in the earliest phases) almost always (if not always) takes place in a context containing conflicting ideas and values, limited resources, a sense of mission and superiority on the part of some (and a need to preserve tradition on the part of others), and a need to protect the setting from outside influences. The social context of the new setting almost always includes (or quickly is seen as impinging on) a large number of existing settings. Yet this matrix of factors is rarely described and discussed by the founders with the clarity required to anticipate how external forces are likely to affect the new setting's development and fate. Project directors routinely fail to ask:

- What were the issues, problems, and conflicts that marked the prehistory of the new setting?
- What reactions might be anticipated as a result of the fact that the new setting will emerge from, and become part of, an existing organization of settings that had long-standing traditions and practices at variance with the new setting (which, if successful, would establish the superiority of its mission)?

There are characteristics of the new setting (such as claims to superiority of mission) and concerns on the part of existing settings (such as ideology and concern for resources) that all but ensure some conflict and competition. As Sarason pointed out, "having to give up part of one's resources is a problem independent of personality, and to be unaware of this is asking for trouble." Inevitably, the new setting will need resources that, until then, had been expended elsewhere. Moreover, through the implication that the new setting has a "superior" mission, the new setting also competes with existing settings in the realm of ideas and values; that is, it disrupts an existing structure or pattern of relationships and causes new questions to be asked about the adequacy of the status quo. Such dynamics are independent of ideology. If the ideological positions of the new and existing settings were reversed, the reaction to the creation of the new setting would, in most cases, remain unchanged.

Sarason illustrated the significance of a before-the-beginning effort to achieve a sense of clarity regarding relationships with existing settings and the confronting of history by using, as an example, the series of events outlined in *Jean Monnet and the United States of Europe* (Bromberger & Bromberger, 1969), which describes Monnet's role in the creation of the European Defense Community, Euratom, and the Common Market:

> What this book does do is to describe exceedingly well how in the earliest phases of the proposed settings every idea and action on the part of Monnet and his colleagues seemed to reflect an exquisite sensitivity to history. It is as if at every step of the way they viewed history as containing forces both for and against them and saw that their major task was to deal with both. Their attention to detail, their use of history to anticipate consequences, and their learning from failure (European Defense Community) are in startling contrast to what characterizes the earliest phases of most new settings. (as quoted in Sarason, 1988, p. 44)

Challenges of the Initiation/Planning Period

The leader of a new setting routinely thinks in terms of forming a core group to whom to delegate responsibilities. Choosing badly jeopardizes the future of the setting. But what does it mean to "choose" a member of this group? If one asks, the most frequent answer given by the leader is that an individual has been chosen to do a certain job—to utilize specific knowledge, experience, and skills. That is to say, there is a match between what needs to be done and what this individual can do. This would be a reasonable answer, except that it ignores the fact that the individual and the leader will be in what is for them a *new* relationship, one that involves far more than is covered by the term *doing the job*. Whether or not they can live together, whether or not their styles are congruent, whether or not their personal needs and goals clash—these are not questions contained in the answers that leaders give about why a person was hired.

The safest and most obvious prediction one can make about the relationship between the leader and individuals in the core group is that there will be problems. When these problems will arise and what their specific character will be are not so predictable, but anticipating the exact nature of a problem is less important than understanding that there will be problems. Ground rules must be developed to deal with them—not to eliminate, but to deal with them. For when two people do not anticipate and discuss in advance how predictable issues affecting them both will be handled, uncomfortable issues too often end up being faced and "resolved" in the worst of all situations: when feelings are high and smoldering conflict and controversy are present. Sarason credited the common failure to anticipate predictable problems to four factors:

- The tendency to view the new setting as different from and superior to other settings generates an enthusiasm and sense of mission that color the future in a rosy way; superiority of ends is confused with superiority of means.
- For both the leader and the core group the attractiveness of the new setting inheres not only in what the new setting promises but in their disappointment in their previous settings.
- Participants do not view the creation of a new setting as a set of developmental problems that are fairly predictable—and about which one can formulate ground rules, so that when these problems arise the element of surprise is diluted and past discussions can serve as a basis for discussion in the present.
- Even when there is some awareness of probable developmental problems, discussion of possible problems at the point when the core group is formed is made difficult precisely because they are problematic, will arouse differences of opinion, and may require decisions and compromises that some may not wish to live with.

Such is the power of these factors that even when the leaders are veterans of other core groups—in which their unhappiness with themselves, their work, and their colleagues reached a high level—they tend to create not a mirror image of their previous setting, but a situation whose resemblance to that setting is unmistakable.

The usual way in which the leader organizes the core group—the arrangements made with each, and the relationships of each with the others—usually reflects several assumptions held by the leader and each of the core group members:

- The appropriate kind and degree of motivation will overcome any and all obstacles, including those encountered by the leader and the core group in their previous settings.
- There is agreement on values and goals (perhaps the first assumption that, in point of time, is invalidated).
- There are sufficient resources, or the promise of them, to allow each of the core group members to realize his or her goals.

From a purely internal standpoint, the major problems of creating a setting center on two related tasks: growth and differentiation, on the one hand, and the forging of a "constitution" by which the setting will be governed. The ambiguities inherent in the usual way of selecting and organizing the core group (ambiguities only later realized as such) are a consequence of the failure to view the creation of a setting as a constitutional problem. Among the most important challenges in the creation of a setting is the anticipation of problems—and the ways they will be handled. The failure to think in constitutional terms maximizes ambiguities, which usually leads to informal, individual kinds of resolutions, such as heightened competitiveness and individual empires.

The Cost of Ignoring Psychological Dynamics

Normally, during the formation and development of the core group the factor that is emphasized (indeed viewed as central) is the job that needs to be done: to provide some kind of service or product for others not part of the setting. The factor that is too often ignored or deemphasized has two ingredients: the professional and personal growth of the setting's members, and the ways in which their mutuality can enhance growth. Usually, in the creation of a setting, these personnel factors have been quite secondary to concern with what is provided for others. Yet the greatest source of disillusionment and disruption within a setting usually arises as a consequence of having ignored or deemphasized these motivational factors. For, to the extent that a setting becomes more and more focused on its relationships to the outside world, it loses sight of what it can (or must) do for its own members. Put in an alternative manner, it is of pivotal importance that members of the core group remember a simple adage: We cannot do for others, we cannot change others, until we learn how to do for and change ourselves.

In its earliest phases, a new setting tends to be suffused with hope, enthusiasm, a sense of mission and unity. The effect is to maximize selective perception. Another factor that inhibits a realistic assessment of what is happening and why (and this is especially true of settings devoted to human service) is that they usually do help others. They do perform functions that others need and value. This result alone has tremendous "reward value," particularly as such a result also serves as the basis for justifying the setting's existence. There is also a more subtle factor: In the early stages of the setting's existence the process of helping others is usually accompanied by a personal sense of growth. The service is not experienced as a routine, without personal challenge and intellectual excitement.

Yet precisely because the value of self-development is not viewed as equal to the value of helping others, over time the sense of challenge and change diminishes; routinization of thinking and action takes place. With the passage of time the members of the setting come to feel locked into their particular function and increasingly experience a disruptive discrepancy between their desire to learn and change (the need for novelty and stimulation) and the perception that this need may not be satisfied. The exclusive focus on doing for others has been maintained at a very high personal price. Sarason noted that the widespread assumption that teachers can create and maintain those conditions that make school stimulating for children *without those same conditions existing for teachers* has no warrant in the history of humans.

Forging a "Constitution"

The creation of a setting is a complicated process containing one booby trap after another. For example, there is a need for openness among participants. Yet this is not a mere matter of open talk or the expression of feeling, as if these were virtues in themselves, not requiring the control and direction of organized conceptualizations. Telling the truth is not the same as being helpful (although it sometimes is), and being helpful is not a simple function of one's desire to help (although it sometimes is). In addition, the issue of openness is intimately related to another issue: How should decisions be made, by whom, and on what basis? Where can help be found when things get off track?

As the setting grows larger and becomes more differentiated, the amount of face-to-face contact between the leader and the core group noticeably lessens. The number of problems increases; the leader must make decisions and resolve issues and conflicts, usually not on direct experience. The leader's knowledge of what is going on is increasingly obtained at second or third hand. There is usually one formal meeting each week between the leader and the core group, which serves two purposes: (a) to bring important issues to the attention of the leader, and (b) to provide an opportunity for the leader to state and clarify policy and direction, as well as to bring up problems. There are many more meetings between the leader and individual members of the core group. These individual meetings usually center on problems that either the leader or the core member cannot bring themselves to raise and discuss in a group or that they regard, on some basis, as not belonging to the larger group.

Sarason noted that he has seen new settings die at a very early age—and even more settings fail rather early in their stated purposes, even though as an entity they survived. In every instance, a contributing factor was some form of strife between the leader and some core members that had never been allowed to surface in a way that could have led to resolution or compromise. The problems were not purely interpersonal; however, the inevitable challenges encountered by the new setting affected and transformed relationships, with effects that were dealt with only in self-defeating, indirect ways. The rate of change in a new setting (as in a newborn infant) is greater than it will ever be again, and this is mirrored in the transformations of relationships within the setting. If the consequences of this rate of change and transformation of relationships are not clearly recognized and dealt with (and they usually are not), substantive and interpersonal differences become fused and confused, rumor and gossip become major vehicles of communication, and the loneliness of everyone is heightened.

Leaders in general are a self-selected group, if only because they actively seek leadership. Leaders who create a new setting may be a somewhat different self-selected group because they strive not only to lead but to create something "out there," the origins of which lie deep within themselves. Yet, regardless of his or her conception of leadership, the leader inevitably remains a private being like everyone else. The degree and content of a leader's privacy become a problem to the extent that she or he has not built into the new setting procedures that serve as external controls against all the errors to which purely private thought and feeling are subject. When a new setting's problems begin to be explained as due to "lack of communication," it is a clear sign that, at the very beginning, the issue of mutuality—or sharing of sentiments—was probably never squarely faced.

The process by which the leader attracts his or her core group almost never permits focusing on how they will live with predictable problems and conflicts. On the contrary, the focus is on the marvelous opportunity the new setting presents for each individual to realize his or her ambitions, within a context of shared values and team effort. Most leaders of new settings have no theory about the nature of the creative process in which they are engaged. What is there to tell them, for example, that in the early stages the verbal commitment to openness is an easy gesture but one that can effectively prevent anticipation of situations that will make openness difficult? That status differences work against openness? That competitiveness among those of similar status, like the core group, also works against openness? That being a leader accelerates the pace of the processes of both self-discovery and self-deception? That absence of conflict may be symptomatic of trouble? This is not to say that leaders must become theoreticians. They are, after all, primarily people of action. They *are* practitioners. However, this does not mean that they are incapable of understanding and being influenced by theory.

The Dangers of "Just Jumping In"

The pressure to "get started" (and to view anything before the "beginning point" as *merely* secondary steps to a primary goal) can have several consequences. First, it can result in a decision to bypass issues, individuals, and existing settings. Second, it can facilitate compromises (made willingly or otherwise) that will shape the future. Third, it can create or exacerbate conflict in the small group that has been formed by the leader to create the new setting. Also, the existence of a fairly definite timetable tends to create a present dominated (and tyrannized) by a future that, when it arrives, is not the one that had been imagined. In most instances, problems arise because of specific factors: the basis and order of recruitment, the absence of problem-solving vehicles, the myth of unlimited resources and an untroubled future, specialization of function, and competition among core members for resources and influence on the leader.

Unconfronted conflicts in the realm of ideas and values can destroy a setting no less effectively than so-called personality clashes. Sarason noted that, in his experience, conflicts in ideas and values are more destructive and that wherever he has been given explanations in terms of personality, it seemed obvious that these obscured conceptual differences. Yet, it is far easier *to see* personality differences than *to hear* conceptual ones. This is one of the reasons why Sarason urged the introduction of an outsider, an external critic, who can supply insights that allow members of the setting to confront and deal with problems before they reach a crisis point. To invite such an outsider in, not just for a day or a week, but as an ongoing source of insight and feedback, is an understandably daunting prospect for the organizers of a new setting. The question that suggests itself is: Why would the organizers want to do that? The best answer might be that those who design settings, like those who design experiments, may not only want to prove something but to learn something. That is to say, they want to experience a sense of growth.

RESEARCH DESIGN

The research project whose results form the core of this book had two goals: (a) to better understand the challenges facing those who create new educational settings, and (b) to better understand the perceptions and concerns that motivate charter school initiators, teachers, and parents. Information was gathered through interviews, on-site observations, and the systematic collection and analysis of archival data. At each school, structured interviews were held with teachers, parents, and administrators. Where opposition to the charter school had been intense, community members who were not members of the charter school community were also interviewed. Classroom visits were undertaken at all schools. School, school district, and state documents, newspaper accounts, and curriculum materials created by teachers were among the archival materials analyzed. However, data collection techniques varied somewhat from site to site, according to the characteristics of that site and the focus of the researcher.

In their respective chapters, Susan Korach and Catharine Perry describe contrasting research studies. Although both made use of the same conceptual framework, the focus differed. Korach compared the early histories of three Colorado charter schools with differing curricular approaches. The first school, which served students in elementary and middle school, had a highly structured curriculum that was based on E. D. Hirsch's Core Knowledge approach. A second school, which served students from kindergarten to 12th grade, offered a highly individualized curriculum based on a successful "open school" in the same school district. The third school, an alternative high school, focused on the special needs of at-risk students. Interviews with key parents and staff at each school allowed Korach to describe the decision-making process that had led to differing policies and outcomes at each school.

Participant observation played an important role in the research of Catharine Perry, whose study focused on the development of one K–8 school. Perry worked regularly as a substitute teacher on-site, attending parent and teacher meetings, including a month-long training workshop held for the school's newly hired teachers during the summer before the school opened. Interviews were held with a wide range of stakeholders, not only at the Model School but also at the elite private university and within the large urban school district that had collaborated in setting up the school.

In contrast, Wesley Elementary had a rich "prehistory" as a regular neighborhood school, having been built during the era of segregation in the South. The school's first principal was a highly regarded African American educator. By the mid-1970s, however, both the neighborhood and the school environment had changed drastically. When Thaddeus Lott became the principal at Wesley in 1975, sixth graders were reading at the second-grade level. By 1980 Lott, who had grown up in the neighborhood, had transformed the school. The standardized test scores of Wesley students ranked with those of affluent suburban schools. Now Wesley Elementary has converted to charter school status. To understand the long and complex history of Wesley Elementary, interviews with a broad range of individuals were needed, along with classroom observations and examination of extensive archival materials.

Whereas the curriculum at Wesley Elementary emphasized a Direct Instruction curriculum, the University of Houston Charter School of Technology made use of a Piagetian approach. Created in cooperation with a large public university, this school was established with the goal of providing a living demonstration in constructivist education. Teacher–child interactions in the classroom were shaped by a strong focus on sociomoral influences. Located in an ethnically diverse neighborhood, this K–2 school admits children on a first-come, first-served basis, based on date of application and the need of individual classes to maintain a balance relating to sex, age, and ethnic distribution. So as to better understand the school's emphasis on teacher–child interactions in the classroom, Barbara Korth made use of extensive videotaping as part of her research at the school.

The final case study included in this book differs from the others in yet another way. The author's involvement with the school was not initially as a researcher, but as an observer and informal consultant. Marblehead Community Charter Public School (MCCPS) was organized in my hometown; my sister, Susan Rundle, was one of the founders. When plans to hire a consultant to help with the charter application went awry, it seemed natural to help out. My role was never a decision-making one. Yet even long-range involvement inevitably has some impact on one's perceptions, as well as one's interactions with interviewees. Thus some might question whether the story of MCCPS ought to have been included in this book. In the end, though, the value of providing something of an "inside view" of the organizational process was deemed sufficient to justify including MCCPS in this group of case studies.

Each case study includes a more detailed discussion of research methods. Chapter 8 compares the experiences of stakeholders at all seven schools, identifying successful—and less successful—strategies that founders, parents, and teachers used in addressing challenges faced by all the schools. Sarason's work on the creation of settings is used as a basis for exploring how evolving theory on the creation of settings might prove helpful to organizers of future schools. Chapter 9 compares results of the present study to previous research on charter schools and shows how charter schools have begun to carve out a middle ground between top-down and market-driven approaches to school reform.

REFERENCES

Becker, H. J., Nakagawa, K., & Corwin, R. G. (1996). Parent involvement contracts in California's charter schools: Strategy for educational improvement or method of exclusion. *Teachers College Record, 98*(3), 511–536.

Bromberger, M., & Bromberger, S. (1969). *Jean Monnet and the United States of Europe*. New York: Coward, McCann, and Geohegan.

Brouillette, L. (1999). Behind the statistics: Urban dropouts and the GED. *Phi Delta Kappan, 81*(4), 313–315.

Burckhardt, J. (1995). *The civilization of the Renaissance in Italy*. New York: Modern Library.

Charter School Resource Center. (1997). *The Massachusetts charter school handbook*, 3rd ed. Boston: Pioneer Institute for Public Policy Research.

Cookson, P. W. (1995). *School choice: The struggle for the soul of American education*. New Haven, CT: Yale University Press.

Crosby, E. A. (1999). Urban schools: Forced to fail. *Phi Delta Kappan, 81*(4), 298–303.

Farkas, S., Johnson, J., & Foleno, A. (1999). *On thin ice: How advocates and opponents could misread the public's views on vouchers and charter schools*. Public Agenda [Online]. http://www.publicagenda.org

Finn, C. E., Jr., Manno, B. V., Bierlein, L. A., & Vanourek, G. (1997). The birth-pains and life-cycles of charter schools. *Charter Schools in Action Project, Final Report, Part II*. Hudson Institute [Online]. http://www.edexcellence.net

Garn, G. (1999, October). The thinking behind Arizona's charter movement. *Educational Leadership, 56*(2), 48–50.

Geske, T. G., Davis, D. R., & Hingle, P. L. (1997). Charter schools: A viable public school option? *Economics of Education Review, 16*, 15–23.

Kolderie, T. (1990). *The states will have to withdraw the exclusive*. Minneapolis, MN: Center for Policy Studies.

Nathan, J. (1996a). *Charter schools: Creating hope and opportunity for American education*. San Francisco: Jossey-Bass.

Nathan, J. (1996b, September). Possibilities, problems, and progress: Early lessons from the charter movement. *Phi Delta Kappan, 78*, 18–23.

National Commission on Excellence in Education. (1983). *A nation at risk: The imperative for educational reform*. Washington, DC: U.S. Government Printing Office.

Office of Educational Research and Improvement. (1999, May). *A study of charter schools: Third-year report executive summary 1999*. Washington, DC: U.S. Department of Education.

Sarason, S. B. (1988). *The creation of settings and the future societies*. Cambridge, MA: Brookline Books.

Stevenson, H. W., Lee, S., & Stigler, J. W. (1986). Mathematics achievement of Chinese, Japanese and American children. *Science, 231*, 693–699.

Stevenson, H., Chen, C., & Lee, S. (1993). Mathematics achievement of Chinese, Japanese and American children: Ten years later. *Science, 259*, 53–58.

U.S. Department of Education (2000). *Fourth-year report of the National Study of Charter Schools*. Washington, DC: Author. [Online]. http://www.ed.gov/pubs/charter4thyear/es.html

Wayson, W. W. (1999). Charter schools: Franchise for creativity or license for fractionation? *Education and Urban Society, 31*(4), 446–464.

Wells, A. S., Artiles, L, Carnochan, S., Cooper, C. W., Grutzik, C., Holm, J. J., Lopez, A. L., Scott, J., Slayton, J., & Vasudeva, A. (1998). *The UCLA charter school study*. Los Angeles, CA: University of California, Los Angeles.

Wells, A. S., Grutzik, C., Carnochan, S., Slayton, J., & Vasudeva, A. (1999). Underlying policy assumptions of charter school reform: The multiple meanings of a movement. *Teachers College Record, 100*(3), 513–535.

Chapter 2

The "Prehistory"
of Charter Schools

> *During the 1980s, educators and employers discerned that America's high*
> *school graduates were not well prepared for college or employment and that*
> *students in other countries, including many "third-world countries," far sur-*
> *passed U.S. students' level of educational achievement. Policymakers also rec-*
> *ognized these shortcomings as major factors limiting U.S. economic competi-*
> *tiveness. (National Governors' Association, 1998)*

This declaration, from the National Governors' Association, makes clear
the concern of state-level policymakers regarding the level of academic
achievement of American students. The overview provided in this chapter will suggest how public education in the United States reached this
impasse. In each state and locality, the story is somewhat different. Yet
general patterns can be recognized. Beginning over a century ago, a
never-quite-resolved national debate on school reform has led many
would-be reformers to spend much of their energy fighting one another
instead of tackling shared problems. As a result, attempts to improve U.S.
public schools have recently been proceeding along two different paths,
with each set of reforms based on assumptions that proponents of the
other set of reforms do not share.

TWO COMPETING VISIONS OF EDUCATION

The current school reform debate has its roots in decisions made during
the closing decades of the 19th century. At that time, the United States was
just emerging as a world power. Until the years just prior to World War I,

Germany was seen as the European country to emulate. Impressed by the growing industrial might of Germany, businessmen worried that the United States might not be able to hold its own in the global marketplace.

> Of particular concern was the excellence of Germany's manufactured goods, an advantage manufacturers attributed to the German system of vocational education. What America needed in their view was a plentiful reservoir of skilled labor similar to what presumably existed in Germany. (Kliebard, 1999, p. 27)

Educators, from kindergarten teachers to university professors, flocked to Germany to study the pedagogical ideas being developed and taught there. German schools and universities were widely considered to be the best in the world.

The groundwork for the German educational system had been laid down by Frederick the Great of Prussia. An enlightened despot, Frederick had in 1763 issued general school regulations establishing compulsory schooling (then a radical idea) for boys and girls from 5 to 13 or 14 years of age. Frederick's minister, Freiherr (Baron) von Zedlitz, supported centralization of school administration under a national board of education. A school-leaving examination for university entrance (the *Abitur*, which still exists in Germany) was introduced. In 1807 Fichte drew up a plan for the new University of Berlin, which Humboldt was able to realize 2 years later. The university was dedicated to a scientific approach to knowledge, to the combination of research and teaching, and to the proliferation of academic pursuits. By the third quarter of the 19th century, the influence of German *Lernfreiheit* (freedom of the student to choose his own program) and *Lehrfreiheit* (freedom of the professor to develop the subject and to engage in research) was felt throughout the academic world.

German industry reaped the benefits of new scientific discoveries. Americans felt that the United States was forced to play "catch up." The 19th century had brought a steady expansion of scientific knowledge, yet the curriculum of most established universities had remained virtually untouched. Although this was the century of the scientists Michael Faraday, Charles Darwin, and Louis Pasteur, most significant research had been done outside the walls of universities. In Great Britain, for instance, it was the Royal Society and other such organizations that fostered advanced studies. The basic curriculum of most colleges and universities remained nontechnical and nonprofessional, with an emphasis on the study of the liberal arts.

Concerns about international economic competitiveness helped to mold educational policies in the United States. The Morrill Act of 1862 established land grant colleges. Federal lands were distributed to support and maintain at least one college in each state. In contrast to the liberal arts tradition that had heretofore dominated American higher education, the instructional focus of the land grant colleges was agricultural and mechanical. The Morrill Act of 1890 broadened the focus to include federal assistance to the states for instructional purposes. In 1917 the Smith–Hughes Act provided categorical aid to public schools for vocational education.

The new vocational and professional emphasis constituted a radical departure from the traditional liberal arts curriculum of American secondary schools and institutions of higher education. This liberal arts curriculum had its roots in ancient times. In the Hellenistic world created by the conquests of Alexander the Great, a "liberal education" had meant the kind of learning that makes the mind free, not subject to the influence of others. In ancient Rome and during the Middle Ages, grammar, rhetoric, and logic (the trivium) and arithmetic, geometry, astronomy, and music (the quadrivium) composed the *artes liberales*, or the arts befitting *liberi*, or free men. In contrast, education for "servility" included all subjects intended to prepare students for a practical trade, as opposed to political or cultural leadership.

In more modern times, the liberal arts had been understood to consist of subjects studied for their cultural and intellectual value, rather than for immediate practical use. A liberal education emphasized intellectual development rather than preparation for business or a profession. Students were exposed to the work of philosophers, historians, novelists, artists, and dramatists whose work encouraged them to ponder such questions as the nature of love and courage, the meaning of death, the proper balance between private and public life, and the consequences of good intentions and mistaken judgments. The arts of expression were taught through enabling students to experience the highest quality work in the arts, in literature, and in speech.

Germany under the Kaiser emphasized other concerns. Social mobility was limited and the aristocracy remained firmly in charge. The educational system was structured so as to efficiently provide highly trained human resources to serve the needs of a booming economy. In the United States, many educators questioned the assumption that human intelligence was just another natural resource, to be harvested in whatever manner seemed to best serve the nation's economic well-being. Supporters of the liberal arts tradition opposed defining education primarily in terms of vocational training, arguing that education should be designed to support the freedom of the mind. Charles W. Eliot, president of Harvard University, declared that educators should not differentiate between "education for college" and "education for life" (Kliebard, 1987).

However, supporters of the liberal arts curriculum found themselves fighting an uphill battle. Many powerful economic and social forces were at work. The transformation of the nature of work and the workplace created a new imperative:

> With apprenticeship in steep decline as a source of training, it seemed obvious to educators, parents, social reformers, business and industrial leaders, and labor alike that education tied to the new workplace was required. The family alone could no longer mediate between the world of childhood and the new and puzzling world of work. A social agency had to intervene, and the schools were the logical choice. (Kliebard, 1999, p. 117)

A growing cadre of professional educators saw in the prospect of an expanded vocational education a chance to make the public school curriculum more visible in the lives of Americans. Not incidentally, the status of educators would be enhanced in the process:

> Education would become not merely a way to master a restricted range of academic subjects and thereby in some vague way promote intellectual development; . . . public education would become an indispensable instrument for addressing matters vital to the national interest and to individual success. (Kliebard, 1999, p. 28)

By the end of the 20th century, these new initiatives and priorities would transform public education in the United States. Yet the goals that professional educators had so enthusiastically embraced as the century began would never be satisfactorily achieved. To understand the reasons why, it is important to understand how things have changed—and why.

Who Should Control the Schools?

> During the nineteenth century the country school belonged to the community in more than a legal sense: it was frequently the focus for people's lives outside the home. An early settler of Prairie View, Kansas, wrote that its capitol "was a small white-painted building which was not only the schoolhouse, but the center—educational, social, dramatic, political, and religious—of a pioneer community of the prairie region of the West." (Tyack, 1974, pp. 15–16)

A century ago, one-room schools across the nation served as natural gathering places where ministers met their flocks, politicians caucused, itinerant lecturers spoke, families gathered for hoedowns, and children competed in spelling bees. School and community were organically related. "Most rural patrons had little doubt that the school was theirs to control (whatever state regulations might say) and not the property of the professional educator" (Tyack, 1974, p. 17). Local citizens provided both the school building and the teacher's salary. Parents had a strong influence on how the school was run. Cultural memories of this era still inform the attitudes of many Americans, creating considerable ambivalence vis-à-vis the more hierarchical and bureaucratic administrative practices that, a century ago, had already begun to dominate urban school districts.

As the 19th century ended, leading educators had begun to argue that a community-dominated form of education could no longer equip young people to deal with the complex nature of citizenship in a technological, urban society. The transition had been gradual. Beginning in the late 1830s, reformers like Horace Mann and Henry Barnard had led campaigns to reorganize public schools. Age-graded classrooms, a uniform curriculum, special training for teachers, and organization of schools into a hierarchical system run by professional administrators were among the reforms introduced. Reformers met with most success in cities, where concentrations of population made age-graded classrooms possible. However, governance remained in the hands of the community members who served on the school board. Urban school boards tended to be large, linked to party politics, and representative of local wards and districts.

In the 1890s businessmen and professionals became disillusioned with the perceived inefficiency of the existing system and sought, instead, to put the governance of schools into the hands of disinterested experts. By 1920, professional school superintendents had gained considerable power at the expense of city school boards. As urban school systems continued to grow in size and complexity, they came to resemble the large business corporations whose efficiency many school reform advocates admired. Meanwhile, pressures to equalize educational opportunity led to increased state control over local school districts. Gradually, larger consolidated schools replaced small schoolhouses, even in rural areas. As the decades passed, all public school districts came to increasingly resemble big city schools in their organization.

Yet the reorganization of public schools along bureaucratic lines brought problems not foreseen by the urban reformers who, during the first quarter of the 20th century, had sought to free schools from the widespread fiscal and policy abuses of 19th-century patronage politics (Iannaccone, 1967). The reformers' aim—embodied in the slogan "Get politics out of the schools and get education out of politics"—was to put policy decisions in the hands of politically neutral educators. Uniform, centralized public school systems gradually evolved out of haphazard educational alternatives. However, much was lost in terms of variety, responsiveness, individual choice, and local control (Kaestle, 1983).

Urban school superintendents began to use the language of social engineers as they sought to replace traditional forms of school governance (in which community members participated in decision making) with a new bureaucratic model where professional educators controlled schools. From classroom to central office, new controls were instituted over pupils, teachers, principals, and other subordinate members of the school hierarchy. Like a factory manager, the superintendent of schools was expected to supervise employees, keep the enterprise technically up to date, and monitor the uniformity and quality of the product (Tyack, 1974).

Unintended Effects of Bureaucratic Structure

Many of the problems for which school systems are now criticized result from the bureaucratic structure that school districts adopted as they increased in size. Max Weber (1922) critiqued the bureaucratic form of organization with its hierarchically arranged levels of authority, within which the activities of "trained and salaried experts" are governed by general, abstract, and clearly defined rules. This emphasis on rules precluded the necessity of issuing special instructions for each specific case. Assignment of roles occurred on the basis of technical qualifications, which were ascertained through formalized, impersonal procedures. Through such techniques it was possible to coordinate the work of large numbers of people to achieve large-scale goals. However such advantages were not garnered without cost.

Organizations have many needs, only one of which is to attain their stated goals (Boyd & Crowson, 1981). Goal displacement, a common malady of bureaucratic organizations, occurs either when (a) the procedural activities that are inherent in organizational life become more important than the goals the organization was created to serve or (b) resources intended for the accomplishment of one task are diverted to another purpose (Sills, 1970). Another common form of goal displacement occurs when the survival of the organization becomes more important than accomplishment of the purpose for which the organization was originally created. As schools became more bureaucratic in nature, they began to suffer from the same ills that plague other bureaucratic systems.

David Rogers (1968) argued in his classic study of the New York City school system that school districts had become so overcentralized that they had turned into "pathological bureaucracies." Decisions took forever. Services were difficult to obtain. More energy was spent working out internal power struggles than on instruction. Incompetent staff found it easy to hide behind patterns of avoidance, blind obedience, compulsive rule-following, and loyalty to internal cliques. Merton (1968) pointed out how the bureaucratic structure of an organization can lead it to act in ways that conflict with the public's wishes:

> The bureaucrat, in part irrespective of his position within the hierarchy, acts as a representative of the power and prestige of the entire structure. In his official role he is vested with definite authority. This often leads to an actually or apparently domineering attitude, which may only be exaggerated by

a discrepancy between his position within the hierarchy and his position with reference to the public. Protest and recourse to other officials on the part of the client are often ineffective or largely precluded by the previously mentioned *esprit de corps* which joins the officials into a more or less solidary ingroup. This source of conflict *may* be minimized in private enterprise since the client can register an effective protest by transferring his trade to another organization within the competitive system. But with the monopolistic nature of the public organization, no such alternative is possible. (p. 257)

There is an inherent tension between the pressure on the employee to preserve a formal and impersonal attitude and the client's demand for personal, individualized consideration. This conflict becomes particularly noticeable when the bureaucracy is an educational enterprise dealing with the idiosyncratic problems and differing needs of young people. Parents worry that their child will be "lost in the shuffle," that his or her particular talents and needs will not be recognized, that school personnel will not keep the parents well enough informed about the welfare and progress of their child. For many students, going to school may begin to feel a bit like "jumping through hoops." Goodlad (1984) described the deadening atmosphere of schools his research team visited, commenting on the possible effect on students:

We do not see in our descriptions, then, much opportunity for students to become engaged with knowledge so as to employ their full range of intellectual abilities. And one wonders about the meaningfulness of whatever is acquired by students who sit listening or performing relatively repetitive exercises year after year. Part of the brain, known as Magoun's brain, is stimulated by novelty. It appears to me that students spending twelve years in the schools we studied would be unlikely to experience much novelty. Does the brain just sleep, then? (p. 231)

THE SEARCH FOR ALTERNATIVES

Charter school parents who were interviewed for this book often mentioned the lack of motivation their child had displayed while attending her or his previous public school; their comments recalled the findings described in *The Shopping Mall High School: Winners and Losers in the Educational Marketplace*. Powell, Farrar, and Cohen (1985) described the situation of the "unspecial" middle 70% of high school students who are left out of the special programs school districts have developed for their most highly motivated as well as their "at-risk" students: "Few characteristics of the shopping mall high school are more significant than the existence of unspecial students in the middle who are ignored and poorly served. Teachers and administrators talk a great deal about the problem" (p.

173). One reason the "unspecial student" can slide through with only a cursory knowledge of the subject matter is the existence of classroom treaties that allow the "unspecial" to avoid work. Little is usually expected of these students, and little is done to change their lot. In such an environment, there is little encouragement to excel: "For the middle students, a school's neutral stance on pushing students has the effect of making minimum requirements maximum standards" (Powell et al., 1985, p. 180).

Such classroom treaties may result from tacit recognition that U.S. public schools have become caught in a contradiction. On the one hand, there are laws that make school attendance compulsory. On the other hand, once students are in the building, there is comparatively little teachers can do to compel a high level of performance. Most children progress through the school system, passing from grade to grade, whether they choose to do much in the way of schoolwork or not. A few may have to repeat a grade. But, on the whole, penalties for academic failure are far lower than in school systems where "seat time" counts for little and where a school-leaving test is used to determine whether or not a student qualifies for university entrance.

The difference is made strikingly clear when one compares U.S. schools to those of other nations. For example, in post-World War II Germany the period of elementary education covers eight or nine grades. After this period, three options have traditionally been available to pupils. They may, after counseling by the elementary school teacher, and on the request of the parents, be placed in a *Realschule*, a *Gymnasium*, or a *Hauptschule* (the last representing a continuation of elementary education). After completion of studies at the *Hauptschule*, the pupil typically enters apprenticeship training. The *Realschule* offers pupils further general education, some prevocational courses, and English-language study. At the age of 16, *Realschule* students conclude their studies and transfer to a vocational school or enter apprenticeship training. If academically qualified, the pupil may also transfer to the *Gymnasium*.

The *Gymnasium*, the third alternative for German youth, offers rigorous academic preparation for higher education. Like the *lycée* in France, the *Gymnasium* is designed for those students who have shown the most academic promise; its curriculum, emphasizing languages, mathematics, natural sciences, and social sciences, requires a high degree of diligence throughout all of the nine grades. Students in the *Gymnasium* must pass an examination, the *Abitur*, if they are to be admitted to a German university. The content of the *Abitur* is adjusted to the focus of the students' studies, such as classical languages or mathematics–science.

Given this curriculum, the role of the teacher in a German *Gymnasium* is rather different from the role of teachers in American schools. In the German system an external exam, over which the teacher has no control, is used to appraise student performance. The teacher's role resembles that of a coach, working together with the student to help the latter acquire the knowledge and skills needed to pass the school-leaving examination. The American teacher, in contrast, must serve both as teacher and as judge, deciding upon the adequacy of student academic performance. If a student receives a passing grade for a semester's work, no further proof of achievement in that subject is required. This can result in a subtle (or not-so-subtle) negotiation process, as students attempt to "wear down" the teacher, subtly bartering good behavior for passing grades, resulting in the kind of "classroom treaties" described in *The Shopping Mall High School.*

Because teachers are evaluated by their principals, there is considerable pressure to avoid situations that may cause trouble or embarrassment. When a teacher gives a large number of students failing grades, uncomfortable confrontations with parents can result. The parents may talk to the school principal. If parents do not get the reaction they desire from the principal, they may go to the superintendent's office. If the superintendent does not react in the desired manner, parents may contact members of the school board. Given that the school superintendent serves at the pleasure of the school board, all district staff employees who are dependent upon the good will of the superintendent generally strive to avoid such an eventuality.

In addition, lawsuits brought by students, parents, and community members have put sharp limits on the power of school districts and state educational agencies to make decisions on behalf of students. Prior to 1950, less than 300 cases involving school issues had been initiated in federal courts (Hogan, 1985). By the late 1970s, however, thousands of school cases were being initiated in federal courts each year. Although the number of cases leveled off in the 1980s, educational litigation in the United States continues to outpace that in any other nation. This has resulted in a steep increase in the number of regulations aimed at schools; for when a school policy or practice is ruled unconstitutional, the judiciary usually charges Congress, the state legislature, or local school board with designing a plan to remedy the constitutional defect. The resulting legislation may then stimulate further lawsuits (McCarthy, 1992). Each regulation put in place further limits the options open to schools.

The Legacy of Conflicting Reform Efforts

In most states local school districts have extensive power to make curriculum decisions (Metz, 1978). Yet the multilayered structure of the U.S. political system—plus the fact that most states and local school districts are in need of federal funds—makes schools simultaneously answerable to federal, state, and local regulations (Bennett & LeCompte, 1990). This division of authority has often put schools in the position of simultaneously attempting to meet two different and partially contradictory goals. For example, a school district might be directed both to tighten graduation requirements and to lower the dropout rate, or a school might be directed to teach a more rigorous core curriculum while at the same time mainstreaming children with ever more profound handicaps.

Goodlad (1984) pointed out:

> Current expectations for schools constitute a hodgepodge, resulting from accumulations of piecemeal legislation. New legislation takes little or no account of existing requirements in the education code. In fact, most legislators are virtually ignorant of these requirements and the potential impact of new bills on the finite time and resources of schools. Principals and teachers are often caught in a paralytic inertia created by the bombardment of changing and often conflicting expectations. (p. 275)

Such a situation can easily become an open invitation to cynicism. Because true compliance is impossible, a premium is put, not on effectively accomplishing a clearly defined task, but on protecting oneself and one's school from any punitive measures that might result from noncompliance.

Even when the school does accomplish one of the assigned goals, what constitutes success to the partisans of one educational goal often constitutes failure to the partisans of another. Therefore, when the tide of public opinion causes one of two competing goals to be strongly emphasized, the partisans of the goal that has been ignored tend to do their best to focus media attention on this perceived failure, thus turning the tide of public opinion in their direction. As a result, there is a tendency for the emphasis of educational policy to lurch from one goal to another, giving the recurrent crises in education a cyclical nature (Cuban, 1990; Kirst & Meister, 1985).

Not only does this turbulence encourage an attitude that dismisses attempts at reform as mere shifts in educational fashion, but it produces another unfortunate side effect. Few educational reforms last long enough for a solid research base to be established on which further rational progress could be built. Thus, when the debate circles around once again, the same debating points are repeated, with everyone hanging on to their original opinion and finding no rational way to settle differences through appeal to mutually acceptable empirical evidence. The constant churning effect created by politically motivated change helps explain why the large sums of money that have been spent on educational research have not brought about meaningful improvement in the way schools are run.

Investigations of the Process of Organizational Change

The bureaucratic nature of the U.S. school district has given an "all or nothing" character to reform efforts. As House (1998) noted: "Over the past 30 years, one of the most persistent features of educational life has been that innovations are advanced, have brief lives, then disappear, without affecting the schools in any significant way" (p. 1). In the aptly named *Tinkering Toward Utopia*, Cuban and Tyack (1997) documented the dynamic tension that has long existed between Americans' faith in education as a panacea and the moderate pace of educational change. The tendency to alternate between lamentation and overconfidence has worked to doom any number of promising reforms. Enthusiasts envision quick and easy progress, only to have their own overoptimistic descriptions thrown back at them when results were slower in coming (and more modest) than predicted. Unwilling to settle for lesser results than had been predicted, school boards and superintendents often prefer to throw the dice again, moving on to the next reform.

Concerned with the failure rate of attempts at innovation, a number of researchers have turned their attention to the change process itself, in hope of making change efforts more successful. Karen Seashore Louis (1992) put together an informative overview of trends in the study of organizational change in education. This research on change in American education began with more than 200 studies conducted at Teachers College, Columbia University, from the 1930s though the 1950s (Mort, 1963). The research looked at diffusion of innovations within the educational system and produced several enduring observations, including:

- Although there is often a burst of action during which a new practice is adopted in many schools at the same time, the spread of a new idea through the entire educational system takes decades.
- Schools vary systematically in their capacity for considering and adopting new practices.
- Interest groups in the schools and community are critical determinants of the adoption process and its outcomes.

These studies drew attention to the fact that innovation diffusion in education is typically an organizational change process, instead of a process of individual decision making.

The comprehensive review of the 1960s literature on planned change carried out by Havelock et al. (1969) identified three streams of research:

1. The social interaction perspective focused on the adoption of specific new practices by individuals, examining the effect of adopter characteristics and social networks on change behavior.
2. The research/development/diffusion/utilization (RDDU) perspective was derived from research on the agricultural extension service, but was used in education to study how to improve the flow of research-based information from the universities to the schools.

3. The problem-solver perspective, based on the work of Kurt Lewin, focused on the process of individual or group change and identified distinctive stages in the change process.

Havelock et al. proposed a model that incorporated elements from each of these and emphasized the need for a linking agent who would deliver technical assistance and facilitate decision making at the school.

Empirical studies in the 1970s (Emrick, 1977; Goodlad, 1975; Louis & Sieber, 1979; Miles, Fullan, & Taylor, 1980) continued to reflect these streams of research. Meyer and Rowen (1977) argued that reform in education is usually imposed from the outside, through changes in social consensus about what schools "should look like," rather than generated from within, through organizational decision processes (Meyer, 1987). In contrast, research influenced by the results of studies of effective schools (Brookover, Beady, Flood, Schweitzer, & Wisebaken, 1979; Clark, Lotto, & Astuto, 1984; Wilson & Corcoran, 1989) focused attention on issues of leadership and design in the change process (Firestone & Wilson, 1985; Huberman & Miles, 1984). In his review of policy research and other literature on educational programs, Elmore (1978) derived the following four models of organizational change.

Systems management strategies grow out of a specific set of assumptions: organizations are goal oriented and operate rationally; organizations are hierarchically structured; subsidiary units can cooperate to maximize overall performance; management by objectives enhances goal attainment. Therefore change processes are enhanced by goal setting, monitoring, and accountability.

Bureaucratic process strategies assume that schools are not tightly controlled hierarchies but spheres of delegated discretion. Therefore, they focus on the need to change organizational routines. Observing that bureaucracies are characterized by the nature of their formal and informal routines, they see examining and altering these routines as the key to effective change.

Organizational development strategies assume that interpersonal relationships dominate organizational life and the change process. This model focuses on individual motivation, the work group as the key unit of change, and the belief that too great a focus on efficiency undermines effective change processes.

Conflict and bargaining strategies assume the centrality of competition for power and scarce resources. Bargaining is seen as the main mode of decision making, and change is viewed as an unstable process of negotiating preferences that rarely results in an overall agreement.

Fullan and Miles (1992) pointed out that "reform often fails because politics favors symbols over substance. Substantial change in practice requires a lot of hard work and clever work 'on the ground' which is not the point of political players" (p. 747). Because the restructuring process is so complex, one cannot know in advance exactly which new structures and behavioral patterns should go together or how they should mesh. Changes in structure must go hand in hand with changes in the school culture. Things seldom go easily during change efforts. Yet it is an oversimplification to attribute unforeseen difficulties to resistance, "variously known as intransigence, entrenchment, fearfulness, reluctance to buy in, complacency, unwillingness to alter behaviors, and failure to recognize the need to change" on the part of teachers and other staff members (p. 748).

THE DEEPER ROOTS OF THE CHARTER SCHOOL DEBATE

The charter school movement represents a different approach to educational reform. Instead of attempting to hold together a district-wide consensus (or even persuade a diverse and opinionated high school faculty to agree on a single reform), the charter school movement allows individuals to gravitate to those programs for which they feel a natural affinity. An assumption is made that different students have different needs and that an approach that does not work well for one may work well for another. In the charter school movement, proponents of different types of educational reform are not put into the position of having to defeat those with differing beliefs in order to put their own ideas to the test. The hope is that school reform can, in this way, be made into a win/win proposition. Although new to education, this approach has deep historical roots.

In medieval Europe, monarchs issued charters to towns, cities, guilds, merchant associations, universities, and religious institutions; such charters guaranteed certain privileges and immunities to those organizations, sometimes also specifying arrangements for the conduct of their internal affairs. Simply put, a charter is a document granting specified rights, powers, privileges, or functions to an individual, city, or other organization by the state (or sovereign). Even today the document that lays out the organizational structure of a city is called a "charter." Therefore, when a city wishes to make changes in its municipal form of government, the debate will commonly center on provisions in the charter.

The most famous charter, the Magna Carta ("Great Charter"), was a compact between the English King John and his barons, specifying the king's grant of certain liberties to the English people. In England, the Petition of Right (1628) and the Habeas Corpus Act (1679) looked directly back to clause 39 of the charter of 1215, which stated that "no free man shall be . . . imprisoned or disseised [dispossessed] . . . except by the lawful judgment of his peers or by the law of the land." In subsequent English statutes, the references to "the legal judgment of his peers" and "laws of the land" are treated as substantially synonymous with due process of law. Drafters of the U.S. federal Constitution adopted the due process phraseology in the Fifth Amendment, ratified in 1791, which provides that "No person shall . . . be deprived of life, liberty, or property, without due process of law."

British colonies in North America were established through charters that granted land and certain governing rights to the colonists, while retaining certain powers for the British crown. Similarly, when a U.S. city incorporates, the state government allows a charter to be drawn up, allowing the people of a specific locality to organize themselves into a municipal corporation—that is, a city. Such a charter delegates powers to the people for the purpose of local self-government. A municipality is therefore the response of the state government to the need for certain public services (i.e., waste disposal, police and fire protection, water supply, health services) in addition to the services available from the county or from other local governments in the area. When the state grants a charter to a school, this allows parents and teachers to organize in such a manner as to provide educational services in addition to those that are available from the school district and existing schools.

Constitutional government has traditionally been characterized by dividing power (between local, state, and federal levels of government or between the legislature, executive, and judiciary) to ensure the presence of restraints and "checks and balances." In keeping with such constitutional precedents, charter schools are not mere subsets within a larger bureaucratic structure, but exist as individual communities in their own right. Much like cities that exist within, but are distinct from, the surrounding county and state, charters offer enhanced responsiveness to local needs. Charter schools also have the advantage of coming into existence already possessed of a nascent social contract, in the form of the school's charter. What this may mean, in practice, is explored in the case studies presented in the following chapters.

REFERENCES

Bennett, K. P., & LeCompte, M. D. (1990). *The way schools work*. New York: Longman.
Boyd, W. L., & Crowson, R. L. (1981). The changing conception and practice of public school administration. In D. C. Berliner (Ed.), *Review of research in education* (Vol. 9, pp. 311–377). Washington, DC: American Educational Research Association.

Brookover, W., Beady, C., Flood, P., Schweitzer, J., & Wisebaken, J. (1979). *School social systems and student achievement: Schools can make a difference.* New York: Praeger.

Clark, D., Lotto, L., & Astuto, T. (1984). Effective schools and school improvement. A comparison of two lines of inquiry. *Educational Administration Quarterly, 20,* 41–68.

Cuban, L. (1990, April). Reforming, again, again, and again. *Educational Researcher,* pp. 3–13.

Elmore, R. (1978). Organizational models of social programs implementation. In D. Mann (Ed.), *Making change happen?* (pp. 185–223). New York: Teachers College Press.

Emrick, J. (1977). *Evaluation of the national diffusion network, Vol. I: Findings and recommendations.* Menlo Park, CA: Stanford Research Institute.

Firestone, W., & Wilson, D. (1985). Using bureaucratic and cultural linkages to improve instruction. *Educational Administration Quarterly, 21,* 7–30.

Fullan, M. G., & Miles, M. B. (1992, June). Getting reform right: What works and what doesn't. *Phi Delta Kappan,* pp. 745–752.

Goodlad, J. (1975). *Dynamics of educational change.* New York: McGraw-Hill.

Goodlad, J. I. (1984). *A place called school: Prospects for the future.* New York: McGraw-Hill.

Havelock, R., Guskin, A., Frohman, M., Havelock, M., Hill, M., & Huber, J. (1969). *Planning for innovation through dissemination and utilization of knowledge.* Ann Arbor, MI: Institute for Social Research.

Hogan, J. (1985). *The schools, the courts, and the public interest* (2nd ed.). Lexington, MA: Lexington Books.

House, E. R. (1998). *Schools for sale.* New York: Teachers College Press.

Huberman, M., & Miles, M. (1984). *Innovation up close.* New York: Plenum.

Iannaccone, L. (1967). *Politics in education.* New York: Center for Applied Research in Education.

Kaestle, C. F. (1983). *Pillars of the republic: Common schools and American society 1780–1860.* New York: Hill & Wang.

Kirst, M. W., & Meister, G. (1985). Turbulence in American secondary schools: What reforms last? *Curriculum Inquiry, 15,* 169–186.

Kliebard, H. (1987). *The struggle for the American curriculum 1893–1958.* New York: Routledge.

Kliebard, H. (1999). *Schooled to work: Vocationalism and the American curriculum, 1876–1946.* New York: Teachers College Press.

Louis, K. S. (1992). Organizational change. In M. C. Alkin (Ed.), *Encyclopedia of educational research* (6th ed., pp. 941–947). New York: Macmillan.

Louis, K. S., & Sieber, S. (1979). *Bureaucracy and the dispersed organization: The educational extension agent experiment.* Norwood, NJ: Ablex.

McCarthy, M. M. (1992). Judicial decisions. In M. C. Alkin (Ed.), *Encyclopedia of educational research* (6th ed., pp. 677–689). New York: Macmillan.

Merton, R. K. (1968). *Social theory and social structure.* New York: Free Press.

Metz, M. H. (1978). *Classrooms and corridors: The crisis of authority in desegregated secondary schools.* Berkeley: University of California Press.

Meyer, J. W. (1987). Implications of an institutional view of education. In M. T. Hallinan (Ed.), *The social organization of schools.* New York: Plenum.

Meyer, J. W., & Rowen, B. (1977). Institutionalized organizations: Formal structure as myth and ceremony. *American Journal of Sociology, 83,* 340–363.

Miles, M., Fullan, M., & Taylor, G. (1980). Organization development in schools. The state of the art. *Review of Educatonal Research, 50,* 121–183.

Mort, P. R. (1963). Studies in educational innovation from the Institute of Administrative Research: An overview. In M. B. Miles (Ed.), *Innovation in education* (pp. 317–328). New York: Teachers College Press.

National Governors' Association. (1998, April). *Preparing students for the twenty-first century.* Washington, DC: Author [Online]. *http://www.nga.org/Pubs/IssueBriefs/1998/980413Students.asp,* downloaded 12/6/99

Powell, A. G., Farrar, E., & Cohen, D. K. (1985). *The shopping mall high school: Winners and losers in the educational marketplace.* Boston: Houghton Mifflin.

Rogers, D. (1968). *110 Livingston Street: Politics and bureaucracy in the New York City schools.* New York: Random House.

Sills, D. L. (1970). Preserving organizational goals. In O. Grusky & G. A. Miller (Eds.), *The sociology of organizations: Basic studies* (pp. 227–236). New York: The Free Press.

Tyack, D. (1974). *The one best system: A history of American urban education.* Cambridge, MA: Harvard University Press.

Weber, M. (1922). *Wirtschaft und Gesellschaft.* Tubingen: J. C. B. Mohr.

Wilson, B., & Corcoran, T. (1989). *Successful secondary schools: Visions of excellence in American public schools.* East Sussex, UK: Falmer.

Chapter 3

Pioneering Change:
The Experiences of Three
Colorado Charter Schools

Susan Korach
University of Denver

In 1993, Colorado charter schools came into being as a result of a grass-roots effort organized by parents and a number of public school teachers, with the support of community and child advocacy groups, a bipartisan coalition of legislators, and Governor Roy Romer. Proponents argued that charter schools would help bring reform to the system of public education by introducing innovations in pedagogy and governance, lead to improved relationships with parents, and provide a vehicle to empower teachers. Initially, the legislation was strongly opposed by the Colorado School Board Association and the Colorado Education Association (the state's largest teacher's union). Questions raised by opponents included: Would charter schools draw the brightest students and most empowered parents away from neighborhood schools? Would they take financial resources away from neighborhood schools? Would they lead to vouchers and the privatization of education in Colorado?

Charter school legislation in Colorado took the form of a compromise: Charter schools could be established, but local school districts would be the sole chartering agencies. The chartering authority vested in the local school district is deeply rooted in Colorado's long and fervently held tradition of local control of schools. However, it creates a natural tension between districts and charter schools. To be granted a contract for a charter school, the applicants have to be approved by the district from which they are trying to break away. Many states have laws that permit local school boards *and* other public organizations—such as the state board of education, public universities, city governments, and others—to sponsor charter schools. In Colorado, charter school applicants can appeal a decision of the local school district to the State Board of Education. As of September 9, 1997, the State Board had heard 53 appeals under the Colorado Charter School Act. Of the first 50 charter schools, 10 (20%) were approved only after the Colorado State Board of Education became involved in the resolution of disputes between local school districts and charter school applicants.

In the first 5 years (1993–1998) after passage of charter school legislation, 50 charter schools were approved in Colorado, serving over 11,000 students. "If the charter schools were combined to create an imaginary school district, that district would be the 18th largest in the state" (Clayton Foundation, 1997, p. ii). The initiating groups that created these schools reflect the grass-roots nature of the charter school movement in Colorado: Of the first 50 schools, 33 of the charters were granted to parent-led groups, 11 to teacher-led groups, 3 to nonprofit organizations, 1 to a for-profit organization, 2 to universities, and 1 to a city.

CONCEPTUAL FRAMEWORK AND RESEARCH DESIGN

This study was designed to examine issues central to the development of individual charter schools in Colorado. Three very different charter schools were followed from the first coming together of the group that eventually applied for the charter, through the creation of a vision for the school, the awarding of the charter, planning for the opening of the school, and the first years of operation. The impact of specific decisions, changing interpersonal relationships among stakeholders, and the school's social and political environment were analyzed in relation to the school's success or failure in implementing its founding vision.

In *The Creation of Settings and Future Societies* (1988), Seymour Sarason provided "an organized set of conceptions" that assisted the researcher in the selection and ordering of data according to the "basic problems confronting the creation of any setting" (p. 21). According to Sarason, the major internal problems seen in the creation of a setting centered on two related tasks: (a) "growth and differentiation" or the impact that new people entering the setting had on the original vision/idea, and (b) the "forging of the constitution by which the setting will be governed" or how power and leadership were distributed and lines of authority and communication were established (p. 141). These problems were explored through an analysis of the history of each site as it progressed from the idea/charter through its first operational years as a school.

The bulk of the data in this study came from semistructured interviews with (and observations of) founders, administrators, teachers, parents, and students. Archival records were also used as data sources. Each school was studied intensively for 1 month during the spring of 1006. During this time the researcher observed each school and its classrooms, gathered historical data, and conducted semistructured interviews with 12–18 past and present members of the school community. Interviewees were chosen so as to represent all constituencies (administrators, teachers, parents, teachers, and board members). Each school was visited 1 year later (1997) to conduct follow-up interviews and observations to verify data. In addition, each school was visited 4 years after the initial visit (January 2000) to ascertain whether significant changes had taken place and to check on organizational health and viability.

Charter School Sample

The three schools chosen for this study represent the diversity of charter schools within the Denver Metropolitan/Colorado Springs area for the period between 1993 and 1997. The names of the schools and the school districts have been fictionalized. Core Academy (CA), a K–8 school, was initiated in 1993 by parents and has a traditional educational design. Passages Charter School (PCS), a K–12 school, was initiated in 1994 by teachers and makes use of concepts long associated with progressive education. Opportunity Preparatory School (OPS), a 9–12 school, was initiated in 1995 by a city employee. This school was created to serve drop-outs and/or students at risk of dropping out of high school.

The following narratives describe the three charter schools chosen for the study. Each narrative includes a detailed description of the school's program and operations, philosophical orientation, and the developmental history of the school as it moved from the original charter idea to an operating school. The focus of this chapter is the similarity of experiences concerning the organizational development and dynamics of leadership observed in the three diverse schools. Since the time of the study, each charter has been successfully renewed and each school has demonstrated a positive impact on students. The data on the schools' impact on student academic and social achievement were omitted from this chapter so that the descriptions of their organizational development could be fully presented, in hopes that new schools will be able to glean insight and learn from their predictable problems.

CORE ACADEMY

Core Academy was the first K–6 charter school approved in the Denver Metropolitan area. This school was created primarily through the work of three women, who were motivated by their perception that academic standards and content in the Arrowhead School District in the early 1990s were inadequate. One of the founders stated that the prevailing philosophy regarding elementary education in the district had been "Don't Worry, Be Happy"; the focus in the school district had been on developing a student's "self-esteem," not on academic content. She believed, in contrast, that the best way to increase self-esteem in students was through academic achievement. Therefore she had tried to change her children's school by proposing to the principal the creation of a "school within a school" that would emphasize content. Her proposal went nowhere. Seven to 8 months later, she learned about E. D. Hirsch's Core Knowledge curriculum. Again, she went to the principal, then to the district, with a curriculum in hand. However, her proposal still went nowhere.

Frustrated, she began to hold meetings in the local library to examine and discuss the Core Knowledge Curriculum with 20 to 30 parents who were also dissatisfied with their neighborhood schools. These parents knew what they did not want; however, they were not as clear about what they wanted. During this period of time, charter school legislation was being crafted in Colorado. By the spring of 1993 it seemed clear that the Charter School Bill was going to be passed and that Governor Romer was going to sign it. A charter school application was quickly written by the organizer of the group that had been meeting in the library and two other mothers. The application, for a K–6 school that would use the Core Knowledge Curriculum, was submitted to the Arrowhead School District on July 14, 1993. After a short period of negotiation, the Arrowhead Board of Education approved the charter application on August 31, 1993. Core Academy opened its doors for students on September 29, 1993.

Growth and Differentiation

As negotiations with the district were taking place, a core group of five mothers created the design for Core Academy. Each of the individuals in the core group had a specific issue of concern. One was concerned about the curriculum. Another pushed for a 17/1 student/teacher ratio. Someone else pushed for a dress code. One founder later stated that "each leader became obsessive about their [sic] own special interest. If you called one of these people and asked them about the school, the first characteristic out of their mouth would be their personal issue of concern." The parents who organized the school gathered ideas from different people, without much thought of how they were going to pull it all together.

The initial mission statement for Core Academy, "Strive for knowledge and truth in all you do," reflects the hasty planning process. This statement did not provide a specific guiding framework for the school. As a result, the special interests of the core group (17/1 student/teacher ratio, student dress code, Core Knowledge Curriculum) grew into the mission. As a dean of the school later stated, "The folks that started Core Academy did not start it out of a greater vision, but an opportunity to get away from their situation. They just wanted a teacher for their children that was away from the public system." Even though these parents did not possess a strong educational vision, they did have unity of purpose; this mobilized them to create a school design, acquire materials, secure a site, prepare the site, hire teachers, enroll students, and open a school within a time span of 2 months.

The time before the school opened its doors was filled with activity and a sense of the "euphoria of a new school." Parents were involved in painting, putting up walls, cleaning toilets, everything. Teachers worked side by side with the parents to get the school building ready. In the beginning, there was a tremendous need for people to work together in order for the school to be ready to open. "People rallied around to get the rock moving. It was such a hard push and everybody was right there because we knew that if it didn't work we were going to have to pull our kids out and put them back into where they were before the charter school."

At the time of the study (1996), Core Academy (CA) was in its fourth year of existence and had received the distinction of becoming the first charter school recipient of the John J. Irwin Colorado School of Excellence award from the State Board of Education. This award is given to Colorado schools that complete an application process and are able to demonstrate improvement in student achievement. The school went on to receive this distinction in two subsequent years (1997 and 1999). Core Academy was housed in a renovated grocery store located in a strip shopping center in a middle- to upper-middle-class suburban area south of Denver. The school that had begun as a K–6 school for 117 students had grown to 324 students in grades K–8. There were 675 students on Core Academy's waiting list after 3 years of operation. In 1998, the school had four significant characteristics that differentiated it from regular district schools: the Core Knowledge curriculum, a student/teacher ratio of 17/1 (later increased to 18/1), a student dress code, and governance by a board of directors composed of parents, a community member, and the dean.

The educational program and design of Core Academy changed somewhat over the first 3 years. Originally the academic program consisted solely of the Core Knowledge Curriculum, which was a spiral curriculum based on specific academic content to be taught in language arts, history, geography, mathematics, science, and the fine arts. Students were grouped by grade level in self-contained classrooms with one teacher. Parents served as instructional aides. Teachers were not involved in determining the initial values or educational philosophy of the school. The only "given" was Core Knowledge. During the first year of the school, teachers had to create everything else they needed to teach their students. Before long the teachers discovered that the Core Knowledge Curriculum did not adequately address reading and math. This lack of curricula was especially troublesome for the inexperienced teachers. After the first year, the school adopted the Saxon math program and Open Court reading curriculum. The school also began to utilize school-wide ability groups for math and reading during specific times of the day. Teachers' pedagogical preferences varied from teacher-directed to hands-on approaches in accordance with the learning activity. Each student had a learning plan that had been written with parent, teacher, and student input. In addition to grade-level classes, students participated in art, music, physical education, Spanish, and technology classes. Students received grades for their work and competed for placement on the honor roll. Traditional disciplinary systems were used, including office referrals, detentions, and suspensions.

As the school entered its second year, the dean began to work on building a vision for the school and creating a team spirit among the teachers. She felt that the teachers had been operating in "cliques" and were not united by a mission. Until this time, the school had been primarily focused on existing, not on its purpose for existence. The process of creating a vision for the school was slow and difficult. The following mission statement was created, approved, and provided guidance to the leadership: "Core Academy provides a challenging academic program based on the Core Knowledge Curriculum that promotes academic excellence, character development, and educational enthusiasm for its students." This mission reflected the areas of emphasis at CA—academics, character, and love of learning. All members of the school community who were interviewed for this study were able to state these three areas of emphasis.

The strength of this sense of mission, even after the school had experienced growth and differentiation, may be a result of the fact that the school's mission was rooted in the past; CA was a return to the type of school with which most parents were familiar. In fact, one teacher said in an interview that teaching at CA was like returning to the fifties. The power of traditional school values and the creation of a tight parental community enabled the school to survive a turbulent history, including two deans within the first 3 years of the school's existence. Core Academy's emphasis on academic content and traditional ideas made the school feel "safe" to parents and resulted in a stable and growing student population, despite the fierce internal struggles that took place as the setting slowly hammered out its system of governance, or its "constitution."

Forging the Constitution and Problems of Leadership

CA grew from a "seed of discontent" that was sown when parents wanted to become involved in developing an "educational platform" (Sergiovanni, 1994) featuring the Core Knowledge Curriculum in a neighborhood public elementary school. Many parents felt that the district was only giving "lip service" to parental involvement. The school and district administrations listened to parents and had developed formalized committees (site accountability committees, etc.) to involve parents in school operations. However, parental involvement took the form of parents volunteering at the schools (recess monitor, paper grader, field trip chaperone, etc.). Parents did not feel they were allowed to enter into a dialogue about educational practices. As a result, some parents felt a betrayal of trust, especially as the district had publicly stated that it strongly supported choice programs and parental involvement. The charter school parents' feelings were exemplified by a comment made by a parent: "I want to be involved; but I want the school to be honest with me and not just tell me what I want to hear."

Because the parents who founded CA had no sense of power in their neighborhood schools, they sought total control of their charter school; they were reluctant to entrust educators with the leadership of their school. In the beginning, there was a sense of "we're all equals" among the founders of the school; "essentially no one was in charge." A board composed of seven members (five parents, one community member, and the dean) governed Core Academy. The parents at CA felt that they had to be at the school daily to enforce their vision, that the board was "entirely responsible for running the school." Each board member had a specific responsibility: teacher review, student advocate, discipline and dress code, and community building. In general, leadership was shared among the board members. However, it was recognized that they needed someone to fill the role of dean. One of the founders had a strong personality, so that when the core group had a disagreement about something they would "defer to her." This founder became the first dean of the school. The governing board of parents was expected to be responsible for the day-to-day operations; the dean would be a "figurehead."

Two months after the school opened the dean left. Until a new dean could be hired, the board members took a calendar and divided the time into weeks when different board members were responsible for running the school. One teacher who was present during this time observed that "during the 'Dean for the Day' period, the school was probably more site based and team managed." The board members would run to the teachers and ask, "Well, what do you think we should do?" She noted that this period helped build relationships between teachers and board members. "Everyone was learning; this [learning] was the one piece that was valid from all directions." The Dean for the Day period lasted 6 weeks. At this point in the creation of the school, board members and teachers were in the same kind of situation; they were all in the learning process about school management. There were no experts; parents, teachers, and board members worked together to keep the school running. During this time, each of the most powerful parents encountered feelings of not knowing how to run a school and they often sought the help of the teachers. Trust between educators and parents began to build.

In mid-December the board hired a new dean who had been heavily involved in a neighboring school district as a parent volunteer and advocate. The new dean had a college degree in education, but her work experience was in business, especially "startup businesses." She and the board felt these skills and experiences made a good fit with the responsibilities of the dean at CA. She would maintain the strong parental voice at Core Academy. Her employment began January 1, 1994. The job description for the dean had not changed; she was to be responsible for overseeing the operations of the school in conjunction with the governing board. The dean continued to have voting rights on the governing board, and there were no clear distinctions between the roles of dean and governing board members. As a result, problems of leadership surfaced.

The issue that led to this second dean's resignation was teacher evaluation and teacher retention/termination. In the beginning a subcommittee of the board, the Evaluation Committee, was responsible for teacher evaluation. The new dean instituted a process in which she and two board members would conduct teacher evaluations by observing classrooms and completing an evaluation checklist she had created. This process was extremely frustrating for teachers. Board members would schedule formal observations with the teachers, then miss them with no communication about the cancellation. According to one teacher, some of the other teachers perceived the board as the "enemy" or "the boss who had too much power." Neither board members nor the dean was a practicing educator; the bottom line was that the parents doing the evaluation had no expertise or even training. One board member who did these evaluations felt unqualified: "I feel that I don't have the skills to evaluate the teacher. I know that I can tell by talking to a teacher how that teacher would be interacting with my child, but I have never felt comfortable making evaluation statements on teachers." This board member stated that there was a growing feeling of need for educational expertise within the governance structure of the school.

Even as the board was feeling a need to have an educator as the dean of the school, the dean was feeling that the board no longer trusted her. She resigned in April 1996 following a board decision to not accept her recommendation for the termination of a teacher. Ironically, the board was in the process of transitioning from a "hands-on" to a "hands-off" governance style, through the approval of a set of by-laws that provided role clarification, lines of communication, and prohibitions for board members. The new by-laws gave much more decision-making authority to the dean than heretofore. However, the governing board retained the final authority in decisions to hire and fire staff. One parent summed up her perceptions about the dean's resignation: "I think that during the struggle to make the change from a parent-run to an administrator-run school, trust was lost. The board and the dean could no longer trust each other, and it was the political forces of making that change that caused the rift. We also reached the conclusion that we needed someone with a stronger educational background to take us forward."

Gradually, the school evolved from a school community characterized by blurred roles and responsibilities to a more formal organization. The underlying issue was recognition of the need for a level of trust between parents and staff. Initially, the parents did not trust the teachers or the dean, as was evident by their practice of micromanagement (teacher evaluations, monitoring dress code, etc.) This lack of trust created tension and threatened to tear down the community. Articulation of clear guidelines and boundaries, through the development of the board of director's by-laws, facilitated development of an increased level of trust by providing a definition of roles (parent-governed, not parent-run, school). This development, along with the realization that they needed to trust an educational leader with the operations of the school—although retaining the right to terminate his or her employment—moved the school to the next stage.

After an extensive and expensive search, the board was able to find a candidate with 15 years of experience in education to become the dean of Core Academy. Under the new bylaws, the dean's position would be filled by a person capable of being the leader of the educational program, in charge of day-to-day operations at the school. The role of the board would be to monitor and assess the dean's and the school's performance. Under the leadership of an experienced dean, parents who had desperately wanted control over their school began to trust their teachers and dean to determine educational practices and take responsibility for day to day operations of the school. Core Academy became a parent-governed school that empowered the teachers and the dean but maintained authority to not renew their contracts if they were not living up to expectations and adhering to the mission of the school.

After a couple of years of stable leadership, concern was expressed that CA might be entering into a stage of complacency. However, before long this school was embroiled in another controversy. Conflict arose between Arrowhead District Administration and the dean of CA. The district was opening several more charter schools and hired a district liaison to handle communications between the five charter schools and the district. Before being hired by CA, the dean had been a dean of an international school and was used to a great deal of autonomy. He did not want to change how he communicated with the district; power struggles began between him and the district liaison. There were also feelings at the school that the decision to adopt the Open Court Reading Program was not a decision that the staff, as a whole, embraced. As a result of these conflicts, the board of directors of CA began to question whether the dean was leading the school in the right direction.

The dean's contract was not renewed for another year and the school community faced another leadership challenge. Once again the school was in crisis. Due to concern over the last dean's authoritative style of leadership, as well as weakened district relations, the board's search committee sought the most collaborative candidate for dean of CA. They chose someone who had a doctorate and administrative experience in private schools. This new dean epitomized the opposite end of the control spectrum. He provided very little leadership and had little impact on the school. The governing board, once again, stepped in and took a more hands-on approach because "things were not getting done." Board members were writing reports and dealing with operational issues, because the dean was not. These board members had not experienced the "Dean for the Day" period, but the result of this hands-on involvement was the same: The board gained heightened appreciation for the administrative function of the school through their close involvement. By March 1999 the governing board knew that it would not be renewing the dean's contract.

This time, rather than seeking administrative candidates from outside the school, they searched within. One of CA's original teachers and a former teacher who had just completed her administrative certification were contracted by the board to serve as co-deans. Originally the board determined their roles and titles: Dean of Students and Dean of Curriculum. However, after a short time, the two deans found this division to be ineffective. They proposed to the board that their roles be changed to Dean of the Elementary grades and Dean of Middle School. The board accepted their plan. Because these two individuals had experienced the school as teachers, before moving into a high-profile leadership position, they were able to earn the respect of staff and school community. They described their style as collaborative and open to input, yet they were there to make decisions. They have made some significant changes.

The school had been plagued by teacher turnover. Only one teacher remained from the first year. There are only a few teachers (3 out of 19) who remain from the 1997–1998 and 1999–2000 staff lists. As a result, the Deans began a staff day care as an incentive to keep and attract teachers. The Dean of the Elementary grades stated that when she was teaching at the school it had concerned her that students were not retaining what they had learned. She devised a new delivery system of the "Core" (Core Knowledge Curriculum). Students "write to the Core" in the morning and "return to the Core" in the afternoon. What this means is that there are writing activities centered around Core Knowledge content that begin the day, and the students return to those concepts in some other way at the end of the day. The Dean of the Elementary grades also is bringing a new literacy approach to Core Academy. Open Court is a basal reading curriculum, and she felt that it did not meet the needs of the students, especially the special education students. She is introducing the staff to The Learning Network, which is a diagnostic approach to reading that is based on individual students' needs. The Open Court books will still be used as reading material, but the program will not be rigidly followed. Many decisions are being made that are based on the deans' prior experiences at the school and the needs of the students and staff.

This school has come full circle when it comes to leadership issues. Initially the founders of the school did not place much importance on school administration because they believed that the school could be, and should be, run by parents. When this proved to be ineffective, they looked for someone from the outside to come in and draw the school community together. This proved to be a very difficult task, especially since the Dean's position was political in nature, with no time built in for the new Dean to assimilate into the culture of the school. Now the school is being led by two people from within the school community. The changes that they have initiated are based on what they knew about the school as teachers.

PASSAGES CHARTER SCHOOL

Passages Charter School was modeled after an established alternative ("open") school that had been in existence in Feather County school district for more than 20 years. The Feather County Open School had a waiting list of approximately 1,000 students, indicating a need for an additional open school in the district. Five teachers, some of whom were also parents, carried the project of Passages Charter School (PCS) from initiation, to planning, to implementation. Their desire was to create a unique school that embraced the philosophical principles of progressive education. They did not wish to create a second campus of Feather County Open School.

This core group met frequently (at least once a week) to make plans and craft the charter application. They had many passionate philosophical discussions; the intent of the core group of PCS was to create a "learning community," where teachers would be involved in their own learning: "sharing their joy and excitement with students and other community members." The intent was for teachers at this school to develop their own Personalized Learning Programs, which would focus on helping students discover "how" to learn as opposed to "what" to learn. Teacher empowerment was an ever-present theme: "Staff members will be involved in decisions concerning the development of the school, and they will make decisions in conjunction with students, parents, and interested community members." After a year of planning, the educational program at Passages Charter School was characterized by multiage learning, experiential education, advisement groups, and parental involvement.

The traditional grade levels, with progress measured by report card grades and Carnegie Units, were replaced by a system of learning outcomes, personal learning plans, portfolios, and graduation by committee decision. PCS students would progress through five "seasons" before they were able to graduate:

Season I.   Kindergarten through grade 3.
Season II.   Grades 4 through 6.
Seasons III, IV, and V.   Grades 7 through 12.

The curriculum for each season was composed of 48 discrete learning outcomes, such as "Understand basic concept of probability and statistics and their possible applications." Each student had a personal learning plan created by the student, advisor, and parent. During the first semester at the school, each student wrote a self-assessment on all 48 learning expectations and (from this analysis) developed, with the help from the advisor and parent(s), a personalized learning plan. Whenever a learning activity was completed, the student was expected to write a detailed self-evaluation and obtain a written evaluation from the leader/teacher of that activity. This self-evaluation was based on the student's documentation of his or her activities and an analysis of his or her performance vis-à-vis the targeted learning outcomes/standards; the result was a document called a transcript.

When student, parent(s), and advisor agreed that sufficient progress had been made on the learning expectations, the student completed a transitional project or "passage," to demonstrate readiness for the next developmental level. This project was interdisciplinary and reflected the skills, work habits, and knowledge students must possess in order to move to the next season. All transcripts and other documentation of student progress were kept in their portfolios. A personal graduation committee, including at least one member from outside the school community, met to consider proposals for the five passages required for graduation: logical inquiry, global awareness, career exploration, creative expression, and adventure. The committee would meet again when the student had successfully completed the passages, fulfilled the learning expectations, and written the final transcript. The final transcript was a personal narrative, written by the student, that summarized his or her entire educational experience at the Passages Charter School. The philosophy of the school was that the evaluation of a student's progress should primarily be the responsibility of the student, with the advisor providing support and facilitation as developmentally appropriate.

Growth and Differentiation

Passages Charter School opened on September 6, 1994, with 400+ K–12 students in a former church in a suburban community west of Denver. It was not long after opening that problems with the original vision of the school surfaced. One cause of these struggles was the myth of utopia referred to by Sarason. Before the beginning, the core group believed that students would come to the school eager to learn and would take advantage of all the opportunities and experiences that the school would be able to provide them. The language of the original PCS philosophy and mission statements was filled with this idealism: "We will promote and be advocates for choice, self-direction, experiential learning, shared responsibility, and lifelong learning." In their planning/initiation stage, the members of the core group did not ask the question: What will we do if we are not able to get students to take advantage of the learning opportunities that we provide? The reality of opening a K–12 school forced them to confront this question.

In creating a charter school, a school of choice, the founders assumed that all who enrolled in the school would have already "bought into" the concept of the school and be prepared to take advantage of it. The founders did not stop to think about the possibility that high school students would probably not be leaving their present schools if there had not been some problems associated with their school experiences. Initially, the founders believed that one-fourth of the student population would be at risk; however, when the school opened its doors, at least half of the student body in Grades 7–12 was made up of students who were there because they were failing, had been suspended, or had been encouraged to leave their existing school by counselors, teachers, and/or parents because of their lack of success. There were also many students who were extremely bright and had made the choice to leave their high school because it was too large and stifling. One student commented, "We had kids from one extreme to the other—brains and rejects."

The high percentage of students who did not choose PCS out of enthusiasm for the program (but enrolled because it was their last chance at a high school diploma) was not foreseen by anyone within the school community. A clear example of this lack of foresight could be seen in the activities planned and carried out during the first few days of school. These activities were designed to build community among the students and the staff of the school. One student stated, "The first day we played sports outside all day; the second day we went to see *Forrest Gump* at the movies, and the third day we went to a lake for a picnic and a swim. I thought 'This is school? I can handle this!' " From the first day of school, students who had little interest in school (beyond knowing that they had to be in some school) got the message that this was a "knock-off school." One student who came to the school as his "last chance" commented that when he went to his advisement his advisor told him, "I just want to let you know that I don't take attendance. You come if you want to come." "I said, 'Cool,' and hardly ever came to school that first year." As a consequence, he made no progress toward graduation that year. Conversations with teachers and students revealed that this student's experience was typical of many students that first year. PCS was not prepared to deal with students who had no interest in school. The founders had envisioned PCS as a first-choice school, where students would want to take advantage of the opportunities offered to them.

During the school's second year, the original philosophy was clarified and transformed into a mission statement: "The mission of Passages Charter School is to provide a personalized preK–12 education in a nurturing and challenging environment which will develop the whole person through the advisory system, choice, self-direction, experiential learning, shared responsibility, and lifelong learning." This mission was much more specific about unique school characteristics and reflected shared beliefs about choice, self-direction, experiential learning, shared responsibility, and lifelong learning. But it did not give much indication about the school's desired impact on its students. The school decided that if the students were to be held accountable, they needed goals that were attainable and measurable. The school community worked on altering the mission and educational goals to show that the school was responsible for providing a certain kind of learning environment, as well as expectations of achievement, whereas the students were responsible for taking advantage of the resources and demonstrating achievement. PCS also created and implemented an orientation process to reduce the number of students who were not prepared for the PCS learning environment. This process consisted of requiring prospective students and parents to attend an orientation meeting and students who wished to enroll to complete an individual project. This helped PCS determine which students and families were really interested in the programs the school offered.

A third version of the mission was approved during PCS's fourth year of existence: "The mission of PCS is to provide a personalized pre-K–12 education in a nurturing environment which will develop the whole person by addressing intellectual, creative, and character development." This version added outcomes (intellectual, creative, and character development) that could be measured. The essence of the mission did not change in any of these versions of the mission statement. But the mission statement evolved as the school matured and stakeholders discovered what their mission statement needed to contain in order to provide clear direction for the school community and for prospective students and families.

Forging a Constitution and Problems of Leadership

The charter application included very little detail about the proposed leadership/governance structure of the school. The school's application stated it would employ a coordinator to facilitate the direction set by the school community of parents, students, staff, and community members. This coordinator would be a lead teacher and would participate on the Peer/Staff Evaluation Teams of other staff, but would not be responsible for all evaluations.

It was clear to the core group that the leader of their group, the one who wrote the application, would become the first coordinator of the school. The comments of core group members revealed that once she became the coordinator of the school the interpersonal dynamics changed; she began to act as if she "owned" the school. Sarason described this conflict between being a founder and becoming the leader of the new organization/school in *The Creation of Settings and Future Societies* (1988):

> The leader's opinions and ideas were expected to be given more weight than he would give to those of others. . . . When the leader begins to use power (in the narrower meaning of that word), it is not difficult to observe how the use can defeat the purposes of the leader and others. (p. 239)

One core group member stated: "She became very autocratic and cut out people she didn't agree with. . . . She wanted to call all the shots. She wanted us all to just sit there and go along with it. She started saying things like 'my school.' " This behavior indicated an excessive feeling of power and desire for control. Sarason explained:

> Some leaders react to the obstacles primarily in moral terms, viewing each obstacle as requiring a compromise inimical to their plans and values. They are so identified with the new setting that each obstacle is not viewed as a problem for compromise but as a moral battle in which the good is pitted against the forces of disillusionment and evil. (p. 194)

Once the school opened and the reality of dealing with their at-risk student population became clear, the coordinator responded by intensifying efforts to control the situation. The dream was not proceeding as planned, and instead of reaching out into the school community for guidance and assistance, the coordinator created more walls around her. These walls took the form of "huge discipline policies" and refusals to allow board members to view the financial books. This leader was not able to transition from the utopian dream of "her school" to the reality of a school that had to adjust to the needs of its students. Responding to pressures, this leader's actions split the school into two factions, "excellence and experiential."

The PCS coordinator and several teachers pushed for stricter authoritarian rules in order to deal with the "out-of-control" students (excellence faction). Opposing this group were teachers (experiential faction) who felt students needed room to set limits for themselves and experience natural consequences. The experiential faction was more aligned with the ideals presented in the charter document and became victorious when the coordinator left before the end of the first year. Her departure was brought on by pressure within the organization to share authority.

During the time preceding the coordinator's resignation, the school was in crisis in most areas—financial, morale, academic, enrollment, and so on. The district began to intervene. In November–December 1994, the coordinator was advised by the district to obtain Colorado Not For Profit Corporation status for the school. In order to do this, the school would have to form a new legal entity—a board of directors. The school opened with an Administrative Steering Committee instead of a board of directors. This committee was originally composed of people (parents, staff, and community members) who had been hand picked by the coordinator. Eventually membership was open to anyone. The meetings of the Administrative Steering Committee (ASC) became a "town meeting forum where people came and spoke out without resolution" because there were neither formal structures nor organization. The ASC was designed to assist the coordinator with decision making, but due to the inability of this chaotic organization to formalize decisions, the coordinator retreated and made decisions herself. The district was very concerned about the financial health of the school and was hoping that the new governance structure, the board of directors resulting from the Colorado Not For Profit Corporation status, would save the school. One new board member received a phone call one Saturday afternoon from the Director of Choice Programs in the district: "She called and said your school is cratering [collapsing from within]. You are on the board of directors. What are you going to do about it?"

The newly formed board of directors followed their by-laws and called a community meeting. They told the school community that they were assuming the authority of the school. According to the by-laws, the coordinator was not a member of this board and had to report her actions to them. The coordinator and board of directors tried to work together for a short time, but power struggles over the termination of a teacher's contract and a request to the district for additional administrative personnel (submitted by the coordinator without board approval) resulted in the coordinator's resignation.

Immediately following the resignation, parents and teachers worked together with an administrator who had been sent by the district to act as an interim coordinator to create a governance system for the school that would achieve a balance of power. The resulting governance structure consisted of a coordinator; a board of directors composed of three parents, three teachers, three students, two community members; and a leadership team consisting of five teachers. The leadership team was involved in teacher evaluations, curriculum review, and most professional issues. The new board of directors, composed of representatives from all constituencies within the school community, created a representative forum through which policies, procedures, and communication could be generated that would foster trust among the school community. This board of directors hired a new coordinator, who believed in the mission and had started an alternative school that embraced similar values. This person had a collaborative leadership style and began to pull the segments of the PCS community together. She did not have a personal stake in any of the prior events, so a level of objectivity was attained.

Passages Charter School approached its second year with a great deal of optimism. "Everybody was kind of renewed. Everybody pulled together and worked pretty hard." The teachers of the "excellence faction" left the school at the end of the first year; there was a new coordinator with experience in running a school. It seemed as if the dark clouds were passing for Passages Charter School. However, the members were not in full control of their future. There was another level of accountability located outside of the school. The Feather County Board of Education was in control of the decision to renew Passages Charter School's contract. The school's contract expired in the spring of 1997; the district commissioned a study on the effectiveness of its two charter schools. The report of the external evaluator (hired by the Feather County Board of Directors to conduct the evaluation of PCS) was not positive. The report stated that many students were "spinning their wheels" at PCS because students were able to stay enrolled without making any progress toward graduation. Prior to this report, it had seemed as if the school was in the beginning stages of solidification with the establishment of the board of directors and the clarification of school-wide academic expectations. This solidification process was halted by the threat of closure.

The school immediately began to work on documents and data analysis that identified students making progress and the positive impact the school was having on the students it served. This year-long justification of the school's existence ended in a very emotional school district board meeting, in which several students, parents, and teachers gave passionate testimony about the value of PCS. The Feather County Board of Directors commended the school for the work it was doing to make the school more academically accountable, but remained skeptical about the school's future and granted PCS only a 1-year contract. PCS was told that the school's contract would not be renewed again without more improvement to the academic program. This was a strong action; many families, especially those with elementary-age children, withdrew from the school. One teacher expressed the following basis for her decision to resign: "This school has dealt with too many stressors. The stress of the first year, the stress of an inadequate facility, the stress of inadequate funds, the stress of an older student population that was not conducive to a younger learning environment, and now the stress of being shut down after one more year. It's just not worth it anymore."

The leadership of PCS did not share in this pessimism. In dealing with questions about the validity of the program and the threat of closure, the coordinator always made it a point to "listen to the critics." She used this strategy to mobilize the school toward refinement and growth, stating that the reductions in staff and students (as a result of the 1-year renewal) actually helped the school. "Those who left were not happy and got in the way of us solidifying our program. We now have a staff and a student body that works better together." As a result of the dire situation, several significant changes were made to the academic program of the school in an environment that strongly valued professional autonomy and collaborative decision making with little disagreement and conflict. The school worked to resolve its dilemma of how to turn at-risk adolescents into self-directed learners by (a) clarifying expectations of staff and students, (b) standardization, and (c) reduction of unstructured time. A standardized portfolio and transcript format was designed. High school students were no longer able to design a daily schedule of several classes, but had to choose one "Intensive" (all-day interdisciplinary course) to take every 3½ weeks. Several students commented on the changes: "I spent last year goofing off and made little attempt to figure out this school. Now it is very clear. There is not as much room to goof around as there was before." The threat of closure seemed to help the school deal with many issues that the initial coordinator of the school had been concerned about; change happened as a result of the entire school community coming to understand the issues and work together toward resolution.

The next year (1997–1998) PCS went before the Feather County Board of Directors and presented the changes and supporting data. The tone of this decision was guarded but optimistic. The district was pleased with the way the school had dealt with its challenge and the significant improvements that were made. As a result, PCS's charter was renewed for another

5 years. District board members, however, raised enough concerns that they required another extensive review to be completed after the first 3 years of the 5-year contract.

Since the time of their 5-year renewal, the school has continued to solidify its principles and program design. With the recognition that self-direction is a developmental process, the philosophy of the school has stabilized; however, its enrollment continues to fluctuate. Students continue to have structured learning experiences; the intensives and the portfolio and passage processes get more refined and systematic each year. The day-to-day operation of the school is in the hands of the coordinator. The board of directors has gone through some significant changes. It is working on becoming more focused on policymaking; however, it does not want to let go of the details.

From the beginning, the culture of this school had been such that change had to happen from within. The staff has always been very involved in the leadership of the school through the Leadership Team and teacher representation on the board. This school has also seen considerable staff stability for a charter school—seven teachers remain from the first year of the school. During the school's fifth year, the staff members on the governing board were expressing leadership fatigue, making comments like "I just want to focus on what I am doing with my students" and "I'm tired of thinking of organizational issues." This encouraged discussion at the board level about altering the management structure in order to make it more efficient. All members of the board of directors agreed that the administrative tasks involved in running the school were becoming overwhelming, but there were divergent ideas about how this problem might best be solved. The coordinator requested the creation of a new position—an administrative assistant who would relieve staff members for special projects. The board president was more concerned about the financial viability of the organization and had formulated a job description for a business director whose duties would include financial management, public fiduciary accountability, facility management, and human resource management. After much discussion and analysis, the board of directors approved the business director position.

The coordinator did not feel that this position fit the needs of the school. But, as a result of board action, a business director was hired. This person hit the ground running and began to make recommendations for cuts in salaries and other things. For example, she suggested that the preschool and kindergarten programs be cut because they weren't cost-effective. The staff was not willing to lose this part of the program. She felt that her role was to save the school money; she did not take time to transition in and to understand the culture of the school. This school was filled with strong personalities, who were passionate about student-directed learning and experiential teaching. As a result of the turmoil created, the business director resigned before the year was finished.

These events also led to the board president's resignation. The staff members had communicated concern over being stretched in too many ways, but they were resistant to creating a more defined management structure. Presently, the school is transitioning between a collaborative organizational structure with loosely defined internal roles and responsibilities to a more clearly defined organizational structure and delineation of authority. This transition comes out of a recognized need for more structure and clarity of roles and responsibility and will be balanced with a desire to minimize any significant loss of collaboration and professional autonomy.

OPPORTUNITY PREP SCHOOL

The founder of Opportunity Preparatory School (OPS) wanted to serve a specific student population; he targeted students (Grade 9–12) who were at risk of dropping out of school or who had already dropped out. The school was located in the heart of Colorado Springs and was founded by a city official whose dream was to create a school that would supply the support services necessary to tear down the barriers between at-risk students and a college education. He believed in the power of education to transform lives; education had transformed his. His dream was that students who were disadvantaged and saw the value in a college education would come to his school and be motivated to achieve. "Give the kids the basic tools and they will find their way. Traditional schools are not giving a lot of the kids the basic tools."

The founder saw students as the "customers" of the school. He felt students should be empowered to make choices; the teacher's role was that of a salesman, making them want to buy the product. He felt that at-risk kids had been shut out of educational opportunities by the traditional system. He wanted to create a school that would give them an advantage. The Opportunity Preparatory School grew from these beliefs and the founder's burning desire to serve disadvantaged or at-risk kids by reengaging those who had dropped out, had been kicked out or "convinced out," and giving them the opportunity to become successful citizens. The founder of this school believed that at-risk kids should be exposed to, and required to master, a high level of academic content. This would give them the means to get to college, which would open the doors of opportunity for these students.

Opportunity Preparatory School opened in August 1995, serving 120 youth, Grades 9–12. The school had a student/teacher ratio of 20/1 and a student dress code. Originally students were placed in the school on a first-come, first-serve basis (later a lottery was implemented) once it was determined that they fit the "high-risk" and/or "at-risk" criteria. Any student who was in jeopardy of dropping out of high school was eligible for placement on the school's waiting list. From the very beginning there has been a waiting list of at-risk students who want to attend OPS.

The creation of this school was the result of an unusual joint venture; the city council joined the local school district to make OPS possible. The founder was the Colorado Springs Director of the Industrial Training Division, which administered the Jobs Training Program funded by the U.S. Department of Labor's Job Training Partnership Act (JTPA). For several years he and his assistant had developed educational programs outside of the school system for at-risk students. They were frustrated by the lack of success of these programs and felt that if they had these students in their own school full-time, they could really make a difference. Together, they crafted the charter application and education design for Opportunity Preparatory School. The school's educational program was ambitious; it consisted of a college preparatory curriculum (44 credits) for all students. The school was located in the same building (a renovated elementary school) as the Industrial Training Division of the City of Colorado Springs. As a result, the students of OPS were able to take advantage of many JTPA programs and support services while they were at school. The school used JTPA services (tutoring, mentoring, etc.) to help students overcome barriers to learning. The goal was to provide at-risk students with the resources that they needed to succeed academically. The unique partnership between a city government and a public school district provided a means to do this.

As briefly mentioned earlier, the curriculum goals and objectives were the same for all students. Students were offered a college preparatory curriculum, with 80% mastery required to receive credit for a course. Forty-four credits were required in categories that included English, math, social studies, humanities, science, and practical arts. Graduation was not contingent upon the number of years spent at the school. OPS used the Comprehensive Competencies Program (CCP) to provide the base delivery system for academics and for assessment of state standards. CCP was a computer-based program, organized by high school courses and assessed by competency tests that followed each unit within the course; it was modified from a program developed for adults to use in preparing for the Graduate Educational Development Examination (GED). The CCP courses were divided into the four content areas (math, English, science, and social studies) with one teacher for each area.

However, the CCP coursework was only half of the students' course requirements. Each course (English I, Algebra I, World History, etc.) also included a seminar that was designed to build critical and higher order thinking skills. This aspect of the school was modeled after the design of the Socratic seminars that Mortimer Adler described in *The Paideia Program*. Thus, OPS students spent a portion of their day working through a "canned program" (CCP) at their own pace, with teachers available to assist them. This aspect of the curriculum was designed to enable a motivated student to quickly make up for lost time, an important consideration for at-risk students who often came to the school lacking the academic background needed for high school success. The other portion of the day was spent in seminars (Paideia Program) centered on projects and interdisciplinary units. Mandatory instructional methods for the seminar classes included didactic, coaching, and Socratic teaching. Experts were contracted to teach courses outside of the core content areas, such as physical education, leadership, Spanish, and others.

The founder's belief that students were the customers of the school was reflected in the school's flexibility in regard to design and accumulation of course credits. The individual student's ability, effort, and desire to earn credits controlled his or her progress. Students would receive a certificate once a credit was earned; a running record was kept of each student's progress toward graduation. In order to address the "at-risk" characteristics of these students, each student developed an Individual Service Strategy (ISS) with his or her advisor. This addressed short-term and long-term social and educational goals. Each student met monthly with his or her academic advisor. Parent/guardian attendance was required at these meetings. Supportive services (child care, bus passes, medical and dental services, etc.) and case management were paid for by JTPA when students qualified for services.

The basic belief behind the creation of Opportunity Preparatory School was that education provided the path out of poverty and into a successful, productive life. This belief was reflected in the practices of the school and in the mission statement: "Provide a quality education in an environment that encourages innovative modes of teaching and learning in order to empower each student to develop academically, socially, and physically as a global citizen of the 21st century."

Growth and Differentiation

This school design and mission statement provided the framework for the opening of Opportunity Preparatory School. However, this mission statement did not fully convey the beliefs and vision of the founder. Terms such as *innovative modes of teaching and learning* did not provide much direction for the families or staff about what to expect from the school. The goal stated in the mission was for students to become global citizens of the 21st century without mentioning the intent of the founder that all students should be prepared to go to college. This omission reflected a lack of consensus about the school's purpose. At the time of the study, there were two prevalent philosophies among staff members at the school:

1. This was a school of last resort, or a "holding tank" for students for whom school was compulsory, either because of their age or because of decisions made within the court system.
2. The school was a fast track to college for students who wanted to accelerate their passage through high school and found the "seat time" requirement of high school frustrating.

Neither of these extremes reflected a great deal of commitment to the founder's belief in the school's ability to transform lives.

In addition to the staff's lack of common vision, many of the students who entered OPS did not have the prerequisite skills to achieve in a college prep environment, nor did they have the desire to go to college. Most students and families saw the school as a means to an end: a high school diploma. This reality led to disenchantment among those teachers who wanted to be able to transform dropouts into potential college graduates. The teachers had come to this school to change lives, whereas most of the students just wanted "credits" to get out of high school. This lack of consensus regarding the mission and purpose of the school caused much conflict and tension in the school.

As with Passages Charter School, the Opportunity Preparatory School was founded on a utopian dream. The founder felt that "Once we give at-risk kids the opportunity to attend a school that is self-paced and filled with supportive services to deal with their barriers they will be able to be successful." This dream was reinforced by assumptions about the results of choice: "All OPS students made a choice to be here, so they will fully participate." This rosy vision kept the founder from recognizing the reality that many kids who are at risk do not see the need of attending school. This is part of the reason why they have been unsuccessful in other school settings. Many parents and students saw the school not as a choice, but as a "last resort." These students entered the school with a "draftee" attitude; for them, school was compulsory, not a choice. They just wanted a diploma and had no interest in attending college. Other students did see the school as a fast track to college; these students wanted to accelerate their passage through high school and found the "seat time" requirements of high schools frustrating. This split in student expectations (approximately 80% "last resort" and 20% "fast track to college") caused the school to develop a dual character.

Most teachers who accepted positions at OPS shared the founder's vision before school began; they felt they would be facilitators for student learning. However, once they encountered the reality of students' educational backgrounds and abilities, some of the teachers began to think of OPS as an alternative school that focused on helping students develop more positive attitudes about school and themselves—instead of a college prep school that emphasized academics. Other teachers struggled to maintain the college prep environment. This duality created confusion for parents, teachers, and students; as one teacher stated, "This school has two faces."

Forging a Constitution and Problems of Leadership

The utopian vision was not modified during the school's first year because the governance structure of the school was located outside of the school itself. Essentially, the Training Division of the city governed the school; all teachers were city employees. Originally, the management team consisted of the principal; later a Dean of Students position was added. There was an accountability committee with parent, teacher, student, community member, and city council representation. However, this committee functioned in an advisory, not leadership/governance, capacity.

The founder became the first principal of the school; however, this role was in addition to his full time job with the city as the director of the Jobs Training Program. At that time he was running approximately 35 programs for JTPA, so the leadership of OPS was 1/36 of his total job. "Starting the school was just a pet project of his; it was just one more project to add on." As a result of his lack of time, once teachers had been hired, the founder possessed very little understanding of how the school really worked. Teachers commented that the kids did not know him; he hardly ever visited the classrooms. His salary did not come from the operating budget of the school but was totally based on grants from the federal jobs program. He felt that success for the school was dependent on its small size, competent teachers, and students with families who had chosen OPS. With all of these things in place, he felt that there was really no need for a traditional principal.

This lack of leader involvement allowed competing visions to flourish in the school. The founder maintained his vision of a college prep school for dropouts, or those at risk of dropping out, because he was not dealing with the day-to-day realities. In contrast, teachers felt that most of the students were not ready to "purchase" the services provided at the school. The teachers had to do a lot of nonacademic work in order to get kids to "buy into" the school and to meet minimal attendance requirements. Some teachers even questioned whether the school would be able to effect a change in the students' future social status. They questioned whether the emphasis should be on giving students life skills as opposed to college preparatory skills. A math teacher began to focus on such things as calculating interest, instead of proving theorems. This approach was far from the "prep school" vision for the school. Absence of leadership aggravated the growing duality of purpose present.

The knowledge that the principal had the ultimate authority over decisions about their work and their jobs created a sense of distrust, because those within the school were aware of his ignorance of their reality. As a staff member said at the time, "We feel that we are disposable. At an Open House [the founder] began to talk to the parents about the fact that he doesn't hire union teachers and that he can fire any one of us at any time." By the end of the first year, 5 of the 18 instructors had quit and 1 had been fired. The leader's unilateral authority, added to the fact that he provided no direct leadership or supervision to the school, created a feeling of helplessness among the teachers. One teacher summed up the staff's feeling: "There is a feeling that we are flying blind with the administration."

The school did create some governance structures in the form of the position of Dean of Students and the creation of a discipline code, but there was no vehicle to deal with grievances. The staff began to have meetings, but the consensus among the staff was that the principal and his assistant made their decisions as if the meetings had never happened. The lack of a school constitution that would delineate powers and provide a vehicle for grievances eventually resulted in the removal of the leader from his position. The city was receiving many complaints about the lack of support, unilateral decision making, and authoritarian leadership present at the school. An investigation was launched and the principal of OPS chose early retirement at the beginning of the second year of the school. This left the school with no one in charge.

The staff member who had been the instigator of the staff meetings became the principal of the school. This new principal had a very different approach to school leadership. She had been a teacher at the school and knew the need for support and direction. She was very visible in the school. Her office was on the same floor as most of the classes. She had regular meetings with the staff and engaged them in an open dialogue about the issues that the teachers faced in dealing with their at-risk students. Staff development was a priority because many of the teachers at OPS were inexperienced; a great deal of time was spent on classroom management. The principal coached teachers and individually counseled them, provided staff development activities, and conducted staff meetings. She and the staff worked on developing course outlines that included both CCP and Paideia requirements for credits. Course outlines with standards and expectations for performance were also written for the contracted courses.

There had been complaints that the former administration made too many promises to students and did not hold them accountable. The new principal stated:

> I think one of the things is that we don't promise the world . . . what we say we can do is what we will do. Before, students were told things like, "You can take any class that you want, take all of the time you want, anything you want to do and then arrangements will be made for you to do it." The kids were then not held accountable for following through with their choices. This has changed. We now follow up on the students and do not promise them everything.

The school was slowly and methodically building the constitutional structures that it previously lacked.

The vision and mission of the school were also clarified. The school is centered around the original mission statement: "Provide a quality education in an environment that encourages innovative modes of teaching and learning in order to empower each student to develop academically, socially, and physically as a global citizen of the 21st century." The college prep component of the school is still present; however, it is now seen as just one option or choice available to students. It is understood that not all OPS students will attend college; teachers are oriented to understand their role as a teacher and advisor. There had been problems where some teachers were getting too connected to students and losing their objective stance. As of 2000, the principal was trying very hard to emphasize the teacher's role of making parents and students aware of expectations and providing them options instead of answers. There is a strong focus on promoting individual responsibility through a balance of choice and structure, along with consistent expectations.

The new principal, with staff input and support, has instituted an incentive program for attendance and has increased the emphasis on typical high school rites of passage, along with symbols and activities like class rings, yearbooks, student council, newspaper, and so on. She stated that these things are really important to these students. "These kids are able to participate in things here that they were not able to in a larger school. Here they can go right to the top."

The school seems to have withstood the leadership crisis well, moving into a stage of solidification and cohesion. The fact that the new principal came from within, and was a person who knew the culture of the school, had a positive impact on the school's ability to move beyond the crisis and into a stage of improvement and growth. The district renewed the OPS charter for another 5 years in February 2000. Now the school is facing a new challenge: The city is no longer responsible for the governance of the school. The school has formed its own board of directors composed of three parents, three community members, one representative from the education community, one representative from the judicial community, and one representative from the city government. The design of the board purposefully seeks to bring resources and expertise into the school as well as to involve parents in school governance. This board takes on the responsibility of governance for the 2000–2001 school year. One advantage that OPS has in dealing with the often turbulent process of school site governance is that, unlike most charter schools, its operations have already withstood the test of time and crisis. Additionally, unlike the other two schools in the study, OPS was created to deal with the social/educational needs of dropouts and potential dropouts rather than out of a desire for a different educational option for the average student. The school thus has a clearly identifiable purpose; each formerly "at-risk" student who graduates is a success story in his or her own right. This strong sense of purpose should guide the development of the governance process.

CONCLUSIONS

Problems of Growth and Differentiation and the Viability of the Original Mission

All charter schools as new settings begin as an idea. This idea may share commonalities (curricular approach, size, student/teacher ratio, etc.) with other schools, but the essence/culture of the school is unique because of its history and the individuals who developed the initial idea. All who enter a charter school, either as students or employees, have an opportunity to examine this idea and make a choice. This study made no attempt to determine which curriculum or organizational structure was "best," focusing instead on the degree to which there was a common set of values/philosophy among those involved in each school and how congruent the present set of values was with the initial vision for the school. As Larry Cuban pointed out in an article entitled "A Tale of Two Good Schools" (1998), "The century-long war of words over traditional vs. progressive schooling is a cul-de-sac, a dead end argument that needs to be retired once and for all."

To what extent had the ideas that created Core Academy, Passages Charter School, and Opportunity Preparatory School remained viable as they developed into mature schools? Seymour Sarason's work indicates that too often in the creation of new settings the power of the initial idea/conception to provide the motivating power to launch the setting is overestimated. Hidden behind the high hopes of the initiation/planning and honeymoon periods are differences in interpretation and priorities that tend *not* to be discussed, lest they lead to discord. Yet these differences cannot lie buried forever. Inevitably, in dealing with the struggles of the day-to-day running of the school, these differences surface, often in circumstances that are not well suited to a rational discussion of choices and priorities. In those settings where no "constitutional" arrangement or rules and procedures for hammering out differences had been agreed on, differences smoldered beneath the surface, causing resentment and discord. Moreover, struggles over the school's vision became worse as organizational growth and differentiation added more people to the core group.

Problems related to growth and differentiation were well documented in all three Colorado charter schools. Each school began as a document (charter) that described the school's mission, educational program, organizational structure, financial plan, facility plan, and so on. This document was the guiding and unifying force for the core group that petitioned the district to grant the charter for the school. Before the opening of the school there tended to be clarity of purpose. However, a school cannot function with only the members of the core group. New teachers, students, and parents must be added. With this growth and differentiation come the greatest challenges of implementation.

One method of determining the impact of growth and differentiation on the original vision for the school is to assess the level of consensus concerning educational values expressed by the schools' constituents. Initially, a sense of consistent values/philosophy was more observable at Core Academy and Passages Charter School (Grades K–6) than at Opportunity Preparatory School. The philosophies of these first two schools were more clearly defined. The families that sought these schools either understood what these orientations meant when their children entered the school or, after entering the school community, reached a decision as to whether or not the school was a good fit for them. The parents at CA desired a content-rich program with more traditional educational outcomes. Many parents of K–6 students at PCS had had their children in Montessori programs or were on the waiting list for the Feather County Open School, which offered a similar educational environment. There were also some PCS families of Grade 7–12 students who sought an "experiential" form of education, although many Grade 7–12 students were just seeking a school from which they could graduate.

In contrast, Opportunity Preparatory School was created for a specific type of student—the disadvantaged, the unsuccessful, the dropout. These students were the focus of the school; however, the adults connected with the school differed as to what was best for them. The founder had a dream that he would be able to provide the *means* (a small, self-paced, college prep school with many supportive services), so that a specific *end* (disadvantaged kids attaining a college prep education) would become a reality. Events during the school's first year indicated that this dream was not shared by a majority of the students of OPS. A similar sobering realization occurred for the founder of PCS. The founders of both OPS and PCS began with a myth of utopia. The founder of PCS believed that the K–12 school would be filled with students who were self-directed learners and had a passion for learning. The original vision of both schools significantly changed in response to the actual student population and the impact the schools found they could have as far as transforming the characteristics of students.

In addition, both PCS and OPS suffered from a lack of structure. As Sergiovanni pointed out in *Building Community in Schools* (1994), in order for a school to be considered a community there must be shared values that provide an "educational platform" (progressive or traditional education, college prep, etc.) on which to build curriculum and relationships within the school. Moreover, this platform alone would not be able to sustain the school; maintenance of a consistent platform requires oversight and management. Oversight/management requires a balance between discipline and discretion. This balance between discretion (freedom) and discipline (rules/structures) could be achieved by providing specific guidelines, often in the form of expectations for student performance, that schools and individual teachers could use to evaluate whether decisions were consistent with the shared values reflected in the educational platform (mission). In order to be effective, the guidelines should be "firm enough and directional enough to shape school and individual teachers' decisions without determining what those decisions will be" (Sergiovanni, 1994, p. 103).

A healthy balance between discipline and discretion eventually evolved in each school. The more student-centered schools, PCS and OPS, increased the level of discipline through more clearly defining their expectations of students and staff. For example, PCS standardized the portfolio and transcript format and expectations, and teachers had to clearly describe the content and student outcomes of each intensive. OPS developed course outlines with specific student performance expectations. At both of these schools, teachers were given freedom to implement their programs as long as they stayed within the schools' established expectations. The more traditional school, CA, also added structures in the form of new bylaws. But the purpose of these structures was to lessen parental control over the operations of the school and allow more administrative and teacher discretion.

Each school spent its first 3–5 years clarifying its mission and/or hammering out how it would go about implementing its values. In each case the founders of the school were so caught up in the euphoria of actualizing a dream that they failed to foresee the struggles they would experience over maintaining, justifying, and developing the school's mission. The passage of time, along with the influence of growth and differentiation, gradually (or, at certain moments, more quickly) altered the original vision of each school.

Lack of a Constitution and Problems of Leadership

As described earlier, problems quickly surfaced after each school opened its door. This led to a high level of conflict within, among, and between the different segments of the school community (parents, teachers, students, staff). Unfortunately, none of the schools in this study had prepared for these inevitable conflicts before the school opened; none had developed operational procedures suitable for dealing with the inevitable grievances, failures of communication, controversies over discipline, and so on that emerged during the school's first year.

Sarason pointed out that this is a possibly fatal flaw of new settings; a new setting must "forge a constitution" (develop rules and procedures) by which all will be governed; the initial vision/mission will not be enough to hold the setting together under the pressures created by normal differences that arise in the course of the setting's day-to-day operations. This constitution would provide a way to deal with unforeseen problems and a forum for examining and resolving them. At CA, PCS, and OPS, the lack of a constitution meant that controversial issues were handled without a shared understanding of procedure and due process. This created an emotionally charged atmosphere where people took sides rather than working together. The forging of a constitution through the development of guidelines, rules, or structures (as well as the definition and boundaries of roles to resolve disputes) had not been addressed by the founders of these settings because they naively believed that everyone who entered their setting would be united around their cause; they assumed that this unity of purpose would maintain harmony. Later on, the founders were too busy dealing with the details involved in opening a new school to consider or give attention to determining lines of authority (roles) and appropriate vehicles for communication.

Each school experienced several leadership changes during its first few years; at each school this led to a period of crisis when the top administrator (dean, educational director, principal) left or was fired. Core Academy has had four deans during its 7 years of existence, Passages Charter School has had two coordinators during 6 years, and Opportunity Preparatory School has had two principals during 5 years. The problems leading to and/or emanating from these crises of leadership centered on the struggle for power within the settings.

Initially, the founding groups at all three schools were not concerned about school leadership; each group chose the most involved, or strongest, founder to lead the school. These decisions proved to be problematic. Sarason (1972) provided an explanation for the lack of success of founders taking on the leadership role within these schools: "In the mind of the leader it will be his setting, an expression of him, a fulfillment of his ideas and dreams" (p. 191). This leader/founder also regarded himself or herself as somehow superior to the group that he or she was going to lead. Feelings of ownership and superiority resulted in leadership behaviors that were naive, controlling, and possessive.

The parents who founded CA had come to feel that they better understood what their children needed than did the professional educators with whom they had dealt. In addition, CA was "their school," where parents were to be in control. This led to micromanagement, conflict, and organizational instability. The founders of both OPS and PCS suffered from the fantasy of leadership described by Sarason (1972): "Everything and everyone will fall into place precisely according to *his* plans" (p. 191). The result was, in both cases, that when faced with the reality of the new setting and the difficulties of drawing the setting together around the original dream, these founders resorted to the exertion of power. The teachers at OPS expressed concerns about "speaking out" during their interviews. Their apprehension was based on the "lurking power" of a principal who was seldom present but held the security of their jobs in his hands. The teachers at PCS who had worked with the founder talked about their plans for "revolution" against her authority. Each new setting had a revolt of sorts when its founder was fired or forced out.

Chris Argyris (1991), in an article "Teaching Smart People How to Learn," stated that business success depends on the ability to learn, but most people/organizations don't know how to learn. They excel at solving problems created by external forces, but they fail to recognize that to learn, one also needs to look inward to one's own behavior. The founders of all three schools were not able to do this; their actions indicated that they thought the problems were the result of a lack of understanding of their vision, not reactions to their behavior. In other words, they did not hold themselves accountable as individuals. However, the growth and improvement seen in the three charter schools after the founders left revealed that all three schools, as organizations, had developed the capacity to learn from their critics.

In each case the organizational capacity to learn was heightened by the state of crisis created when the leaders left. The schools had to rally around and develop more structure to fill the void. The results of their efforts were seen in Core Academy's development of by-laws; Passages Charter School's development of the board of directors, its revisions to the mission statement, and its revised expectations of students; Opportunity Preparatory School's staff development efforts and delineation of course expectations. The crises forced each school to work toward clear and accountable roles as well as the creation of a method for all those within the school community to share concerns and criticisms productively; thus the process of building a "constitution" had begun. Sarason used the U.S. Constitutional Convention as an example of a new setting that was successful because it developed a process by which individuals would be able to disagree without being reduced to destructive power struggles.

The experiences of Core Academy demonstrate the difficulty that parent-governed schools may experience in finding suitable educational leaders. The history of CA shows that ground is often lost when a new leader enters the school. Each new dean at CA brought in his or her own conception of what the school needed, or didn't need, and altered the school's forward progression. The school's last leadership decision may be the most significant one. Instead of seeking for answers from outside the school community, they sought within. The decisions made by the two new deans of the school reflect purposeful change based on the school's prior experiences. Both PCS and OPS have had consistent leadership since the departure of the founder, and both schools have shown progress toward consistent goals and the development of educational structures. As of January 2000, individuals who have lived the history and culture of their respective schools continue to serve as administrators at all three schools.

RECOMMENDATIONS

The original mission statements of the three schools proved inadequate because they lacked operational definitions and prioritization. A mission statement should be based on educational beliefs and values and answer the questions: What is the purpose of this school? What are we trying to accomplish? If the resulting statement of purpose (mission) contains multiple elements, the elements need to be prioritized. This prioritization will help those involved in governance of the school with their decision making. Prioritization provides direction and rationale for decision making. Decisions and policies will be seen as more purposeful and reasoned by the school community. Without prioritized goals, a governing board struggles to make consistent decisions and may be tempted to take arbitrary actions. For example, if a strong academic program is given a higher priority than athletics, then a proposal to build a climbing wall will be put on the back burner if one of the academic programs has a stronger need.

The terms used in the mission statement to describe the school's purpose need to be clearly defined. Often phrases and terms used in mission statements have multiple connotations, which can lead to multiple perceptions of how they should be put into practice. For example, to some an emphasis on creating "lifelong learners" may mean providing the students with strong skill-based instruction so that they will be comfortable in academic settings; for others it might mean making learning situations fun, so that children are motivated to learn. One way to achieve more clarity about the educational program of a school is to write a narrative that answers the following questions about terms used in describing the mission:

- What do we mean by ____?
- What will ____ look like?
- How will we know if we attain our mission?

The answers to these questions will provide a more comprehensive picture of the aims of a particular school because they require one to consider how the mission will be put into practice. Discussions about mission and practice should occur before the charter school opens its doors (initiation/planning stage) and again after the school has opened (implementation stage). The transition between idea and practice is often problematic; discrepancies between vision and reality should be examined on a regular basis (twice a year), so that the school is able to make minor adjustments along the way regarding either mission or practice.

All schools benefit from strong leadership and clearly defined missions, but the need to develop a "constitution" also seems to be critical for new settings. This need was clearly seen in all three schools. Without clear roles and divisions of authority—and a process to deal with problems and grievances—power struggles developed, bringing on a period of crisis. Achieving an effective balance of power can be especially problematic for charter schools because they are created by constituents who were not typically in positions of power within the public school system (parents, teachers, community members) and who were therefore seeking power and control.

The establishment of constitutions (by-laws and policies of the board of directors) in two schools within this study (CA and PCS) allowed trust to develop and the power struggles to subside. What is a constitution? A constitution is a set of rules by which the organization will be governed. Constitutions should define:

- Lines of communication (Who you go to for . . . ?).
- Grievance procedures for parents, teachers and students (Who you talk to when you have a problem or a concern?).
- Roles and responsibilities of administration.

- Roles and responsibilities of board of directors.
- Roles and responsibilities of staff.
- Roles and responsibilities of parents.
- Roles and responsibilities of students.
- Roles and responsibilities of committees.

Most of the problems having to do with balance of powers occurred, in the charter schools in this study, between the administration and the board of directors. New charter schools should assume that they will encounter difficulty with governance issues. These problems often center on blurred lines of authority (What is the role of the board? What is the role of the administration?) and multiple roles (some parents are board members, administrators, or teachers as well as parents). Many school administrators are not used to reporting to, and answering directly to, a governing board. Similarly, most charter school board members are new to this role. Given their unfamiliarity with this type of school site governance, the administration and board should perceive their work as involving shared leadership with the school administrator responsible for management and the board responsible for accountability. To prevent unnecessary conflicts, boards and administrators should spend a great deal of time discussing their expectations and defining their roles. The governance texts by John Carver (*Boards That Make a Difference,* 1997a, and *Reinventing Your Board,* 1997b) provide a framework to assist a board with the delineation of a constitution. There are also many resources for nonprofit boards that are referenced on the National Center for Nonprofit Boards web site (http://www.ncnb.org).

An example of what the governance section of a hypothetical charter school constitution (listing and defining roles and responsibilities) might look like is provided in Table 3.1. Each school should design its own constitution based on its mission, beliefs, history, demographics, etc. The process of delineating a list like the one above can be as beneficial as the outcome. Through dialogue about roles and responsibilities, collective understanding is increased. The documentation of the constitution is essential for the continuation of the governance structure after the original parties are no longer on the board and/or at the school.

The purpose of these structures and protocols is to diminish power struggles and to create a sense of professional community by clarifying expectations and accountability. Once established, the constitution should be published and consistently followed. The constitution should be reviewed periodically to determine if it is providing enough structure to allow the balance of power and degree of trust that are necessary for the members of the school community to work together in pursuit of their mission. Establishment of a constitution will not prevent conflict, but

TABLE 3.1
Governance Section of a Hypothetical Charter School Constitution

Board of Directors Roles and Responsibilities	*School Director Roles and Responsibilities*
Mission/direction	Mission/direction
• Establish, support, and monitor the school's mission, charter, goals and objectives, and contract	• Provide input and data to the governing board concerning the implementation of the school's mission, charter, goals, and objectives
Accountability	Accountability
• Establish and monitor the desired results, priorities, goals, and objectives for school performance	• Provide leadership for the annual accountability process, work with the governing board to establish priorities, goals, and objectives for the school, and collect, analyze and report data to evaluate performance according to the priorities, goals and objectives
Curriculum	Curriculum
• Establish academic and nonacademic goals for student performance	• Coordinate and lead the faculty in the design, implementation, evaluation, and critique of the school's curriculum as a means to accomplish the desired academic and nonacademic goals
Personnel	Personnel
• Hire and evaluate the performance of the school director according to the policies of the governing board	• Establish and implement the hiring, appraisal, and dismissal procedures for the teaching and support staff in accordance with policy, as determined by the board of directors
Budget	Budget
• Set priorities for and provide a process (calendar) for the approval and periodic review of the annual school budget	• Develop operating budget that is reflective of board priorities and provide financial management of the approved budget on a daily basis
Management	Management
• Develop, implement, and monitor board policies that define board process and authority over the school	• Develop, implement, and monitor staff and student policies that are aligned with governing board policy

rather will provide a means for conflict to be dealt with in a constructive way so that the school can continue to focus on the pursuit of its mission.

Charter schools begin as an idea, based on an educational philosophy or a vision of schooling. This study examined the issues that three schools faced in making the transition from vision to practice. It is hoped that the information provided in this study will provide insight into the problems faced by the founders of charter schools and ease the transition from paper to practice for initiators of future charter schools. It is noble to plan an educational environment that will make a difference, but it is foolish to proceed without becoming aware of, and planning for, the predictable problems encountered by those who have gone before.

REFERENCES

Adler, M. (1984). *The Paideia Program: An Educational Syllabus.* New York: Collier Books.
Argyris, C. (1991, May–June). Teaching smart people how to learn. *Harvard Business Review,* pp. 99–109.
Carver, J. (1997a). *Boards that make a difference.* San Francisco: Jossey-Bass.
Carver, J. (1997b). *Reinventing your board.* San Francisco: Jossey-Bass.
Clayton Foundation. (1997). *1997 Colorado charter schools evaluation study.* Denver: Colorado Department of Education.
Cuban, L. (1998, January 28). A tale of two good schools. *Education Week,* p. 48.
Sarason, S. (1988). *The creation of settings and the future societies.* Cambridge, MA: Brookline Books.
Sergiovanni, T. (1994). *Building community in schools.* San Francisco: Jossey-Bass.

Chapter 4

Politics Versus the Best of Intentions: A Case Study of a School–University Collaboration

Catharine T. Perry
University of Houston

> *Practices like graded classrooms structure schools in a manner analogous to the way grammar organizes a language. Neither the grammar of schooling nor the grammar of speech needs to be consciously understood to operate smoothly. Indeed, much of the grammar of schooling has become so well established that it is typically taken for granted as just the way schools are. (Tyack & Tobin, 1994, p. 454)*

As Tyack and Tobin pointed out, the basic "grammar" of schooling, the regular structures and rules that organize the work of instruction, has remained remarkably stable over the decades. At every level and subject, teachers have been expected to monitor and control students, assign tasks to them, and ensure that they accomplish them. Periodically, innovators have challenged the accepted model of schooling, proposing that individualized instruction replace batch processing, or that specialized subjects be merged into core courses, or that the textbook-centered approach be replaced by a more experiential style of teaching. However, most of these challenges to the accepted grammar of schooling have soon faded or become marginalized. Why?

This chapter uses a case study approach to investigate the organizational dynamics that can cause innovative schools to revert to the familiar patterns. The focus of the study is a Model School set up as a collaborative effort between a highly selective private university and a large urban school district. The goal of the collaboration was to alter traditional educational patterns in two fundamental ways: (a) by replacing age-graded, self-contained classrooms with multiage grouping and teachers who worked together in teams, and (b) by bringing together K–8 educators and university professors in an attempt to strengthen teaching and improve student learning in the humanities and the sciences. Extensive effort went into the planning of the Model School. Foundations and corporations provided extensive resources. Nationally recognized experts were brought in as consultants during the 3½-year planning period. Arguably, if any new school were able to break out of the traditional mold, this one had that potential.

CONCEPTUAL FRAMEWORK

So, what happens when an "irresistible force" (a high-powered school–university collaboration) meets an "immovable object" (the established "grammar" of schooling)? The account that follows explores the fundamental paradox inherent in any attempt to establish a creative new setting within a bureaucratic, custodial organization. The lens is supplied by Seymour Sarason's book *The Creation of Settings and the Future Societies* (1988), which describes predictable stages in the growth of a new setting. These stages are loosely characterized as Initiation/Planning, Honeymoon, Implementation, Crisis, and Aftermath.

Sarason argues that when a new setting fails, not only were the seeds of that failure probably existent in the beginning stages, but the setting's chances of success could have been predicted. Internal problems encountered in the creation of a setting are seen as centering on two related tasks: (a) the "forging of the constitution by which the setting will be governed," or determining how lines of authority and communication will be established, and (b) "growth and differentiation" or the impact that new people entering the setting have on the original vision/idea. Too often the need to nurture the personal growth of all participants is ignored. External problems center around the fact that a new setting "can arise from and exist within a context of existing settings over which it has little, and frequently no, control" and where competition for resources and prestige can render relations with existing settings extremely problematic.

How the Model School dealt with these internal and external challenges during each of the five stages outlined by Sarason forms the heart of this study. Interviews, on-site observations, and archival materials were used to examine whether the early history of the Model School followed the predicted pattern. However, the literature on school–university partnerships, along with that on the culture and politics of school districts, also provided valuable insights into the challenges that the creators of the Model School had taken on.

BUREAUCRATIC AND SOCIAL CONTEXT

New public schools are continuously being established across the country, many of them incorporating cutting-edge educational theory concerning empowerment, community, motivation, and teaching techniques. This process of creating new settings is critical to a society; it is the means by which a society renews itself (Gardner, 1981). Moreover, collaborative efforts, such as that described here, offer one of the most tempting avenues for such social renewal.

> What we need, and what seems to be emerging in some of our communities, is something new—networks of responsibility drawn from all segments coming together to create a wholeness that incorporates diversity. (Gardner, 1997, p. iii)

The Model School described here attempted to do just that, bringing university faculty and K–8 teachers committed to innovation together with a highly diverse student population.

Partnerships between schools and institutions of higher education have existed since the beginning of public education, usually in connection with the activities of teacher training institutions. In recent years there has been a trend toward fostering contextualized theory and theoretically informed practice by developing professional communities between schools and universities (Darling-Hammond & McLaughlin, 1995). The Holmes Group (1986, 1990, 1995), a consortium of universities with teacher training programs, has encouraged the organization of "professional development schools," where collaboration between professionals, university faculty, and students can make possible supervised clinical experiences for teachers and other education professionals. Such centers provide opportunities for preservice preparation and career-long professional development, as well as for collaborative research.

Lawson and Hooper-Briar (1994) noted that the ideal behind creation of the land grant universities was to build institutions that would be responsive to societal needs and aspirations. These institutions would seem particularly well suited to address public school education. However, institutional norms do not facilitate collaboration. Knapp and others (1993) noted that collaborative interprofessional practice challenges the fundamental assumptions underlying professional education in the university. Disciplinary loyalty and allegiance, along with conflicts arising from the way status and rewards are apportioned, work to thwart collaborative efforts. As long as criteria for promotion and tenure within the university encourage a single-minded focus on publishable research, faculty members will be hesitant to put too much time into collaborative efforts that may reduce their chance of reaching important career goals.

Formidable roadblocks to collaboration also exist in the central administrative offices of school districts. Tyack and Hansot (1982) asserted: "Public school leaders in the past have mostly been able to absorb the demands for change by accretion. . . . As a result, American education has been both faddish in particulars and resistant to change in its basic mode of operation" (p. 252). Cuban (1988) noted that superintendents have traditionally managed, rather than led, because their positions were originally conceived as administrative; they were socialized and trained to perform a management function; it was more convenient to manage; management helped reduce conflict; and education had ambiguous effectiveness indicators.

Traditionally, control and communication within school districts have been a one-way, largely top-down phenomenon. Central office personnel have worked to manage those within the system and create buffers against external intruders. This sort of administrative culture creates habits of mind in central office staff that make it difficult for them to effectively support organizational developments like decentralization or collaboration. Yet if reform is to be successful, central office people in positions of authority must begin to think and behave as service providers, not deliverers of policy and procedure. Stoll and Fink (1992) described the district role in restructuring as that of working with school staff to develop a vision, providing development support in implementing that vision, and encouraging school-level change efforts. But what happens if change is occurring only in a few isolated parts of the larger system? Fullan (1993) argued persuasively that "What is especially missing and needed in the research on districts is not research on districts qua districts but on the changing role relationships between schools and districts" (p. 146).

Community attitudes can also become barriers to reform. When there is a poor fit between a reform strategy and a community's culture and expectations for schooling, actual change is unlikely even if it is desired by educators (Cohn & Distefano, 1984). Local community members influence the implementation and persistence of change, establishing a climate that influences adoption and decision making (Farrar, DeSanctis, & Cohen, 1980). In large urban school districts, competition for resources and power frequently focuses on the schools, exacerbating tensions. Such districts struggle with a shrinking tax base, citizen disillusionment, a declining share of federal funds, and huge social problems stemming from the persistence of poverty and racism. If the challenges facing such districts are to be successfully met, the need for flexibility is clear. Yet, in the face of complexity and uncertainty, individuals and institutions too often become rigid in their behavior, clinging to that which gives a feeling of continuity, consistency, and stability.

RESEARCH METHODOLOGY

The ethnohistorical case study summarized here covers a 5-year span, from the initiation of the planning process for the Model School through the first year of implementation. Participant observation played a key role. The author observed the evolution of the school, firsthand, both as the mother of a student at the school and as a designated substitute teacher, among the first called when a regular teacher was absent. Time spent in formal and informal observation at the school exceeded 1,000 hours. In addition, data was collected through 65 semistructured, open-ended interviews conducted with students, parents, teachers, administrators, and university staff. Teacher, parent, and student samples were stratified by grade level and ethnicity. Written surveys and archival records were also used to acquire, clarify, and verify information.

BEGINNING AN EXPERIMENT IN INNOVATION

With quiet pride a task force, originally composed of three district and three university designees (later expanded to include over a hundred community members), issued the result of its 3½-year planning effort in early fall. The new school was to open the next August. The document, which outlined a full slate of cutting-edge innovations, included separate reports from the six committees: assessment, curriculum, governance and staffing, parental involvement and community resources, professional development, and student grouping. It was an idealistic vision of a cohesive learning community that would include multiage grouping, dual-language immersion, alternative assessment, a teacher-led and student-oriented organizational structure, extensive involvement of parents, and the establishment of a professional development program to serve the urban district in which the school was located.

In the background, unmentioned, loomed complex factors tied to the social and political context of the school. Located in an upper-middle-class neighborhood adjoining the university, the school would fill a dual purpose. It would both serve as an overflow school, relieving overcrowding at the existing neighborhood school, and also serve as a quasi-magnet school, drawing students from all parts of the district. Children of the university faculty were given guaranteed slots; the remaining students would be chosen by lottery. Roughly half of the lottery students would be drawn from adjoining, largely Anglo, areas where the schools were overcrowded. The other half would be chosen from the remainder of the district. Moreover, the at-large applicant pool would be stratified so that approximately half of the students chosen would be African American and the other half Latino. This was done to bring the demographic profile of the school somewhat closer to that of the district, which was only 12% Anglo.

The planning document satisfied all the necessary constituencies. University faculty were assured that the academic program at the school would be rigorous. Advocates of bilingual education were promised a dual-language immersion program in grades K–2. Educational reformers were told that the school would incorporate multiage grouping and alternative assessment, as well as a teacher-led and student-oriented organizational structure that featured extensive involvement of parents. Social activists reveled in the promise of a multiethnic school that valued equity and diversity. Lacking, however, was either a prioritization of this plethora of goals or guidelines as to the how and when of their implementation. Nor was there an organized system for discussing differences and negotiating a settlement should deep-seated philosophical disagreements or scarcity of resources lead to conflict.

Emergence of a Leader

For the moment, it seemed enough that the Model School had the leadership of a widely respected administrator who was willing to lead the charge. As one of the three district-appointed members of the original Core Planning Committee, this leader had decades of experience in education, including administrative experience in both university and public school settings. She had worked her way up through the school district's administrative system by, as one colleague put it, "doing everyone's work, letting them take the credit"—and subsequently coming to be seen as indispensable. Her pattern was to pick strong and independent employees, demonstrate personal confidence that they, as professionals, would do their job efficiently and thoughtfully, and then allow them to do just that. This leadership style allowed her the freedom to keep up with her assigned administrative duties within the district central office while also pouring energy into the planning of the new school.

This administrator became the Model School's first principal, resigning her district position 6 months before the school opened. She had an unmistakable air of authority, spoke plainly and forcefully, and inspired enthusiasm among staff and parents alike. However, she was not able to cut enough red tape within the district to acquire the necessary funds to hire teachers in the early spring, as the Task Force had recommended. The bulk of the hiring had to be delayed till May and June, with the school due to open in late August. This situation provided only one short month for orientation, development of a shared knowledge base among teachers, and sketching out a "constitution" or a road map providing guidelines on how the setting would be governed. This time crunch limited opportunities for social and professional bonding among a staff that would be expected to operate within a team-oriented and highly consensual framework, and also curtailed development of implementation plans consistent with the vision of the school's planners.

Construction of the Building

Architecturally, the new school building had a grand and slightly playful air. Construction costs were said to have come in under the budget allowed for a traditional school. However, this could not be guessed by looking at the school, a fact that would fuel resentment among other school district constituents, who would pointedly ask why so many resources had been spent on a school in an affluent Anglo neighborhood at time when school buildings in poorer neighborhoods were falling further into disrepair. Designed by three talented graduates of the collaborating university, the building won an Architectural Award for Excellence. According to one of the designers, the building was meant to impart the feeling of a small village. Triple-wide hallways, bathed with indirect light from atrium ceilings two floors up, resembled boulevards. The library was located in the center of the complex. The classroom area consisted of 10 "clusters," located on two levels. Each cluster consisted of a large common room with five classrooms radiating from it. All classrooms had large windows, overlooking the landscaped grounds or airy interior spaces.

THE HONEYMOON PERIOD

The time between the hiring of teachers through the first months of school can be roughly designated the "honeymoon period." The newly hired teachers were excited and enthusiastic, "all on cloud nine." However, as Sarason pointed out, this temporary paradise is often bought at the expense of confronting vital issues that may later disrupt the euphoria. These issues include true consensus on goals, reconciliation with existing settings, the inevitable shortage of resources (requiring a prioritization of goals), realistic timelines, an agreed-on governance structure, and the development of a shared knowledge base. For now, though, the newly hired teachers felt that "our visions just connected" and trusted that all implementation problems would be overcome by enthusiasm, hard work, and a worthy purpose.

Due to the exceedingly short timeline and the unexpected eruption of political crises elsewhere in the district, the principal spent much of the summer out of the building, putting out various political fires, making sure that the building would be finished on time, and finally dealing with health problems that limited her mobility. In her absence, most of the people who ended up working with the newly hired teachers during the precious 1-month window of summer planning time were employees of the district's in-service department. Potential theoretical gaps in the teachers' knowledge base were the most thoroughly covered areas. The teachers spent hours sitting through presentations derived from stock in-service curricula that, although thought-provoking, had little application to the teachers' immediate needs. For example, one session included a comparison of two cities where magnet schools had an ethnic mix that exacerbated the segregation at other schools, a situation that was applicable to this district's situation, but hardly in the purview of teacher responsibility.

With the exception of some team building and filling in of conceptual holes, many teachers began to feel that little of substance was being accomplished. As opening day neared, they became increasingly anxious to make more practical plans. One teacher fretted, "We needed to be setting up a discipline management program for the whole school—across the board. We needed to talk about the schedule, anticipate problems, discuss flexibility in fine arts. . . . Where do we rehearse? How often meet? Space contingencies. . . ." As a participant noted, "The teachers kept saying: 'Leave us alone! We need time to plan and talk to each other.' " But little time was allotted for teachers to formulate specific cluster goals, plan cohesive interdisciplinary units adaptable to multiage grouping, or even prepare their individual classroom spaces. Yet in spite of all the omens, excitement remained high. When there was grumbling, it was done with resigned humor. After all, they were in it together, and the school was "a place that was open, new, and going to try new things."

External Relations With Existing Settings

The power of inertia, growing out of the historic mind set of the district, had been largely ignored by the planners. However, school district politics became an ever stronger force as the opening of the school came closer. Although the planning document described a teacher-led school, the district continued to view teachers as the bottom layer of a steep bureaucratic hierarchy, as low-level employees who could not be trusted to use nonscheduled time in a beneficial manner. The vision gap was exemplified by the didactic instruction delivered to teachers at a school that had been planned to emphasize quite a different type of learning experience.

Ironically, it was breakdowns in the administrative areas supervised by the central office staff that would cause the most confusion during the school's first weeks. Transportation issues headed the list. There had been no adequate planning as to how school buses would go about picking children up all over a large urban area. Child monitoring and discipline became formidable problems. The proposed school uniforms also became a major logistical headache. Uniforms were ordered late, not arriving en masse until October and November. Technology, an alluring facet of the curriculum for many of the parents, was slow going online. Symptomatically, although a corporate grant had bestowed 1,100 computers on the school, the school board did not approve the behest until January.

University Frustrations

Relations with the collaborating university became increasingly strained. During the 3½-year planning period, the university had brought in a number of nationally prominent experts on school reform. But it had never been made clear how the theoretical underpinnings that supported the task force planning document would be absorbed into the culture of the evolving school. University faculty members who had been slated to be part of the training process felt that their expertise was not fully utilized. The university instructor in charge of technological training for teachers explained that he had not been able to accomplish much because he did not have the power to require teachers to attend. Another frustrated university faculty member complained that "the university role is nebulous, we can only advise." A university curriculum developer recalled: "I was given one day with the [content] specialists to create a [discipline specific] curriculum and then one day to create a common vision with the teachers." As another university faculty member noted, "There has been resistance by some [teachers], and I think it is because they were not asked when it started. . . . I don't think anyone told the teachers that the job entailed collaborating with [the university]."

Theory Meets Practice

As the teachers entered into the implementation stage, practical, hands-on experience with the innovations that the school had promised to deliver was scant. To the outside world, the image that had been projected was of a break-the-mold school, brought into being through the work of elite specialists, a fait accompli. However, the lack of hands-on training for teachers, the laissez-faire structure, and the scanty resources available for instructional purposes precluded any such reality. For example, in the area of multiage grouping, which was to be the most substantial innovation attempted in the first year, many teachers had little in the way of practical experience and few materials adapted to teaching children with widely varying levels of knowledge in the same classroom. There was not even much consensus as to what multiage classrooms would look like. The majority of teachers still struggled with the concept. As one teacher poignantly noted, "It was an ego boost to be chosen to teach here. But it got so hard when the kids came."

Competing Agendas

On the day that the school opened, it had no name. Planners had anticipated that the students would name the school, decide on its mascot, and determine the discipline rules. Staff members were holding their breath, unsure of what would happen next. As one teacher explained, "Everyone had all these expectations." Indeed, the expectations seemed to be a critical factor. The school's faculty had been recruited from all over the nation, each attracted by different aspects of the vision laid out in the planning document. The initiating motivation for the university administration had been to promote a "school of excellence," a model for future curriculum. The affluent Anglo parents who lived in the neighborhoods surrounding the school expected high performance standards, a rigorous academic life, and spectacular achievement gains for their children. Social activist faculty at the university, with the support of minority school board members who desired these benefits for a broader range of children, had seized the opportunity to create a "school of equity," with dual-language immersion in grades K–2, and an ethnically diverse student body.

Both the advocates of excellence and the advocates of equity held out admirable visions. However, setting up a school where equity and the nurturing of social skills are given primary importance—when at least half the parents and most of the faculty at the collaborating university are expecting an emphasis on technology and academic excellence—is to set the stage for considerable controversy. The principal and a handful of teachers represented the only real bridge between the task force members who had written the planning document and the teachers responsible for implementation. Most current stakeholders agreed with parts of the total vision, but not necessarily with others. As one of the task force members later reflected, "The problem that I see is that we never agreed on what [the school] would look like, so sometimes I felt like different people were making different schools."

Divisions in the Parent Community

The Model School had originally been conceived as a K–5 overflow school, with a homogeneous group of parents from an upper-middle-class, primarily Anglo, neighborhood. The school from which most of the overflow students would come had a turbulent history of interaction with parents who were highly active and perceptive politically. This overcrowded school was known for raising incredible amounts of money through silent auctions, carnivals, and grants. The parents had the leisure time to become highly involved. They were used to wielding power in the business and economic arenas, and this attitude carried over to their involvement with their children's schools. Principals at the school tended to have short tenures and knew they had to appease the parents. The Gifted and Talented Program, designed to provide enrichment for 3% of the nation's students, and funded by the state to include no more than 5% of the student population, for several years enrolled 85% of the students at this school.

In response to political pressure, a decision had been made at the district level to expand to a K–8 school, half of whose students would be ethnic minorities. However, there was a skew in the distribution of minority students: Grades 6 through 8 were well over 50% minority, whereas the elementary grades were substantially less than 50%—a situation that would, within 2 years, produce a predominantly Anglo school. Moreover, from the angle of exercising power within the school's governance structure, minority parents labored under several disadvantages: Few of these parents knew each other; they were geographically dispersed throughout the city; their children were often bussed an hour one-way from their homes. Also, most of the minority households had working mothers, without leisure time for heavy involvement in school affairs.

The director of a community interfaith activist group said he could see the power struggle "coming a mile away." For, although the Anglo population was far richer in "social capital," the African American parents at the school were generally well educated, concerned, and activist. The very process of learning about the school, then supplying the necessary paperwork and following it through the bureaucratic channels, had selected for just that characteristic. Many of these parents were accustomed to proactive, sometimes negative, encounters with the public schools. Dispersed geographically, they took several months to develop a working community. But after this, their presence was strongly felt. In contrast, the Latino population, often drawn by the prospect of a bilingual atmosphere for their child, was heavily dependent on oral communication, often requiring that communication to be in Spanish. Their interest centered on the happiness of their child and keeping that child out of trouble. Yet when they were asked to help, and language was not a barrier, they were very responsive.

THE VISION MEETS THE STUDENTS

The selection process assured that the students would be ethnically diverse, with widely differing educational experiences and attitudes. Children who had previously attended schools in low socioeconomic status

(SES) neighborhoods often had trouble making the transition. As one staff member explained, some of "the kids did not know what to expect and brought a lot of emotional baggage with them—they were used to teachers yelling at them and were on the defensive here at school. They tried to recreate what they knew." Nor was the school ready to deal with students whose experiences up to this point had caused them to view teachers and administrators with suspicion. As of opening day, it had been decided that discipline procedures within the school would be handled by the Parent and Child Advocates (newly created positions within the administrative staff), but no set procedures had been established.

The teachers also seemed unprepared for the problems that some of their students brought with them. This discrepancy was particularly marked in the seventh and eighth grades, where the students were predominantly minority. Many of these students had left their established places at other middle schools because of discipline, gang, or emotional problems. One teacher recalled, "I heard that principals in some schools gave troubled kids the application forms and said 'This school is for you.' " The attendance/records clerk at the Model School said that her counterparts at other schools had asked her, "How do you choose your students?" After learning what they meant, she would ask, "How many of your discipline problems did we get?" One school told her, "Nine." A middle school teacher quipped, "It was not the demographics that were unexpected, it was the behavior." Another middle school teacher, who left during the first year, recalled, "A lot of teachers said that this was the worst group of kids they had had. . . . There were a lot of disturbed kids, who needed someone with more training than I."

The cultural chasm that divided the student body was amusingly described by a middle school teacher: She mimed some students looking at her and thinking "Oh—a teacher!" (she acted out taking a pencil in hand and taking notes frantically), whereas other students looked at her and thought "Oh—a teacher!" (she mimed walking quickly toward the door). The teacher explained: "Not only were the teachers not prepared for the great diversity of achievement levels of the students, but [they were] not prepared for the diversity of attitudes toward learning."

Complex Interactions

It should be stressed that most stakeholders, if asked, would have said that they supported all of the task force goals wholeheartedly. The problem came when decisions about priorities were necessary, or when proposed courses of action involved a conflict between differing philosophical positions. The most stressful conflicts involved the structure of the multiage classroom and the locus of decision-making power. Table 4.1 describes the competing groups, with their concerns and their interactions.

TABLE 4.1
Interactions of School Groups

Relationship	Characteristic	Result
Between administrative personnel	Loosely coupled	Lack of consistent policies
Administration to teachers	Mixed signals about empowerment	Confusion concerning functional authority
Administration to parent	Lack of dialogical structure	Exclusion of some parental subgroups, confusion
Teacher to administration	Requests for more centralized direction	Administrative impatience with lack of teacher autonomy
Teacher to teacher	Difficulty with teaming and multiage grouping	Regression to old ways, competition
Teacher to parent	Lack of dialogical structure, teachers caught in "cross fire" among parent groups	Teacher defensiveness; initial parental confusion, followed by anger
Parent to school community	Competing agendas	Power struggles
University to school district	Clash between school district and university priorities, cultures	Withdrawal of university faculty from the school

The first visible casualty of the evolving power struggle was the dual-language immersion program. Although supported by Latino school board members, the main support for dual-language immersion came from the Spanish-speaking teachers hired for Grades K–2 and from university task force members who explained that the district currently had "an Hispanic majority. Twenty-five to fifty percent speak Spanish at home, so we were going to reflect that." That coalition fought a losing battle to keep the Spanish immersion program. The problem they faced was that teachers in Grades 3 through 8 had little fluency in Spanish. Nor did they have time to improve their foreign language skills. Spanish translators at meetings were slowly phased out. Documents that originally had gone out with translations began to go out without translation. As the dual-language thrust lost power, its supporters worked toward the more modest goals of retaining dual-language stipends for the teachers and maintaining a modicum of Spanish language instruction.

As the dynamics reflected in Table 4.1 began to make themselves felt, building administrators commented on the tendency of teachers to retreat to the familiar. The teachers, hesitant to admit regression, preferred to talk instead of "seeking stability" or "accommodating" or doing things "temporarily." One teacher said: "I thought this would be a purely constructivist school. That is what excited me. I have found that it is more eclectic in its being. Teachers are unable to completely buy in because they are unable to let go of their own power in the classroom; it scares them. So some teachers got really excited in the summer, went to all these workshops, and got into the classroom and BOOM [fist smashes into open palm]—they are back to their old ways. They are back to children walking in straight lines, and children sitting down and being quiet, and raising their hands. I've had teachers yank children out of class to bring to me, 'He called out an answer in class.' Well, for me, that shows excitement." She continued, "Yet, I understand that it cannot change overnight. It may take a whole new generation of teachers who are not used to the old way. Like . . . you can't teach an old dog new tricks—well, you CAN, you CAN, but the old dog does the new tricks with a little bit of the old twist."

CRISIS: THE LEADER LEAVES

Sarason told us that the crisis period is when enough reality has penetrated to a critical mass of participants, so that they have come to realize that (a) all dreams will not be fulfilled, and (b) they are engaged in an ongoing process, one that requires consistent hard work and will never produce the initially envisioned stable end state. Inevitable power struggles ensue as opposing subgroups, not reconciled to working together, seek to control the setting. If the power struggles produce a winning subgroup that gains control of the setting, then that setting is off on a new path, with a new set of leaders; essentially it is a new setting. This is true even if the name and external legitimacy of the setting are maintained, as is common in institutional settings. However, if the competing subgroups are able to accept and commit to a new covenant (not the usual course of events), then the setting continues to develop. Eventually, participants come to know that they can only approach (not achieve) their goals, in the process enduring conflicts, fear, failure, and sometimes painful personal and institutional growth. They learn that constant attention to accommodating participants and maintaining community is needed; there will be no permanent rest periods.

   The departure of the leader often catalyzes this critical period, if indeed the crisis has not been the immediate cause of the leader's departure. Frequently such a departure signals the perhaps tacit, but still real, failure of the founding vision. Yet, despite this failure of vision, in the case of public organizations, like schools, the skeleton of the organization often remains—frequently evolving into exactly the sort of traditional setting that the original vision sought to replace. In the present case, however, although the leader was having her problems—and her departure signaled the familiar signs of failure (indeed, the event did catalyze the crisis period and its accompanying power struggle)—the crisis turned out to be cathartic.

Teacher Reactions: Shock, Fear, and Withdrawal

The announcement of the leader's decision to resign was made at a faculty meeting that was called 30 minutes before the end of the school day on a normal January afternoon. An announcement, asking the faculty to gather for a short meeting, was made over the public address system. Teachers entered in groups of two or three, wondering what the meeting was about. The principal stood up and briefly described the opportunity, necessity, and obligation to accept a new position, as a career move. She spoke only a couple of minutes and then attempted to make a hasty exit back to her office. Though she had strategically placed herself near the door, her retreat was very slow. Faculty crowded around, many with tears, some hanging on her shoulder. She responded in her customary fashion, mirroring the sad, resigned, pragmatic, or cynical attitudes that individuals expressed toward her.

For the first week following the announcement, the teacher reaction was primarily one of shock. As one teacher put it "When she said she was leaving, I was SHOCKED OF COURSE." When the shock wore off, the pervading feeling was that there had been a sudden loss of grounding, the removal of a secure base from which to operate. There was a sense of restrained panic. Almost to a person, the teachers had felt dependent on the leader to protect them from parents, higher administration, or arbitrary program changes. One teacher said, "Now that [the leader] has left, the teachers are quite vulnerable. Things that are going to be changed will be changed now, nobody can stand up to people the way [the leader] could. We are vulnerable from all sides—the parents can come in and say this is how we want you to do things." Another teacher, referring to the panic he observed, explained, "I think it just came from fear, that people were not comfortable themselves with what was going on, that [the leader] would take, [the leader] *was* taking a lot of the heat from that, and I felt that people thought: 'Well, now who is going to stand up for us, who is going to take the heat for us?' "

Teachers feared losing their feelings of empowerment and losing the personal and programmatic arrangements they had made with the leader. Teachers that had been recruited personally by the leader, representing perhaps 20% of the faculty or more, felt some measure of anger and decried the lack of stability. "A lot of people came because [she] is such a charismatic leader. No matter who the leader was, continuity, especially of the instructional leader, is imperative. It is a real shakeup." Others used the word "betrayal," but no one seemed able to pin it to the leader. Instead they tended to blame the district. A typical teacher comment follows: "But why could she not finish the year? Is there something we are not being told about? Why not wait another three or four months? In the end, I felt angry with [the district], and their not explaining. I'm happy for [the leader]. I don't think she had much of a choice." Many could "accept that she is going, but not the lack of explanation."

Parents: Shock, Fear, and Unrest

The parents also seemed to go into about a 3-week period of shock. However, once their shock subsided, they exploded, stepping up pressure on the teachers and consolidating power among themselves. Complaints voiced by parents, upset that the evolving school did not look like their vision, that their children had too much homework or not enough, that children were not challenged or were discriminated against, began to invade the classroom. One cluster of classrooms was studying recycling and so had decided not to hand out Valentine's Day cards because it wasted paper. The parents were aghast. A teacher remembers that he "felt real animosity" from the parents, explaining, "It has a lot to do with [the principal's] leaving, they are scared." As the parents became increasingly vocal and invasive of the teachers' claimed domain, the teachers, perceiving themselves as under attack, without a strong leader to back them up, tended to support more traditional paradigms of parent involvement: the out-of-sight, cookie-baking role. But the door had been opened and proved hard to close.

Meanwhile, the social agenda contingent resurfaced, powerfully challenging the agenda of the self-declared proponents of excellence. Near the end of the first semester, upset by exclusion and emboldened by the chaos, the African American community began to coalesce. Ethnic factionalism took place; polarization began to develop. Accusations of racism were voiced. In late January, a popular local radio talk show broadcast a conversation with an unidentified caller who vociferously accused the whole school of being racist, relating racial and personal gossip over the air. Others called in to support the accusations. In February, partially in response to the onslaught of complaints, an active Black History Month program was instigated at the school, at the behest of the district, which gave the school administration a mandate to involve minority parents—or the district would intervene.

African American parent leaders were asked by district and school site administrators to head the Program Committee. The effort was used as a springboard to draw African American parents into the school. Indeed, participation by Anglos was discouraged by the program organizers. The effort succeeded in bonding the African American community within the school. Some members of the school community found the Black History Month program (which featured sets of drummers, with lip-synching and dancing to pop tunes, and with small children of all ethnicities reciting one-liners in a litany of African American leaders and innovators) to be refreshingly eclectic and culturally oriented. But the program was also criticized heavily by some parents and teachers, both for the amount of time that was taken away from academic pursuits and for the suggestive nature of some of the dances. One group of teachers sent a scathing letter of criticism to the principal. When this letter was intercepted, defensive African American parents reacted as a block, sending written complaints to their attackers and to the administration.

Regression to the Mean

The immediate effect of the leader's departure was shock, followed by an escalation of the power struggle and a speeding up of the process of regression that a lack of common vision had already begun. The new interim principal (the former assistant principal) explained the dynamics of this regression: "People had been of the faith of 'Let them come, see how it flows.' If there is no problem, why address it? Let the school develop its culture, its whole atmosphere. But, when they have nothing to fall back on, they fall back to the traditional way. That's what happened. Everybody went back to what they knew."

While the protective first principal was there, the teachers had felt safe, had trusted that problems would eventually be solved and that their tentative efforts toward learning new paradigms would be supported and protected from criticism. In the absence of this support—and in the face of two strong, somewhat angry and aggressive parent populations—there was an increased impetus to regress to a "safe" environment, traditional practices and expectations, both by the new leader and by the increasingly insecure teachers. Classroom management, discipline, assessment, and curriculum delivery became increasingly traditional. After all, most of these teachers had been successful, if unsatisfied, in that more traditional world, and the parents seemed more comfortable with a system they recognized.

AFTERMATH AND REGROUPING

After about a month and half, the fog lifted. The tale of a setting in the throes of failure began to be rewritten, with the teachers taking the lead, still regressing to be sure, but regrouping, finding stable ground and making a stand. The unification was catalyzed by the perception of a common "enemy," whose presence caused warring factions to work together for a common purpose. The threatening force was the school district, which had been severely criticized for removing such a popular principal at such a critical time. That resentment was quickly transformed into an apprehension that the district would now arbitrarily assign a new principal, who would not understand—or would be ineffective within—the contentious but fertile milieu that the school had now become. In spite of all district protestations to the contrary, the school community felt it was fighting, with the force of adolescent panic, for its identity and independence from a parent organization that was perceived as exerting pressure for conformity and obedience. As one parent expressed it, "The pressure we get from [the district] is standardization."

The first principal had left a powerful legacy. Paraphrasing the words of an active parent: She had assembled an awesome staff and placed them in an awesome building, with a mandate for innovation, consensus, and a wider definition of community. When the principal left there was a vacuum—and a lot of apprehension about the future. Yet the strong foundation that she had so laboriously laid remained. A renaissance of sorts ensued. A school/university gathering was organized for the main stakeholders by members of the quasi-administrative staff. One of the organizers explained, "It's been awhile since we have sat down and talked about the vision of the school, so we gave out invitations to [administrative staff]. It was fantastic. Everyone showed up. [Faculty name] represented the teachers. [University name] was there. We met at [administrator name's] house from 9:00 a.m. to 5:00 p.m. We led the whole thing. [Organizer's name] cooked gumbo for everybody and played guitar."

Members of the community began talking to each other, searching for points of consensus, and finding them. At a parent curriculum meeting, the suggestion by administration to invite an experienced principal (later to become the new principal) to speak on multiage grouping was met with unanimous approval. The meeting ended in rare applause. Again the school reaped the benefit of university resources, this time in the form of a knowledgeable and active faculty member, a university representative on the Model School's governing council. He had quickly become trusted and respected at the school. Now he led the group in grappling with the issue of finding a new principal, winning from the district an unprecedented degree of freedom in conducting the search process. During the last month of school, the decision was announced. The new principal had 10 years of experience in one school. Her school had been the first school in the district to develop multiage grouping and had been successfully implementing multiage grouping for the last 4 years. Moreover, the school where she had long served as principal had a naturally triethnic composition. For several years running, she had been selected as the most popular principal in the district, as determined by the school community.

CONCLUSIONS

Sarason's description of the predictable problems that arise in the course of creating a new setting was found to be a useful guide to understanding why developments followed the pattern that they did. The critical importance of considering historical and cultural context, gathering a sufficient knowledge base, allowing for a realistic timeline, establishing adequate vehicles for criticism, realistically assessing the resources available, and nurturing the personal growth for all participants was confirmed. At the Model School described in this case study, the early failure to identify an overarching vision, to prioritize a set of concrete and realistic goals, to clearly transmit purpose and goals to potential participants, and to routinely refer to these goals when decisions were made severely handicapped the school during its first year of operation.

Problems were exacerbated by the failure to hammer out a mutually agreed on way of resolving the differences that inevitably arise among any group of people working closely together, what Sarason referred to as a "constitution." These issues prevented the school from capitalizing on one of the major advantages of a choice school, the opportunity to create a cohesive community around a common purpose. Other setbacks resulted from a lack of attention to the problems associated with what Sarason referred to as "growth and differentiation." The hiring process and student recruitment were strongly influenced by political factors, without due attention to the fact that who is hired or attracted constitutes a de facto decision on the path the school will take when you have a shared decision-making system. Inadequate attention to the need for open and honest communication also resulted in regression and conflict.

In addition, the Model School was continually buffeted by forces originating in the existing context of settings, over which it had no control. Specifically, this study confirmed that there is considerable potential for conflict in collaborations between public schools and universities because the loosely coupled, political nature of these entities results in a tendency to avoid specific discussion—in advance—of the role each will play and the expected reciprocal benefits. This study confirmed the findings of other researchers concerning the extreme difficulty of creating an innovative setting within an established bureaucracy. Although the Model School had been planned as a professional development school that would generate change throughout the school district, at the end of its first year it had taken all the energy the school could come up with just to avoid being, itself, transformed into just another traditional school by the forces of inertia generated by the school district.

IMPLICATIONS

As Tyack and Tobin (1994) made clear in their reflections on the "grammar" of schooling, the organizational patterns that shape instruction are not ahistorical creations etched in stone. "They are the historical product of particular groups with particular interests and values at particular times—hence *political* in origin" (p. 476). Specific reforms have faded for differing reasons, but two problems have recurred. One was that leaders lacked political savvy and fell out of touch with the opinions of school boards and parents. Focused on convincing their professional peers, they did not cultivate the kind of broader social movement that might nourish educational and social change. The second was the problem of turnover and burnout among the reformers themselves.

Both problems surfaced at the Model School. The task force that drew up the original planning document dedicated its time to discussion of desired reforms, without engaging in the sort of networking that would be needed to enlist the support and ideas of the broader community. This led to an inevitable clash between the vision outlined in the elaborate planning document and the parents' notion of a "real school." Burnout became a problem because changes in basic organizational patterns created considerable strain on teachers, who were not only required to replace old behaviors with new, but also had to persuade pupils, colleagues, parents, and the district's central office staff to accept the new patterns as normal and desirable. That many teachers regressed toward the familiar was, under such circumstances, understandable. After all, teachers cannot be expected to create and sustain contexts for productive learning if such contexts do not exist for them.

Can a way out of this conundrum to be found? The answer, ironically, may lie in the reasons why the Model School collaboration proved so frustrating for the university. The bureaucratic inertia of a large urban school district proved to be more than a match for the best of intentions on the part of individual university faculty. The political realities of school reform clearly require a more measured, collective approach. Although the reforms now being proposed in public education are of a very different character than those undertaken at the beginning of the 20th century, there may be much we could learn from the collaboration among leading universities—not just among their departments of education—that was then instrumental in bringing about educational reform. Many of the institutional arrangements that are now an accepted part of the "grammar" of schooling were originally introduced through the coordinated intervention of influential university presidents, gathered through the efforts of Henry S. Pritchett, President of the Carnegie Foundation for the Advancements of Teaching.

The trustees who gathered at Carnegie's mansion in New York on November 15, 1905, were a stellar cast of university presidents, including such luminaries as Charles Eliot of Harvard, Woodrow Wilson of Princeton, Arthur Hadley of Yale, and David Starr Jordan of Stanford. These elite educators were determined to reform from the top down a system of schooling that they regarded as chaotic and ineffective. They saw Carnegie's grant as an opportunity to raise standards in American secondary and higher education through unifying and centralizing academic practice. (Tyack & Tobin, 1994, p. 461)

These days many reformers see the "Carnegie unit" system of academic credits and the type of academic courses recommended at that time as major stumbling blocks in the road to reform. That the reforms of the past have proved insufficient to present-day needs is hardly surprising. What we too easily forget is that these reforms also laid the foundation for an educational system that enabled generations of immigrants to enter the American mainstream. Now the problems we face are different. However, there is—as there was a century ago—considerable unanimity about the need for reform of a public school system that is widely perceived to be "chaotic and ineffective."

Colleges and universities are obvious stakeholders in, and can exert a powerful influence on, the system of public education. There is a pressing need to cultivate, not just in departments of education, but within the university community as a whole, an understanding of the role that colleges and universities can play in reforming the system of education. No other segment of our society has such a vested interest in fostering meaningful school reform. However, the needed collaboration can only happen if we are willing to set aside institutional and disciplinary rivalries, joining in an effort to create a shared vision powerful enough, and inclusive enough, to overcome the inertia that has doomed so many reforms in the past.

REFERENCES

Cohn, M., & Distefano, A. (1984). The recommendations of the National Commission on Excellence in Education: A case study of their value. *Issues in Education, 2,* 204–220.

Cuban, L. (1988). The district superintendent and the restructuring of schools: A realistic appraisal. In T. J. Sergiovanni & J. H. Moore (Eds.), *Schooling for tomorrow: Directing reforms to issues that count* (pp. 251–270). Boston: Allyn & Bacon.

Darling-Hammond, L., & McLaughlin, M. (1995). Policies that support professional development in an era of reform. *Educational Leadership, 76*(8), 597–604.

Farrar, E., DeSanctis, J., & Cohen, D. (1980). Views from below: Implementation of research in education. *Teachers College Record, 82,* 77–101.

Fullan, M. (1993). Coordinating school and district development in restructuring. In J. Murphy & P. Hallinger (Eds.), *Restructuring schooling: Learning from ongoing efforts* (pp. 143–163). Newbury Park, CA: Corwin.

Gardner, J. W. (1981). *Self-renewal: The individual and the innovative society.* New York: W. W. Norton.

Gardner, J. W. (1997). Foreword. *Boundary crossers: Community leadership for a global age* (pp. i–iii). College Park, MD: Academy of Leadership Press.

Holmes Group. (1986). *Tomorrow's teachers.* East Lansing, MI: Author.

Holmes Group. (1990). *Tomorrow's schools.* East Lansing, MI: Author.

Holmes Group. (1995). *Tomorrow's schools of education.* East Lansing, MI: Author.

Knapp, M., Barnard, K., Brandon, R. N., Gehrke, N. J., Smith, A. J., & Teaher, E. C. (1993). University-based preparation for collaborative interprofessional practice. *Politics of Education Yearbook,* pp. 137–151.

Lawson, H., & Hooper-Briar, K. (1994). *Expanding partnerships: Involving colleges and universities in interprofessional collaboration and service integration.* Oxford, OH: Danforth Foundation and Institute for Educational Renewal.

Sarason, S. B. (1988). *The creation of settings and the future societies.* Cambridge, MA: Brookline Books.

Stoll, L., & Fink, D. (1992). Effecting school change: The Halton approach. *School Effectiveness and School Improvement, 3*(1), 19–41.

Tyack, D., & Hansot, E. (1982). *Managers of virtue: Public school leadership in America, 1820–1980.* New York: Basic Books.

Tyack, D., & Tobin, W. (1994). The "grammar" of schooling: Why has it been so hard to change? *American Educational Research Journal, 31*(3), 453–479.

Chapter 5

Beating the Odds in the Inner City: Wesley Elementary Becomes a Charter School

Long before it achieved charter school status, Wesley Elementary School confounded expectations. In the early 1990s the *Houston Chronicle* observed: "Wesley Elementary, in the poor, black Acres Homes neighborhood, has continuously out performed elementary schools in the city's more affluent neighborhoods on standardized tests" (Editorial, 4/16/91, p. 12A). A decade earlier, in 1980, William Broyles, Jr., editor of the *Texas Monthly*, had noted:

> Wesley is located in Acres Homes, a pocket of semi-rural poverty on the far North Side, seven miles from the glittering prosperity of downtown Houston. Its student body of 750 is 99 per cent black and ranks economically in the bottom 15 per cent of Houston's schools. It would be hard to imagine a school more likely to be dominated by hopelessness and failure, more likely to confirm the image middle-class whites have of black schools as inferior. Five years ago, those assumptions would have been correct.

At the time Broyles wrote, Wesley Elementary was one of the few bright spots on Houston's educational horizon. Between 1970 and 1980 the White student population of Houston's public schools shrank from 49% to 27%. News stories focused on White flight, drugs, discipline problems, plummeting test scores, a jeremiad of dissension and decay.

Prior to the arrival of longtime principal Thaddeus Lott, Wesley Elementary School had been caught in the same downward spiral that had ensnared many other urban schools:

In 1975 Wesley's third graders scored 2.7 (second grade, seventh month), a full year behind the national average, on the Iowa Tests of Basic Skills. Last year, however, they scored 4.4 (fourth grade, fourth month), or almost a full year ahead of the national average. That score beats those of the third-graders in most of the elite districts surrounding Houston. (Broyles, 1980)

Under the leadership of Dr. Lott, now a legendary figure in Texas public education, Wesley students established a long-standing and enviable record of academic achievement that has continued into the 1990s. Yet this rise in academic achievement is only part of the Wesley story.

For Wesley Elementary School had not always been the demoralized inner city school it had become in 1975. Before the court-ordered desegregation of public schools in Texas, Wesley Elementary had been under the leadership of a highly regarded African American educator. The school had served a tight-knit Black working-class community. The arrival of Dr. Lott, who had grown up in the neighborhood, enabled Wesley to become, once again, a focus of community pride. Yet the school's striking record of achievement over the next two decades did not prevent Wesley Elementary School becoming a lightning rod for controversy.

RESEARCH PURPOSE AND METHODS

This historical case study looks at how shifting educational priorities at the local, state, and national level affected one urban elementary school, tracing how the unintended results of policies mandated by decision makers far removed from the target neighborhood eventually led the school to seek charter school status. Data for this study were gathered through a combination of interviews, observations, and archival data. Interviews were held with past and present members of the leadership team at Wesley, with teachers and parents at each grade level, and with knowledgeable community members and school district employees (and former employees). Observations were carried out in selected classrooms. Moreen Thompson and Lindsey Pollack provided pivotal help with interviews as well as many insightful observations. Archival data used in this study included school records, newspaper articles, and descriptions written by other researchers who have visited the school.

THE INFLUENCE OF SOCIAL CHANGE

At the time when Thaddeus Lott was attending school there in the 1940s, Acres Homes was still an all-Black unincorporated community in a rural setting. Two-parent families were the norm. Residents owned their own homes. Many, including the Lotts, kept hogs and livestock, planting their own gardens to stretch the food budget. Lott recalled the atmosphere: "The houses were poor, but there was pride in ownership. And a house was a home. The children wanted to be home. Parents wanted their children to have an education beyond high school." While Dr. Lott was growing up, the Acres Homes community was safe; houses were rarely locked. However, the educational facilities were "bare bones." Lott described his elementary school:

> What we had was a pot-bellied stove that we put coal in. The coal bin was at the end of the building. Outdoor toilets. When I went to elementary school, it was from '40 to '46. It was primitive. No cafeteria. A little old lady used to bring hot food, soup from home on a little wagon she pulled. We used to get books that came from white schools. They were hand-me-downs.

Dr. Lott's father, Andrew A. Lott, founded the Wright Grove Missionary Baptist Church and was known in the local community for getting things done. For instance, Andrew Lott got electric lights installed in Acres Homes. Other parents, too, had a strong commitment to community involvement. Dr. Lott commented: "The parents, when we came along, sponsored the Cub Scouts. You could depend on them. They were involved in Boy Scouts. They were involved in P.T.A." At that time, when Acres Homes children went to middle school, they were bussed to Houston's First Ward. Lott explained that the bus "was owned by a private individual; it broke down as much as it ran. Many afternoons we walked the streets, trying to get home." Yet, in spite of the lack of services, the children had good teachers. Lott recalled:

> We did have teachers that were committed. I mean, they would not let you become less than you were capable of becoming. You didn't get by. We had some very good ones. They used to come out here through all that rain and mud. There were no streets, really. No black-top streets; they were shell. There were no streetlights.

After desegregation, however, the relationship between school and community changed. Many African American educators were displaced. White administrators downtown now had "final say" on matters of curriculum policy. School practices in newly integrated schools did not take into consideration the cultural backgrounds of African American students (Watkins, 1996). The linkage between home culture and school was lost. White teachers often took a distant, impersonal attitude toward Black students. Members of each community felt uneasy, unsure of what to do, how to act. Black children often felt alienated, adrift in an oddly impersonal world that contrasted painfully with the warm relations they had known in the all-Black schools they had attended previously.

African American parents felt at a loss as to how to help their children. No longer could they talk informally with their child's teacher at church or in the checkout line at the neighborhood grocery store. No longer were the administrators who ran their children's school people from their own community. When Black parents voiced concerns, there was not the same feeling of having been heard and understood. For many, the neighborhood school began to feel like foreign ground. At the same time, a bifurcation had begun to develop in the Black community. Before desegregation, African Americans who achieved economic success remained in their neighborhoods. Desegregation allowed the successful to move to more affluent areas. New avenues of opportunity were opened for individuals with adequate education, support, or mainstream ties; meanwhile, the less successful often languished in deteriorating surroundings.

In the 1960s, many African-American young people without adequate family and social network support, mainstream skills, and attendant confidence were unable to enter a mainstream economy that was becoming increasingly complex. The difficulty was compounded by the tendency of employers to use education level as an indicator of personal discipline and reliability, even when the job did not require a high level of education. (Comer, 1997, p. 132)

Thaddeus Lott graduated from Houston's Booker T. Washington High School in 1952. When he returned to Acres Homes in 1975 to serve as principal of Wesley Elementary School, the neighborhood where he had grown up had changed dramatically. Many of the people Lott had known as a child had moved away. The children who now lived in Acres Homes were far more likely to come from chaotic home environments. Dr. Lott recalled: "There was not this reverence for education that my parents had. We knew that education was our passport to a better life, in a better world." Comparing his own childhood memories to the experiences of many children in low-income families today, Lott observed: "There are things in life that made us what we are, and we are failing to pass that on to the generation following us."

Yet Lott was determined to reestablish roots in his old community. "I wanted my kids to know their grandmother." Lott's seven children grew up in a home within blocks of Wesley. He noted that "the principal who was my childhood principal at Highland Heights Elementary was the same person who was the principal at Wesley until 1964. She lived to be 99 and was a sage in education. . . . So I'm honored to be sitting in the same office as my childhood principal." As a veteran teacher at Wesley explained, "These are *his* children here. This is *his* neighborhood."

Turning Expectations Upside Down

> To look at Wesley Elementary from the street, you wouldn't guess that there was anything *too* extraordinary about the place. It's a long, low, red-brick one-story building with a flagpole in the front. . . .
> Once inside the classrooms, Wesley appears a spectacular school. Our first stop was Earlene Alexander's first grade. I counted 20 kids. She was working on a phonics reading and spelling drill with half of them, and those ten responded lustily to every slashing motion of her hands. Fine. It was the other ten kids who startled me. They had been given a writing assignment, copying words over and over, and every one of them was working without supervision . . . in every class we visited, I found the same thing. . . . And on the level of sheer vibe, they seemed happy to be at it. (Theis, 1991, pp. 32, 33)

When they arrive at Wesley Elementary, after driving down narrow black-top streets with no sidewalks, past sagging houses with peeling paint, among the first things visitors notice are the clean and pleasant surroundings. Dr. Lott explained: "Some children don't have a lot going for them from the standpoint of a home, a place to stay, a residence that's beautiful and well taken care of. . . . I feel like school should be the one place that children enjoy coming to. If anything is going on right, anywhere in a child's life, it should be at school." But Wesley Elementary School was not always such a pleasant place to be. A teacher who came to Wesley at the same time as Dr. Lott described the situation that she encountered that first day:

> When we went into the faculty meeting I remember putting my purse on this old wooden cafeteria table. It had the extra border . . . a piece of wood that went around it as trim, and when I turned around and looked, roaches were coming out that border and up my purse. I moved it to the floor and I said "Oh my God! What have I gotten myself into?" . . . [It was a] nasty school . . . but before the children came he had the floors polished, the walls painted. I mean everything looked clean.

Asked how he brought about that seeming miracle, Dr. Lott explained:

> [The school district] used to have a little program wherein, if you had a specific amount in your activities fund, the district would match it. In some instances you'd go out and get your own carpenter to come in and do the work, just so it'd pass code and all that. . . . So, a lot of that, I did.

The first years were a struggle. A teacher recalled: "I had children that were much bigger than me! They had been retained maybe three, four, or five times. They were men, some of them, and women." The sense of failure these students had absorbed over the years made them resentful and difficult to teach. A teacher described one incident: "I had at least thirteen 14-year-olds . . . and I remember one day I had to run to the restroom and somebody was supposed to be watching the classroom. When I got back one boy and one long-legged girl had their legs wrapped around each other, just rolling on the floor, because they were in to a fight." The can-do attitude Dr. Lott brought into this situation is described by a veteran teacher:

> When I tested my sixth graders, I had one child that could read at the sixth grade level. The rest of the children (I think there were about thirty-nine children in the classroom) thirty-seven of those children read at the second grade level . . . I had a non-reading boy, and I'll never forget his name. His name was Walter. I turned my results in to [Dr. Lott]. Of course, I only had sixth grade literature books out there to use. He took his station wagon over to Brock [Elementary], where he had been before, and borrowed second grade books.

Maintaining order became a school-wide priority. One teacher explained:

> [Dr. Lott] started that immediately. No children would be locked out of the building. All children . . . report to the cafeteria first thing in the morning. There they are to sit and they're monitored. They are called out by class, in the beginning, and later by grade level, once they are organized.

Not all teachers were pleased with the changes. Before Lott's arrival, staff discipline at Wesley had been exceedingly lax. As a teacher explained: "When we first came here everybody was doing basically whatever they wanted to do. . . . The secretary was using a pad like you would use to write orders for a meal at Denny's, to do her books. When she wanted to tell you something, she would yell from her secretary's desk. . . . They would just eat . . . the office was unbelievable!" A teacher remembered being told by local residents that, before Dr. Lott came, teachers would "almost race the children out the door" when the school day was over. Some staff members opposed the changes the new principal insisted upon. Lott recalled:

> I had one of the teachers' husbands go down to Billy Reagan, who was then [Houston Independent School District] superintendent. I just said, "Your wife is probably going to want to get a transfer. But I'm not changing." I don't know what all he and the superintendent talked about, but [the superintendent] said: "He's the principal out there."

The greatest problem, however, was what to do for the large number of nonreaders at the school. Dr. Lott had visited a school in Bay City, Texas, that used DISTAR. He had been impressed. At the school he visited, special education students had been mainstreamed into regular classrooms and were keeping pace with their classmates. Dr. Lott commented: "It blew my mind! When I visited, I couldn't tell special education [students] from regular education. I couldn't! So I was sold on it." However, it was difficult to get funding to buy the DISTAR materials. Lott explained: "That was a terrible hurdle for us to conquer, having enough money to buy materials for these children, inasmuch as we were not using the state-adopted material." A teacher recalled:

> I think he got [DISTAR] in the second year, by using Chapter 1 funds. So he only trained the Chapter 1 teachers. Ironically . . . by December the bottom group was out-performing the children who had scored in the top percentile on the Metropolitan test. . . . These [DISTAR] children had maybe 68 words and [the top group] were struggling with twelve. If it wasn't for those twelve words they couldn't read anything.

Learning the "Wesley Way"

At the time DISTAR was first introduced at Wesley, the program was not part of the approved curriculum. Lott was only able to buy enough materials for a few classes at a time. A teacher explained: "He had to implement in stages and he was only trying it in our worst scenario, where we had children who couldn't read at all." Dr. Lott commented: "The only way that you could get anything would be to have an outside activity—like selling candy and having different kinds of movies—to buy the material. So, by whatever hook or crook we could, we started buying those kits." There were also many teachers who resisted using DISTAR. A staff member recalled: "You know, they would say they were teaching it when they weren't teaching it. And if he didn't stand in the room it didn't get taught, sometimes."

Still, in the early 1980s, Thaddeus Lott's approach was very much in tune with the general direction in which the Houston Independent School District (HISD) was moving. Houston Superintendent Billy Reagan had started life as one of eight children in a White East Texas tenant-farming family. He was a master of the country-boy school of political leadership, which he combined with shrewd practical management. Reagan instituted a system of competency-based education, insisting that students be competent in certain basic skills, publishing the test scores of every school. Houston Deputy Superintendent Larry Marshall, an African American, insisted:

The kids want us to give them structure. . . . Our poor kids don't get much structure at home. We've got to give it to them or they'll be lost. And we've got to teach them there aren't any free rides. And you know what? Once we stiffened up and took the heat and failed some kids, we found out that it worked. (Broyles, 1980, p. 6)

Thaddeus Lott described the educational philosophy that helped him to turn Wesley around: "Philosophically, I've always believed in standards. I believe that teachers should know what's expected of them. . . . A teacher should know, at grade level, what it is that they're supposed to be teaching. Parents should know. If your standards are user-friendly, a parent can read them." Having grown up in the Acres Homes neighborhood, Dr. Lott had a comfort level in communicating with parents that was quite different from that of the principal he had replaced. His approach made clear just what the expectations were:

If a child is not able to read fluently without mistakes, and comprehend the first grade basal by the end of first grade, he's not promoted to second grade. I've always been in favor of retention, if necessary. But, retention only if the child is going to receive another [teaching] method or technique.

The classroom scenes described by Broyles in 1980 still typify Wesley Elementary today:

In a first-grade classroom, most of the children were practicing handwriting while seven students sat in a corner with the teacher, reading aloud. . . . Whenever they came to a new word, the teacher would drill them on it. In this case the question was why the *i* in "fine" was pronounced differently from the one in "fin." "Because it ends in *e*!" the kids shouted all together. The teacher kept the lesson moving, clapping her hands, asking questions, pushing. A second-grade class was using an orange impaled on a pencil to study how the earth rotates on its axis and what causes the seasons. A third-grade class was going over the muscles of the body ("Triceps!" "Deltoid!"). (p. 5)

The highly structured curriculum at Wesley relies for its success on warm face-to-face interaction between teachers and students. Teachers are on their feet, interacting with students, all day long. The results can be spectacular. One of the most challenging roles at Wesley is that taken on by the third-grade teacher who works with students new to the school, using a direct instruction program called Corrective Reading. Most children who transfer to Wesley come from low-performing schools. Many enter the Corrective Reading class as nonreaders, often not knowing all the sounds of the alphabet at the beginning of their third-grade year. Yet these children, who might well have carried a "learning disabled" label for the remainder of their years in school, usually end the year reading at or near grade level.

However, the task undertaken by Wesley teachers is arduous. The direct instruction scripts usually require teachers to ask 300 or more questions in six small-group sessions each day. Teachers also must perform reading checks every 5 or 10 lessons to ensure that students achieve 100% mastery. Daily quizzes are given and corrected in five content areas. Wesley teachers typically put in 10-hour days. Perhaps for this reason, most Wesley teachers are young, with many having come to Wesley directly out of college. Often teachers stay only 2 or 3 years. As they enter that time of life when they begin to think seriously of starting families of their own, many of these young teachers leave Wesley for schools in more affluent neighborhoods where less energy is needed to enable children to achieve at a high level.

Professional development plays an important part in getting each year's new teachers "up to speed" at Wesley. This is true not only for teachers but for paraprofessionals, who play a large role in the Wesley academic program, working one-on-one with struggling students. During the first 4 to 6 weeks of school, new teachers and paraprofessionals at Wesley work directly with the school's instructional supervisor, who helps them to fully digest the direct instruction strategies. Lead teachers at each grade level work extensively with the new teachers throughout their first year. In this way, the powerful work ethic apparent in the Wesley staff is continually reinforced as new teachers see how their colleagues impart their own sense of dedication and focus to the children in their care. As Dr. Lott observed:

> Results come both from the quality of the program and the character of the person implementing it; that is equally true whether you are talking about a teacher in the classroom or a principal looking after a whole school. The traits, characteristics and values of the principal are important. The principal has to be constantly monitoring what is happening in the school and keeping up with the children. So, it is not just the program. Implementation is just as important.

WESLEY ELEMENTARY AND THE "PHONICS WARS"

As mentioned earlier, when Lott first took over at Wesley, his goals were in alignment with the objectives of long-time HISD superintendent Billy Reagan. After Reagan retired, however, a new superintendent, with quite different priorities, took over. Another Houston elementary school principal described what the resulting policy changes had meant for his own school.

When Charles Taylor was principal of Crawford Elementary School six years ago, its reading test scores topped the charts.

At the time, Taylor's teachers used a highly structured phonetics program to teach reading. But in 1988, the Houston Independent School District stopped funding that program and required schools to use a literature-based whole language approach. That approach teaches children to read by first recognizing words in the context of a story.

Crawford's reading scores dropped. And Taylor, who was transferred to Dogan Elementary a year later, was frustrated.

"The main question that will always linger in my mind is why we changed," Taylor said. "We had something that hadn't been broken, and we decided to fix it, for whatever reason."

Now Taylor, along with seven other HISD principals, will have a chance to prove that the strong phonetic approach works. The school board voted this fall to provide funds for eight schools to use the program, called Direct Instruction Teaching Arithmetic and Reading, or DISTAR. It was this program that gave Wesley Elementary School Principal Thaddeus Lott the reputation of being a maverick principal. Despite pressure from higher level administrators to change, Lott spent his discretionary money on the phonetic materials and kept using them.

"Many of us stopped when we were directed to. Thaddeus just put his helmet on and kept going," Taylor said. (Markley, 1991b)

Lott's resistance to using the new reading program caused tensions between Wesley Elementary School and school district administrators. The incident that finally brought the situation to a head was described in an April 15, 1991, article in the *Houston Chronicle*.

The teacher was in tears.

Someone—and no one would say who—had accused her of cheating while preparing her first-grade class for a standardized test.

Two Houston Independent School District administrators arrived at Wesley Elementary School to investigate. They moved her students to the library, pored over materials for most of the day, took copies and left. All they found were practice sheets from a store-bought book.

To the teacher, India Williams, the investigation was upsetting, embarrassing and out of the blue.

To others, it appeared to be part of a pattern.

Wesley, a high-achieving minority school in Houston's impoverished Acres Home neighborhood, has a maverick principal whose teaching methods are different from what the district prescribes. Some higher-level administrators, they say, would like to discredit him.

Gayle Fallon, president of the Houston Federation of Teachers, said for four years HISD administrators have questioned whether the school cheats on tests. They're suspicious, Fallon said, "because many of our white administrators cannot conceive of poor black children performing better than the (wealthier) southwest schools, and that is what is happening at Wesley."

George Scott, an associate of the Tax Research Association, was at the school the day that Williams was confronted with the cheating claim, "I don't think the issue was cheating at Wesley," Scott said. "The issue is intimidation." (Markley, 1991a)

Why should district-level administrators care so much about what was happening at Wesley? In 1988 almost 73% of Houston's public schools were ranked in the bottom 25th percentile on the state-mandated skills tests, compared with 7% in the top quarter, according to figures released by the Texas Education Agency. Of HISD's 234 schools, 170 scored in the bottom quarter and only 17 in the top, giving Houston the worst showing among the state's eight largest districts. In comments published in the *Houston Chronicle*, the city's largest newspaper, the president of the Houston school board pointed to Wesley Elementary (one of the 17 Houston schools ranked in the top 25th percentile) as evidence of what schools that served neighborhoods with a high percentage of low income students could achieve, insisting, "Wesley's performance provides proof positive that educational excellence is possible in our inner-city schools" (Greene, 1988).

Two years later, in November 1990, the *Houston Chronicle* ran a story asserting that if the board of trustees determined that the current school superintendent was "not following their directive to improve education, her days in Houston could be numbered." The school board president declared that no final decision had been reached about the superintendent's evaluation, but that the board's question to the superintendent was: "Do you have our vision and are you on the same wavelength?" The same article made prominent mention of Wesley Elementary:

A case in point is Wesley Elementary School, a high-achieving school in the impoverished neighborhood of Acres Home.

For years, Principal Thaddeus Lott has bucked the system, broken the rules concerning what and how his teachers should teach and turned out students who, despite their poverty, score high on achievement tests.

Lott has been criticized, reprimanded and passed over for promotion. Educators from other states and other school districts have visited Lott's school to better understand why he is so successful. But Lott has gotten no recognition from his own HISD supervisors.

Despite the school's extraordinary achievement, Raymond had never set foot inside it until a board member persuaded her to visit two weeks ago. And when the *Chronicle* ran a story a year ago about Wesley's glowing success, Lott said, the superintendent never acknowledged it.

"The point is, the people who are getting the most results and the best results are people who are not doing what the status quo and the bureaucracy says," he said. "I will not get promoted doing what I'm doing."

. . . Lott's situation has not gone unnoticed by board members who believe the district's job should be to encourage and reward educators like him, rather than burden them with rules and criticism. Trustee Rod Paige considers Lott an inspiration.

"Thaddeus is interested more in the performance of his children than in compliance with the rules," Paige said. "He is willing to take the consequences of non-compliance in order to get the kind of performance he needs for his students." (Markley, 1990)

Trustee Rod Paige, quoted here, was then the Dean of the College of Education at Texas Southern University. In 1994 he would become the first African American to serve as HISD superintendent. Early in his tenure as superintendent Dr. Paige would initiate the process by which Wesley and three other schools in its feeder school pattern would gain charter school status under the leadership of Dr. Lott. In 2001 Dr. Paige left HISD to become the United States Secretary of Education.

Direct Instruction in Action at Wesley Elementary School

A squat brown building flanked by rows of pale, wooden expansion classrooms, Wesley comes across as a well-tended but colorless outpost of public education. Yet the preK–5 school plays host to as many as 600 visitors a year: teachers, administrators, board members, camera crews, all wanting to know just why Wesley kids score so well academically. (Rose, 1997, p. 10)

The article quoted here (from the May/June 1997 issue of *American Teacher*, published by the American Federation of Teachers) describes the paradox that Wesley presents today. Visitors wonder: How could children at *this* school, where about 80% of students qualify for free or reduced-price lunch and about 88% of students participate in standardized testing, consistently outperform students in the affluent suburbs, sometimes by one or two grade levels? One possible answer, "('They cheat!') fell by the wayside after numerous investigations and even a few classroom shakedowns in search of pre-test subterfuge in the early 1990s" (Rose, 1997, p. 10). Yet there remains considerable resistance to crediting the school's use of direct instruction.

This resistance centers on the scripted nature of direct instruction, which is characterized by rapid-fire question-and-response that children at Wesley often perform at the top of their lungs. The result can sound like

a scripted patois that is somewhere between combat training and a catechism: "What do we call a place with lots of fruit trees?" "An orchard!" "Very good! We said *an* orchard because, what does an orchard begin with?" "A vowel!" "Very good. Do we say *a* orchard?" "No!" "No, because, What does orchard begin with?" "A vowel!" (Rose, 1997, pp. 10–11)

The scripts are written, tested, rewritten, retested, polished in a cycle of classroom field testing and revision that ends only when trials show that 90% of students grasp a lesson the first time that it is presented. Every concept to be learned, every step in the learning process, is preplanned and carefully laid out.

TAKING OFF OUR CULTURAL BLINDERS

As Pulitzer Prize-winning syndicated columnist William Raspberry pointed out, descriptions of what goes on in direct instruction often sound "awful" to people who have never watched skillful teachers, adept at using the program, use direct instruction in the classroom:

> "It sounds awful," the woman wrote in response to my column praising the results a Houston elementary school has attained with something called direct instruction. "Direct instruction," as she accurately understood, heavily involves set questions and scripted responses to any answer a child might give. Only in the most unusual circumstances does it allow for anything that might be called teacher creativity. It is almost like a computer program in an if-this-then-that mode. It does sound awful. But it works. (Raspberry, 1998)

As Raspberry goes on to observe, "according to those who have visited Wesley . . . the test scores don't begin to tell the whole story . . . the eager learning, the purposeful noise as the children respond to teacher's questions in choral fashion." How could this be? What would account for the "eager learning" of children engaged in this sort of scripted instruction?

Although the shouting, clapping, and stomping often heard in Wesley classrooms may sound like unnecessary noise to an outsider, students clearly enjoy it. The rhythmic delivery of many Wesley teachers—and the choral responses of their students—contain a kind of vocal styling that makes the exchange something much more complex than mere rote repetition. Often the call-and-response interactions have an almost musical sound. When children recite in this manner their response becomes far more than a mere display of rote memory; it is also an act of self-expression, even an affirmation of group unity. Teachers at Wesley have transformed the scripted reading lessons into an enjoyable daily ritual.

In the hands of an able teacher, direct instruction can become both reassuring in its familiarity and motivating to children, who quickly begin to take pride in the daily growth of their reading repertoire. For an urban school, unable to offer the salary and benefits competing suburban district can afford, the advantages are clear. As Raspberry (1998) commented: "Some teachers are very good at improvisation; many—including many of the unsuccessful teachers—aren't." For affluent suburban schools that can afford to hire only highly trained and/or experienced teachers, mandating a curriculum that requires a high level of teacher improvization may not present a problem. At a school like Wesley, however, a curriculum such as DISTAR makes possible a level of school-wide teacher performance that would otherwise be exceedingly difficult to attain.

Direct instruction also offers distinct advantages to students who are not exposed to standard middle-class English at home and thus have not had an opportunity to internalize the rules of grammar, pronunciation, and social interchange that students in more affluent neighborhoods may have absorbed in the course of their daily lives. Direct instruction systematically teaches these children the rules of middle-class language usage they will need to know if they are to succeed at higher levels of schooling. At the same time, students build a sense of confidence in their own abilities as learners. Speaking up is the norm. Because all recite aloud together, there is no need to make a self-conscious choice to be "the one" to raise one's hand or to speak up in class.

Where Did DISTAR Come From?

Direct instruction (DI), or DISTAR, is a system of teaching that attempts to control all of the variables that make a difference in the performance of children. Originated by Siegfried Engelmann and his colleagues at the University of Illinois, this approach was developed for small-group instruction of disadvantaged children (Bereiter & Engelmann, 1966). The first series of reading and arithmetic programs carried the name DISTAR, an acronym that originally stood for Direct Instruction System for Teaching Arithmetic and Reading. The program became widely popular, in part because of the results of a major federally funded study was undertaken in the late 1960s in response to concerns about the poor educational outcomes for disadvantaged students.

Entitled Follow Through, this study was designed to determine which methods of teaching would be most effective for disadvantaged students throughout their primary school career. This study followed the early-intervention project Head Start, which had as its goal the overcoming of educational disadvantage prior to school entry, at the preschool level. Follow Through was a huge study—involving 75,000 children in 180 communities over the first 3 years of their school life. It remains the largest educational experiment ever undertaken, extending from 1967 to 1995, at a cost of almost a billion dollars.

Follow Through looked at nine major competing sponsors, covering a broad range of educational philosophies. These included child-directed learning, individualized instruction, language experience, learning styles, self-esteem development, cognitive emphasis, parent-based teaching, direct instruction, and behavioral teaching. The models can be reduced to three distinct themes: those emphasizing basic academic outcomes, cognitive development, or affective development. The targeted basic skills included reading, language, spelling, writing, and math. The models that emphasized the systematic teaching of basic skills (direct instruction and behavior analysis) performed best. In reading, the direct instruction model (which also has a strong phonic emphasis) had the most impressive results in both academic and affective areas.

There were criticisms that variability in implementation across Follow Through sites made judgments of model superiority dubious and that overall effects were too small to be pleased about (House et al., 1978). Nevertheless, when the data were reanalyzed by several groups (Bereiter & Kurland, 1981; House et al., 1978; Meyer et al., 1983), the direct instruction (DI) model still produced the best gains. Follow-up studies (Becker & Gersten, 1982; Gersten, Keating, & Becker, 1988) were completed over the following 10 years and added support to the argument that the superiority of the direct instruction model was real and significant.

The DI model has been criticized (Schweinhart, Weikart, & Larner, 1986) for its strong emphasis on teacher-directed, scripted lessons; critics have alleged an overreliance on teachers and an inability on the part of students to self-direct learning. However, follow-up studies of the DI students showed "strong consistent long term benefits in reading" 3, 6, and 9 years after students completed Follow Through (Gersten et al., 1988, p. 326). The effects were evident in higher achievement, fewer grade retentions, and more college acceptances than in comparison groups that had been given a traditional education in the same communities. Research is, however, often less powerful than politics in determining what programs will be adopted by school districts.

Although widely popular when first introduced, DISTAR fell into disfavor with the growth in popularity of whole-language instruction. Where DISTAR proved strongest was in those situations where inexperienced teachers were called upon to work with children who came to school without a command of the sort of middle-class language they would need to succeed in school. DISTAR systematically taught them everything they would need to know, telling the teacher just what to do and say during each lesson on each day. As demonstrated at schools like Wesley Elementary, this approach could be highly successful when enthusiastically embraced at the school site level.

The problem was that, during the period of DISTAR's initial popularity, its use was often mandated by a school district. Experienced, highly skilled teachers who had no need of such scripts were told that they had to use them. This caused understandable resentment and anger, also making it likely that the teachers involved would not have much investment in making the DI approach "work" in their schools. In the minds of many, DI became associated with a lack of respect for teachers as professionals and with the stifling atmosphere that can take over in a classroom when teacher and students are trudging through a series of activities, the value of which is not evident to anyone present. Certainly, if the teacher has no enthusiasm for a lesson, there is little likelihood that the students will enjoy or value what they are doing.

Where Did "Whole Language" Come From?

Steven Stahl (1999) noted that the first experiment with what became known as "whole language" can be traced to the activity-based educational approach originated by Col. Francis Parker in the late 19th century. According to Parker, reading should be, first of all, interesting to the learner; in order to be interesting, it must enter the child's stream of thought (Parker & Helm, 1902). The first trial of Parker's method was in the city schools of Quincy, Massachusetts. Later he brought his methods to the Cook County Normal School.

> Parker disdained the use of textbooks, but instead sought out children's books, boasting of a library of over 13,000 volumes in the Cook County Normal School, which he ran from 1883 to 1899. The school had a printing press that was used as the primary source of reading material for the first 3 years of school and as a source of sight word learning and phonic analysis. (Stahl, 1999, pp. 13–14)

The relative effectiveness of Parker's approach cannot be assessed, given the lack of data available. However, the ostensible reason for his leaving Cook County was concern about the low achievement of the children in the school. Never the dominant view among educators, Parker's techniques were adopted in a handful of school systems, then died out. Not until the 1960s, with the arrival of the language experience approach, did such ideas gain widespread popularity. Language experience approach included two distinct styles: that of Roach Van Allen and that of Russell Stauffer. In its pedagogy, the language experience approach (LEA) resembled what we now call "whole language."

> LEA began with the children's own language, captured by dictation, to use as material for reading instruction. Although the use of experience charts is the common stereotype of language experiences approaches, in their original conception they included a great deal more, including copious reading aloud to children, oral discussions, individual reading and writing, and reading of selected books. . . . The major differences between LEA and whole language are in the use of invented spelling and Big Books. Also,

there were explicit procedures recommended for embedding phonics and sight word instruction in the reading of the charts. These procedures received greater emphasis by Stauffer (1970) than by Allen (1976). (Stahl, 1999, p. 14)

The whole language movement, as such, might be traced to a talk given by Kenneth and Yetta Goodman at a conference at the University of Pittsburgh in 1976. In this talk, entitled "Learning to Read Is Natural," the Goodmans laid out the basic premises of the whole language movement: that learning to read can be as natural a process as learning to speak and understand oral language; that it should take place in an environment rich in literacy where written language serves a function and is used for authentic purposes; that in such an environment children will learn to read and write naturally. This idea proved to have wide appeal and the movement burgeoned. In the late 1980s, journals such as *The Reading Teacher, Elementary School Journal*, and *Teacher Magazine* devoted entire issues to whole language instruction.

Even so, it can be difficult to establish just what is meant by the term *whole language*. When Bergeron (1990) reviewed articles that used the term and examined commonalties among definitions, she found that "whole language was defined differently in each of the 64 articles reviewed" and "little consistency was also found in the descriptions of those attributes thought to be the focus of whole language" (p. 312). Still, there is a set of beliefs that tends to be accepted by most whole language practitioners:

Among these are that language (oral and written) is used for authentic purposes, including communication, information, and so on (K. S. Goodman & Y. M. Goodman, 1979), and that children will learn language (again, oral or written) best if it is learned for authentic purposes. In the classroom, this involves the use of authentic reading and writing tasks using whole books, and not looking at parts of language (e.g., sound–symbol correspondences) for their own sake or using artificial tasks such as worksheets or even the specially adapted stories found in basal reading programs. (Stahl, 1999, p. 15)

The Genesis of the "Phonics Wars"

During the first years of the whole language movement, there was a widespread belief that explicit instruction in phoneme awareness, phonics, structural analysis, and reading comprehension strategies was unnecessary because oral language skills provided the reader with a meaning-based structure for the decoding and recognition of unfamiliar words (Edelsky, Altwerger, & Flores, 1991; Goodman, 1996). This assertion did not hold up under scientific scrutiny, however. In an article entitled "Why

Reading Is Not a Natural Process," G. Reid Lyon, chief of the Child Development and Behavior Branch of the National Institute of Child Health and Human Development (NICHD), pointed out that nearly four decades of scientific research on how children learn to read support an emphasis on phonemic awareness and phonics. This research challenges the belief that children learn to read "naturally." What is meant by this?

To learn to decode and read printed English, children must be aware that spoken words are composed of individual sound parts termed phonemes.

> Phoneme awareness and phonics are not the same. When educators assess phoneme awareness skills, they ask children to demonstrate knowledge of the sound structure of words without any letters or written words present. For example, "What word would be left if the /k/ sound were taken away from cat?" "What sounds do you hear in the word big?" To assess phonics skills, they ask children to link sounds (phonemes) with letters. Thus, the development of phonics skills depends on the development of phoneme awareness. (Lyon, 1998, p. 00)

Phoneme awareness is critical in beginning reading. If beginning readers have difficulty perceiving the sounds in spoken words—for example, if they cannot "hear" the /at/ sound in fat and cat—they will have difficulty decoding new words. Yet many children have difficulty in developing phoneme awareness. When we speak, the individual sounds within words are not consciously heard by the listener. This is because spoken language is seamless, an overlapping bundle of sound. We don't get any "natural" practice breaking words into smaller, abstract sound units. To learn to decode and read printed English, the beginning reader must learn to detect the seams in speech, unglue the sounds from one another, and learn which sounds (phonemes) go with which letters.

Reading research by NICHD and others reveals that "making meaning" requires more than phoneme awareness and phonics. Children must also acquire fluency and automaticity in decoding and word recognition. However, if beginning readers read the words in a laborious, inefficient manner, they cannot remember what they read, much less relate the ideas to their background knowledge. This is a mater of importance, not only to educators but to society at large.

> If a youngster does not learn to read in our literacy-driven society, hope for a fulfilling, productive life diminishes. In short, difficulties learning to read are not only an educational problem, they constitute a serious public health concern. (Lyon, 1998, p. 00)

Moreover, the risk is greatest in the case of those children most dependent on the public schools, those children whose families lack the resources to seek out other help should their children not become fluent readers as a result of the instruction offered at their neighborhood school.

Whole language approaches have frequently been criticized because of their apparent ineffectiveness with at-risk students (Bateman, 1991; Gersten & Dimino, 1993; Stahl, 1990; Stahl & Kuhn, 1995; Vellutino, 1991; Yates, 1988). Henry (1993) argued that whole language's lack of explicitness regarding phonics militates against at-risk learners, as they are the students who are least likely to develop their own phonic generalizations. Unlike children who routinely hear middle-class English in their home environment, these learners may not simply be seeing a word on the page and saying to themselves "So that is what it looks like in print!" Systematic access to useful phonic principles is needed if these learners are to be given a firm basis for mastery. Moreover, there must be enough massed and spaced practice for incorporation to occur.

BEYOND THE IDEAL OF "ONE BEST SYSTEM"

Sociolinguist Deborah Tannen (1998) insisted that we live in an "argument culture" in which issues tend to be constructed in terms of diametrically opposed extremes. Every issue, no matter how complex or benign, is seen as having two sides—and only two sides. Tannen didn't suggest that disagreement, even strong disagreement, is a bad thing. But any field that divides itself into warring camps is unlikely to provide the conditions necessary for the development of fruitful new ideas. For example, Tannen pointed out that always positioning issues as two-sided provides no space for imagining multiple points of view. Are "phonics" and "whole language" the only possible stances one can take on the reading issue, for example? Recent research would suggest otherwise. The problem is that understandings limited to two sides make it difficult to create the middle ground needed for compromise. This makes some policy questions—for example, what curriculum ought to be taught in the nation's public schools—appear to be nearly insoluble.

As long as public education is structured in the present "winner takes all" manner, there will be a strong incentive for those who believe strongly in a specific curriculum or course of action to bend their efforts toward winning the policy debate at all costs. The reason is simple. Where the accepted practice is to adopt one curriculum or policy, district-wide or even state-wide, those attempting to influence policy tend to fall into a all-or-nothing mind set. The progression of the rhetoric within what became the whole language movement demonstrates what can happen. As any number of outsiders have pointed out, there is no commonsense reason why the teaching of reading cannot include both the teaching of phonemic awareness and immersion in stimulating children's literature. Indeed, the "balanced approach" currently recommended by most scholars does exactly that. The more interesting question is why the "both/and" approach that is now seen as optimum was, at the height of the "phonics wars," hardly discussed as an option. How did educators come, for a while, to treat the teaching of phonics and of children's literature as incompatible, forcing an either/or choice?

A Tale of Unintended Consequences

Back in the 1960s, the language experience approach (LEA) pioneered many of the practices now used by whole language teachers. LEA came out of a political impulse that was similar to that which led to the development of direct instruction (Bereiter & Engelmann, 1966). At the time, LEA was but one of many approaches that had been developed as a means of enabling poor (especially Black) children to become better readers and thus participate on a more equal basis in the economic life of the nation. For example, Serwer (1969) argued that LEA was the best approach for working with disadvantaged children because it used their language and their dialect instead of trying to teach Standard English and reading simultaneously.

The whole language movement grew out of the conviction on the part of many teachers that schools had gone too far in the direction of teaching isolated skills. They wanted to switch the emphasis to reading-to-enjoy (Stahl, 1999). Whole language instruction emphasizes the personal response of individuals to quality literature. This in itself is hardly controversial. The emphasis on children's response to literature, as opposed to their recall or comprehension of stories, is somewhat more so. However, what made whole language highly controversial were the claims made by some advocates that direct instruction in phonics was unnecessary. Since that time the debate has become politicized. Research has not backed up claims that phonics was unnecessary. Moreover, Stahl and Miller (1989) could not find a single comparison of language experience or whole language instruction with children labeled as "disadvantaged" that favored whole language instruction.

Optimally, educators should be able to take what is useful from the whole language approach and amalgamate it with approaches that are useful in meeting other goals. Yet the political nature of educational policymaking has tended to produce an all-or-nothing mind set.

The rise and decline of the whole language movement is a prime example of what Slavin (1989) likens to swings of the pendulum, in which an approach becomes widely accepted before its effects have been studied. When the results of the program become known, the program is dropped and another approach, often the opposite, is hastily adopted. (Stahl, 1999, p. 21)

At present, there is a swing "back" to phonics instruction. Yet to swing to the opposite extreme is hardly the answer. Children need to gain a certain level of phonemic awareness if they are to learn to read. But "Enough is as good as a feast." Children need to know lots of other things, as well. Phonics is necessary to beginning readers, but a knowledge of phonics is not sufficient to produce fluent readers.

The sad irony is that the current bureaucratic structure of public schooling creates a "winner takes all" climate, in which a single curriculum is mandated throughout a school district (or even a whole state), creating a strong motivation for advocates of a specific curriculum to stridently compare the best aspects of their favored curriculum to the worst aspects of competitors. As is true in politics in general, negative campaigning can at times be highly effective; but it cannot be said to serve the common good. Dudley-Marling and Murphy (1998) pointed out, citing Deborah Tannen's (1998) concept of the argument culture, that this sort of politicization has the effect not only of promoting extreme positions but also of driving out new ideas.

Wesley Elementary School's struggle to hang on to its hard-won success speaks, in a most profound way, to the dilemmas that confront other inner-city schools. Not only do such schools face the challenge of helping children from hard-pressed urban neighborhoods to compete academically with their more privileged peers, but these schools often must carry out their mission within a highly charged political environment. What is defined as "success" one year may be seen quite differently should another political faction gain the upper hand. These days Wesley has gained a measure of protection from such pressures by becoming a charter school. The charter school movement holds forth the promise of making school reform more of a win/win situation. However, before looking at the circumstances that surrounded the decision to seek charter school status for Wesley, it is useful to look at the school from another perspective.

Schools as Engines of Community Change

To understand the importance that Wesley Elementary School has come to have within Houston's African-American community, it is necessary to consider that community's history. Prior to the 1954 Supreme Court decision in *Brown v. the Board of Education,* in which "separate but equal schools" were found to be unconstitutional, many African American students attended segregated schools with inadequate facilities. These schools often had to make do with materials discarded by schools serving

European American students. This situation clearly did not provide African American children with equal access to a high-quality education. For example, during the 1931–1932 school year, the nine states that had 80% of the U.S. Black population had a per pupil expenditure that was three to seven times higher for Whites than for Blacks (Comer, 1997). Yet despite these disadvantages, the commitment of African American teachers was not questioned by those they served (Walker, 1996).

> During the nineteenth century no group in the United States had a greater faith in the equalizing power of schooling or a clearer understanding of the democratic promise of public education than did black Americans. . . . Practically every black voluntary group, almost all black politicians, rated the improvement of educational opportunities near the top of priorities for their people. (Tyack, 1974, p. 110)

In the years following the Civil War, the job ceiling in White institutions and the poverty of Black communities severely restricted careers for the Black middle class. Teaching had great prestige in the African American community and frequently attracted highly educated men and women. A substantial number of African American graduates of leading northern universities found careers in Black high schools. Both in elementary and secondary classrooms, "black teachers served as important role models for their students, visible proof that in education, at least, there could be a ladder of success for the ambitious black child" (Tyack, 1974, p. 118). During the first half of the 20th century, the segregated schools attended by African American children in the South were often centers of community pride.

In *Waiting for a Miracle* (1997), psychiatrist James P. Comer, MD, described the pivotal role that families and local institutions play in holding neighborhoods together and creating a constructive, supportive culture for children. He recalled his own childhood: "My family and its primary network, the church culture, made achievement possible in the absence of full opportunity in the larger society" (p. 33). Comer went on to describe the three networks that influence the development of the growing child. These can be imagined as three concentric circles with the child at the center. What goes on within these networks promotes or limits the development, and the ultimate sense of power or security, of the child at the center.

Primary network: The innermost circle comprises the family, the extended family, their friends, and the institutions selected by them and accepting of them, such as their places of worship or fraternal organizations.

Secondary network: The middle circles embraces services and opportunities such as the workplace, health activities, recreation, and schools.

Tertiary Network: The outer circle is the policymaking circle that includes local, regional, and national legislators, as well as business, social, and religious leaders.

Those who are the elders within the primary, or family, network take the lead in interacting with secondary or tertiary networks to secure what they need to help their children to develop the capacities that *they* will need.

At the beginning of life, the baby relies completely on the parents. The child's sense of self begins with the simplest of accomplishments: crawling, walking, talking. Children are pleased when the powerful adults on whom they depend are pleased, and are motivated to master those skills that win praise. How the adults react thus profoundly affects the choices that children make. But socializing young children is a long, tough journey. Young children scream, bite, scratch, and do whatever is necessary to manage fear and insecurity of all kinds. How adults cope with such behavior has far-reaching effects, encouraging self-control and creative problem-solving—or creating defensive resentment, repression of a necessary level of assertiveness, or loss of self-regard.

If all goes well, by the age of five, good childrearing should have led to significant thought and language development, desirable social skills, ethical foundations, and emotional development. However, when children have not had home experiences that prepared them to meet the expectations they will encounter at school, they are made anxious by the challenge of the tasks assigned in class. If they don't experience success, they feel frustrated and, as a result, sometimes act out in disruptive ways. Children may fight because they have not been taught to negotiate for what they want. Or they may fight for power and control through teasing and provocation. Often the reaction of the school is to clamp down, creating a cycle of punishment and rebellion.

This is where the curriculum and disciplinary methods in use at Wesley give the school an advantage. In addition to the academic program, the staff members at Wesley struggle to provide the sort of developmental experiences many children living in a demoralized inner-city neighborhood might not otherwise have had. Not only is the academic program at Wesley rigorous, but there is a continuing dialogue regarding cooperation, consideration, what it means to be a part of a community. As the kindergarten teacher announced to her class the first day of school: "Rule #1 is: 'We are all friends!' " Discussions of pushing, shoving, name calling, and other interpersonal frictions were based on that understanding. How would a friend treat a friend in this situation? Teachers at Wesley immediately confront students who harass their peers, or treat others with disrespect, letting the students know that such behavior is unacceptable, helping students find alternative ways to relate to classmates.

As Thaddeus Lott explained: "You have to be firm. You have to say what you mean and mean what you say. The students understand that we don't tolerate disruption. They know that fighting and hitting are out." School discipline is seen as having two goals: to ensure the safety of all concerned, and to create an environment conducive to learning. Disruptions interrupt lessons for all students, with disruptive students losing even more learning time. Lott, a passionate defender of the potential of Black children, insists that with proper teaching the vast majority of children can perform on grade level and go on to become constructive, committed members of their community.

Still, absorption in the work at hand is a habit that many children entering Wesley for the first time have yet to learn. Often, when new students enter the school, their eyes scan their surroundings, alert to excitement or threat. Unaccustomed to sitting quietly to listen to a story or complete a painting, they could easily become disruptive, pushing and shoving, talking out of turn, constantly looking for attention, not staying in their seats. New teachers, entering an inner-city school where the unmet needs of the students are so apparent, are often tempted to ask little of their students, to settle for just trying to be friends. The culture at Wesley demands that teachers do much more. But the outsider, entering the school for the first time, may misinterpret what he or she sees.

"They all looked like little robots!" one HISD teacher from another school exclaimed when asked about a visit she had made to Wesley. This teacher was referring to the Wesley tradition of asking children to cross their hands in front of their chests when walking in line, so as to keep pushing and shoving to a minimum. She assumed that this must feel demeaning to the children. Yet the meaning, for the children, might have been quite different than an outsider might surmise. A former Wesley staff member explained:

> Imagine you live in a little shot-gun house, up on cinder blocks. Sometimes you hear gunshots at night. . . . The only defense you have is to learn to shift, instantly, into an in-your-face, fighting attitude. For kids like that to let down their guard, school has to be a place where harassment just does not happen.

Wesley Elementary now serves a more transient population than lived in the close-knit working-class neighborhood that Dr. Lott experienced growing up in the 1940s. Families have fewer ties to church or extended family. The school, as part of the secondary network surrounding the child, can provide many resources not available in the child's primary support network. However, there are limits to what a school, alone, can do. Families may not be able to provide the secure and orderly environment children need for optimum development; parents who do not have adequate resources and support may retreat from the demands of parenting. Children may engage in out-of-school activities that do not support their development. All these things affect school achievement—as well as the life chances of students after they leave the school.

Policy decisions made at the tertiary level, beyond the Acres Homes neighborhood, have had a devastating effect on the neighborhood's secondary network (jobs, family services). Social changes in the 1960s and 1970s triggered the abandonment of this neighborhood by many of its former residents. Those families left in Acres Homes were less able to afford basic needs such as health and child care. Comer (1997) pointed out that, although some individuals can function adequately even when the three networks of influence work against them, such people are rare. Most of us are what we are by virtue of the support for development that we received, the opportunities that were made available, our own effort—and good luck. Comer insisted: "A modern society probably cannot thrive for long with conditions that require exceptional performance from large numbers of people who have not had reasonably adequate developmental experiences" (p. 99).

Imparting a Sense of Connection

In the eyes of its constituency, one of the most valued characteristics of Wesley Elementary School was the caring staff. A former Wesley student spoke movingly of how the care and interest shown by her teachers when she was at Wesley had been pivotal to shaping her attitude toward school, creating a desire to succeed and a conviction that success was possible. A parent commented:

> The school realizes that we are partners, parents and the school. . . . We have to work together, so that we can be a good team and help the kids. The bottom line is helping the kids, and if the parents are not involved, then the kids do not do well.

Again and again, parents mentioned the importance of feeling welcome, of feeling at home within the school community where their children spent so many of their waking hours:

> I'm always feel welcome at this school. I always get a big smile or a big firm handshake. I always look forward to going there and just seeing those little kids having fun . . . they are so attentive to what they are doing. It's like being in a world by themselves.

I visit anytime I feel like, 8 in the morning, noon, 2 or 3 o'clock. It never matters.

I have come here many times and talked to her teacher about certain things. I feel really comfortable about that.

Parents also spoke of the importance of establishing norms within the parent community that supported the mission of the school:

As Black parents, we need to make time for our children because it's very, very important. . . . If you show that you care what they are doing and get involved, they know you care about them. And they are going to do the best they can, because they don't want to let you down.

They need parents to get involved to help support those other parents, and encourage the kids to come to school.

On a daily basis, the most important support activity in which parents were involved in was the supervision of homework. Dr. Lott explained, "We have a preponderance of parents who have to work, in order to help support their children. The definition for us, in a setting like this, of parent involvement is that parents are supporting what we are trying to do and the way we are educating their children." Parents and grandparents spoke about the homework issue:

I have tried to keep her from watching too much TV until she does the work that needs to be done, until she reads her assignments. I think that motivates her to get her work done before she does anything else. She is not allowed to do anything else until she is done.

When we get home, we get a little snack and after that he starts to do his homework and read a book and explain what he didn't put down on his paper, tell me how he did it, how he got the answer. And then his mom comes home, and he has to tell her the same thing.

No TV during the weekdays. . . . There's no TV, so what are you going to do? You might as well do something constructive.

She gets home from school in the evening and she wants to start her homework, even on Fridays. It's nice to see her so involved and trying to get those things out of the way.

Not all Wesley parents were as involved as those who volunteered to be interviewed. Lott spoke forthrightly of the challenges the school faced: "We are committed to do what we are supposed to do, and that is to teach the children and to teach them regardless to what their social-economic background is, whatever their problems are at home. We are committed to not using that as an excuse not to teach." Still, the challenges posed by the school's social environment could not be denied. The dangers children faced outside of school were made poignantly clear by a tragic incident described in the *Houston Chronicle*:

> Last June, when Roland was 10, he spent those first, lazy weeks of summer cutting grass. He needed a new bike—he'd had two that had been stolen—and he and his parents agreed it was time for him to buy his next set of wheels. Painstakingly, he earned the $75 he needed. As soon as he had the money, July 10, his mom took him to Wal-Mart, and he picked out a blue 10-speed. Late in the afternoon, he asked if he and a couple of friends could ride to the convenience store three blocks away.
> Reluctantly, she said yes. Her parents had been strict. When she was a kid, they wouldn't let her off the block.
> A few minutes later, a robber was holding a gun to Roland's ribs. . . . A young man had been lurking in the convenience-store parking lot. He'd seen the bike, tags still on, and he wanted it.
> Roland resisted briefly, but by the time he let go, it was too late.
> The robber shot the child in the left side. The bullet punctured a lung and kept going. Roland fell to the ground, stunned. He couldn't feel anything from midchest down. (Feldman, 1998)

The newspaper article went on to describe how ramps had been installed at Wesley Elementary to make classrooms wheelchair-accessible for Roland, now a paraplegic. Two of Roland's friends now took turns packing his bookbag and carrying his lunch tray. He has learned to play wheelchair basketball. Roland's plight stands as a deeply affecting reminder of the limitations on what a school, alone, can do. Their experience at Wesley does not make children immune to the problems that beset students in inner-city neighborhoods. The challenges faced by Wesley graduates who stay in the neighborhood are formidable. As a result, when their child finishes fifth grade, many Wesley families attempt to get their children into magnet or private schools. Some have even had their children stay with grandparents and attend middle school in another school district. But could another answer be found? In this question lie the roots of a unique charter school district.

CHARTER SCHOOL STATUS

The Houston Post, on the front page of its Sunday Style section on February 23, 1992, listed a number of indicators that made clear the tensions that, at that time, existed between central administrators in the Houston Independent School district (HISD) and Wesley Elementary:

- In 1989 a first-year Wesley teacher, who asks to remain anonymous, was called into an HISD area office where three administrators first accused her of cheating because her students performed so well on standardized tests. They then told her there was a way she could avoid being the "sacrificial lamb": "They wanted me to say that Mr. Lott was passing out test answers." They were looking for a way to fire him, the teacher says.
- During the Raymond (Superintendent Joan Raymond) regime, while more than 100 Houston schools were receiving corporate sponsorships, Wesley received none, despite Lott's repeated requests.
- In 1990, a district instructional specialist visited Wesley and voiced her disapproval over the school's ambitious kindergarten curriculum. She said the children had no need for requested maps, reading lamps and other reading concept materials. She complained that kindergartners were using too much paper. (pp. E1, E6)

Houston Federation of Teachers President Gayle Fallon is quoted in the same article, saying of Lott: "He doesn't meet with their belief system," especially the belief "that poor minority children will not perform as well as other children, and here's a school outperforming many middle class schools." Fallon accused the HISD bureaucracy of perpetuating an "institutionalized form of racism" by lowering expectation levels for minority children: "This guy (Lott) blows all the excuses. He raises the question: 'Why aren't they performing as well elsewhere?' which is a real ugly question" (p. E6).

At the same time, the teachers union president noted, "He's probably the hardest person in the district to work for." She commented, "I have members who hate him and members who love him. There's very little in between. One of his teachers once told me she'd wake up early every day, just to cry. She later fought to stay in his school" (p. E6). Teacher Lenore Payne commented, "When I first started working here, I thought it was 'The Stepford Teachers,' and Mr. Lott was a dictator, but when I saw what the kids were accomplishing, I became a believer. You want to do more." Payne also observed: "Mr. Lott runs his school like a business. He looks at the bottom line. At the end of nine months, he wants to see nine months growth." Fallon, whose 4-year-old son was enrolled in Wesley's pre-K program, believed the school offered a good balance of DISTAR and "higher types of learning. They (the Wesley staff) just believe you should get the basics first. The kids I've seen go through Wesley have done well in higher grades."

Elsewhere in the district, however, critics characterized the program at Wesley as too structured, rigid, and "rote." Opponents asserted that direct instruction stifled reasoning and creativity. Dr. Rheta DeVries, professor and director of the Human Development Laboratory School, a training ground for early education teachers at the Universtiy of Houston, said,

"(DISTAR students) can often give the right answers to paper and pencil tests as a result of rote drill and practice, but you're not sure they're really reasoning or understanding" (*Houston Post*, 2/23/92, p. E6). Differences in perception and philosophy stood out clearly. Lott agreed wholeheartedly that children should be taught to reason, but cautioned, "You don't want them to reason and think and then not have the skills to do what they need to do."

Lott argued that it is necessary to look in an unsentimental way at what was going on in the larger society: "We are either going to teach these children now or we are going to teach them in the penitentiary. We're going to pay for it now or pay for it later." During an interview, Lott grabbed a copy of *Retarding America: The Imprisonment of Potential* by Michael S. Brunner (1993) from a shelf using it to illustrate his point. Written by a visiting research fellow at the National Institute of Justice at the U.S. Department of Justice, *Retarding America* reviewed research literature linking academic failure and delinquency, including the following:

> Low reading levels tend to predict the likelihood of the onset of serious delinquency. Longitudinally, poor reading achievement and delinquency appear to mutually influence each other. Prior reading level predicted later subsequent delinquency . . . [moreover] poor reading achievement increased the chances of serious delinquency persisting over time. (Huizinga et al., 1991, p. 17)

> The causative chain starts with the fact that the child is not taught reading properly and that his reading disorder is not corrected early enough. Such a child may feel that he is stupid and that he will never be able to achieve anything worthwhile in life, and in this way slide into delinquent behavior. The reading disorder comes first and is the major cause of such a child's violent or otherwise delinquent behavior. (Mosse, 1982, pp. 284–85)

> Compulsory school attendance law . . . facilitates delinquency by forcing youth to remain in what is sometimes a frustrating situation in which they are stigmatized as failures. . . . The longer learning disabled students stay in school, the more likely they are to become involved with the police. (Gagne, 1977, p. 13)

Brunner argued that delinquency is brought about not by academic failure per se, but by sustained frustration that results from continued failure to achieve academic goals. When frustration can find no resolution into constructive activity, one predictable response is aggressive, antisocial behavior. Citing Pavlov's clinical demonstrations that frustration can cause antisocial aggression in animals and humans, Brunner (1993) asserted that in a classroom where reading instruction is ineffective:

All the ingredients necessary to create this anti-social aggression through sustained frustration are present: There is an unachievable goal, in this case academic achievement. It is unachievable because the means of achieving it, the ability to read and comprehend text material, is, in many cases, absent due to whole-word reading instruction. Though the means of achieving the goal are absent, the student, nevertheless, is continually pressured to achieve it by teachers, parents and peers. As a result, frustration ensues. Finally, the student not only has no alternative for achieving the goal, but he is not allowed to leave the failure-producing environment as a result of compulsory attendance laws. (p. 31)

In Brunner's view, it is difficult for those who do learn to read to grasp the magnitude of resentment and hostility that is generated in non-readers, over time, as a result of unrelenting frustration from which there is not escape. In addition, because meaningful employment opportunities go hand in hand with literacy, opportunities for economic independence are also cut off. Brunner quotes literacy researcher Jeanne Chall regarding the tragic irony involved:

Whole language . . . seems to say that a good heart goes a long way, and the less teaching, the better teaching. It fears rote learning more than no learning. . . . These views attract many teachers to whole language. . . . It is a romantic view of learning. It is imbued with love and hope. But, sadly, it has proven to be less effective than a developmental view, and least effective for those who tend to be at risk for learning to read—low income, minority children and those at risk for learning disability. (Chall, 1991, p. 25)

Unfortunately, the strong belief of some educators in the validity of whole-word teaching methods may cause them to assume that when a child does not learn to read using this method, there must be something wrong with the child. Tests are used to "diagnose" the problem may appear to affirm this. However, as Keith Stanovich (1986) pointed out:

Slow reading acquisition has cognitive, behavioral, and motivational consequences that slow the development of other cognitive skills and inhibit performance on many academic tasks. In short, as reading develops, other cognitive processes linked to it track the level of reading skills. Knowledge bases that are in reciprocal relationships with reading are also inhibited from further development. The longer this developmental sequence is allowed to continue, the more generalized the deficits will become, seeping into more and more areas of cognition and behavior. Or to put it more simply—and sadly—in the words of a tearful nine-year-old, already failing frustratingly behind his peers in reading progress, "Reading affects everything you do." (p. 390)

Needless to say, arguments such as those offered by Brunner are not viewed with enthusiasm by persons who are strongly invested in the whole-word recognition approach. Even after former Superintendent Raymond left the district, tensions remained between Lott and many HISD middle-level district administrators. The contrast between the viewpoints of Wesley Elementary School supporters and its critics are many and stark (see Table 5.1). During the administration of Superintendent Frank Petruzielo, who succeeded Raymond, tensions between Wesley Elementary and members of the HISD central administrative staff remained high, despite Superintendent Petruzielo's public support for Thaddeus Lott. However when former Trustee Rod Paige, himself an African American, became HISD superintendent, he made it a priority to find a way to resolve the long-simmering tensions.

On January 5, 1995, the Houston Independent School District trustees approved a plan that gave Dr. Thaddeus Lott unprecedented control over

TABLE 5.1
Views of Wesley Elementary School Supporters and Critics

Issue at Stake	School District and Its Allies	Wesley Elementary Supporters
Whether teaching methods should be chosen by school or by district	School board, as elected representatives of the people, should decide matters related to what will be taught and how	Curriculum decisions should be made on basis of proven effectiveness, not political maneuvering at district level
Whether charter schools are an effective approach to reform	Charters "cream off" best students, and drain funding away from neighborhood schools, thus are a drag on the system	Charters provide innovative ways of solving problems that have eluded solution within existing public schools
Explaining low-achievement level of African American students	Many socioeconomic factors have impact on learning of these students; schools doing best they can in a difficult situation	Decisions made by district have not served Black children well, but Black children's lack of success shrugged off by district
Whether the curriculum at Wesley should be seen as successful	No; test scores of Wesley students begin to drop by third grade; no long-term follow-up study of Wesley students has been done to validate success over time; many former Wesley children struggle later on in middle and high school	Yes; Wesley children reading when peers in similar neighborhoods are not; many Wesley students choose magnet or non-HISD schools after Wesley; for those who stay in neighborhood, social factors often overpower all else

a small group of HISD campuses that included Wesley Elementary, Osborne Elementary, Highland Heights Elementary, and M. C. Williams Middle School. The plan was approved before the Texas legislature approved a new education code that paved the way for more schools to sign charters. Under the new state code, there would be two kinds of charter schools: campus charters like Wesley that were granted by school boards, and open-enrollment charters (which were limited to 20 statewide), which were state-approved and usually designed from scratch.

Radically Differing Perceptions

Given the controversy that has swirled around Wesley Elementary for over two decades, it is not surprising that the school's newly acquired charter school status is perceived differently by different groups. Most striking is the stark contrast (see Table 5.2) between the perceptions of African Americans and European Americans. (Wesley staff members of European American descent were not included in this analysis as their perceptions differed systematically from those of other European Americans.) Differences were noticeable on a number of levels. For example, when Whites referred to past injustices they tended to explain them in terms of individual bigotry and opportunism, rushing to point out that Houston now had a Black superintendent. The implication was that things were different now.

In contrast, African Americans saw far less evidence of change. They saw the educational opportunities open to most Black students as far from adequate. Moreover, they credited this inequality to deep-rooted social causes, including a power structure that systematically disadvantaged Blacks. That an African American now headed the school district was seen by Blacks as a step forward. However, they pointed out that the superintendent had to deal with an entrenched bureaucracy. Many of the superintendent's subordinates, who would play key roles in implementing policy, had personal agendas of their own. There were even some Black respondents who saw the choice of an African American superintendent to lead a school district that had routinely failed to promote Blacks to other major district-level posts as a somewhat cynical ploy by the school board—a way to create the perception that things had changed, while leaving the "usual suspects" holding the reins of power.

From the viewpoint of many school district employees, recent changes in the reading curriculum had addressed the primary criticisms put forward by Dr. Lott and his supporters. In their eyes, this negated any need for Wesley Elementary to seek charter school status. The situation seemed quite different to many Blacks. They argued that, given the volatile politics involved, both the current superintendent and the curriculum he advocated could be gone in a short time. African American respondents em-

TABLE 5.2
Race-Related Attitudes Vis-à-Vis Wesley Elementary's
Need for Charter School Status

Perception of:	Viewpoint Common Among Whites	Viewpoint Common Among Blacks
Reasons for past lack of support, resources from district for Black schools	Result of mean-spirited actions taken by individuals who in past held positions of power, funneled resources to their own community	Result of institutional practices, individual attitudes, cultural assumptions that continue to systematically disadvantage Blacks
Prospect of improvement without significant change in existing system	Structures are now in place to remedy past problems; new curriculum has been mandated; Houston schools currently improving	System still operates to limit opportunities for Blacks, whose failure is explained as due to factors beyond control of public schools
Power of African American superintendent to change existing system	As top official in school district, the superintendent has great power to shape policy, influence school board actions	Majority of school district bureaucracy is unchanged; superintendent dependent on board support, cooperation of subordinates
What is required for real school reform to take place	Reform requires all groups concerned to work together to bring about desired goals	Reform requires concerted effort to change system in which Blacks have little voice
Best chance of bringing about meaningful reform	Enabling professionals with requisite knowledge to spearhead school reform	Putting real power in the hands of those who will defend the interests of Black children

phasized the need to put real power in the hands of those who would stalwartly defend the interests of African American children. They insisted on the need to change a system in which Black voices were too often silenced. Charter schools were seen as providing one way for the Black community to begin to "have some say" in the way that Black children were educated.

Taking Another View of the Data

There is, however, another angle from which the interview data can be viewed. The analysis already offered has two major limitations:

1. The sample of the European Americans interviewed was far from random; most were, or had been, professional educators.

2. The viewpoint of Dr. Lott differed in a systematic manner from the views of many other African American respondents.

Moreover, beginning with his first days at Wesley, when he had used money from his school activities fund to hire carpenters to repair the run-down building, Lott had shown a striking spirit of independence. When the district would not furnish funds to buy needed DISTAR materials, he had sponsored various fund-raising activities to obtain money. Setting up the charter school district was but a further extension of the entrepreneurial mind set Thaddeus Lott had long exhibited.

That Lott was not averse to experimentation was clear from the moment he took over at Wesley. The curriculum Lott gradually put together for Wesley was the result of trying one thing, then another, until he found something that worked. Eventually, adequate solutions were found for many of the challenges the school faced. During Lott's early years at Wesley, his problem-solving approach was viewed as acceptable, as long as it brought results. After the retirement of long-time HISD superintendent Billy Reagan, however, the climate within the school district became hostile to Lott's entrepreneurial approach to school administration. The incentive structure for principals changed. The new superintendent had an emphatically top-down leadership style. Principals were not expected to be innovators, but implementers of policies chosen at the district level; ideological alignment with the superintendent's views was emphasized.

Suddenly Lott was considered a "maverick." Criticism mounted. No longer was his school one to which the district pointed with pride. The high level of student achievement at Wesley was now explained away as "ephemeral." The tide of professional opinion had turned, not only in Houston, but nationally. DISTAR was distinctly out of fashion. Yet during this same period, publication of A Nation at Risk (1983) and other studies had focused public attention on the low achievement levels of many American students. Therefore, even as Lott fell out of favor within the school district, he found himself suddenly becoming a focus of attention among education-oriented business leaders, who began to point to Wesley as an example of what should be happening in other inner-city schools.

Under attack within HISD, Lott was able to use his growing support outside the district to generate the kind of publicity that made it difficult for district administrators to move against him without clear cause. Indeed, the attempt to find evidence of cheating at Wesley may have had its source in the frustration of district administrators who found this sort of "freelancing" a threat to their authority. When the incident garnered national news coverage, district administrators were forced to apologize. However, dynamics of the struggle had their costs for Lott, as well. For

there were elements within the Black community who reacted with suspicion to his close ties with members of the White business community.

SOCIAL JUSTICE SEEN FROM DIFFERING PERSPECTIVES

Going back at least as far as the publication of sociologist E. Franklin
Frazier's seminal 1957 study *Black Bourgeoisie: The Rise of a New Middle
Class,* suspicions have been expressed within the African American community that successful Blacks have accepted "unconditionally, the values of
the white bourgeois world" and that they "do not truly identify themselves
with Negroes." Thaddeus Lott's strong ties to the Houston African American community have been underscored again and again, as local Black leaders have rushed to defend Wesley and its principal. Yet there have also been
activists within the African American community who have criticized Lott.
For example, a few Black respondents in this study complained that Lott
had hired too many White teachers at Wesley. Others expressed distrust of
Lott's ties to members of the White business community.

There were also members of Houston's African American community
who felt Lott's continued "harping on" the issue of low academic achievement among inner-city children in Houston was a case of blaming the victim. They thought this focus on test scores pulled attention away from
much that was going right in the Black community. Lott himself shrugged
off such criticism, insisting that he was not blaming the children but the
adults who were failing to provide them with a real chance to succeed in
life. He argued that if an effective way of turning around the nation's inner-city schools was not found, millions of students might find that their
future had been foreclosed. Similar arguments had been made by the late
Hilde L. Mosse, MD:

> When a disorder affects so many people, one calls it an epidemic. An epi-
> demic is always caused by external forces, not by defects in the individual.
> This applies to psychologic disorders as much as to physical diseases. When
> so many children are affected by the same disorder, the explanation cannot
> possibly be individual psychopathology. Adverse social forces must be inves-
> tigated as the common cause. (Mosse, 1982, pp. 261–62)

To Lott, what mattered was addressing the problem at hand; it made
little sense to turn away potential allies, White or Black, who offered help
in dealing with the current epidemic of academic failure in the inner city.
Recent research has tended to confirm the daunting nature of the situation facing low-income and minority children. Currently 40% of the na-

tion's fourth graders cannot read at basic levels—68% in schools serving
children from low-income families (Lieberman & Colvin, 2000). A study
released by the Civil Rights Project at Harvard University (Colvin, 1999)
reported that in 1997, nearly 70% of Black students and 75% of Latinos attended schools that were primarily Latino and/or African American. Such
schools were far more likely to serve poor students, be overcrowded, and
have poorly trained teachers. Nor was there much that school districts
could do on their own to change the situation, as the recent rise in segregation had been tied to economics, immigration, and housing patterns.

What the school districts could do, Lott insisted, was focus on the task at
hand, realize that the ethnicity of the children sitting in the classroom was
less important to academic success than the quality of the teaching. Moreover, despite the presence of the dissenting voices referred to, Lott enjoyed the support of an overwhelming majority of Houston's African
American community. A newspaper article published just after a new
Houston school superintendent, Frank Petruzielo (predecessor to current
superintendent, Rod Paige), had arrived in town to replace the controversial Raymond provides considerable insight into the nature and effect of
that support.

> The story of Houston's Wesley Elementary School and its maverick princi-
> pal, Thaddeus Lott, was replayed Thanksgiving night on ABC's Prime Time
> Live, but with an update at the end.
>
> After the news segment depicting how the school had been shortchanged
> during former Superintendent Joan Raymond's administration, anchor-
> woman Diane Sawyer announced that much had changed at the school since
> the segment first was broadcast in June.
>
> For one thing, the school had received hundreds of calls and some
> $20,000 in donations, Sawyer said. And she pointed out that Raymond, who
> had clashed with Lott, was gone.
>
> Viewers saw film footage of new Superintendent Frank Petruzielo hug-
> ging Lott at a church service. Sawyer also noted that the Houston Independ-
> ent School District had spent $75,000 to transplant Wesley's reading pro-
> gram to seven other schools.
>
> Furthermore, Sawyer said, the school was no longer short of supplies, and
> Lott was no longer an outcast. In fact, she said, he had been in great demand
> to speak to business groups and educational groups all over the country. The
> Prime Time Live piece was first aired June 6, about two months after a
> Chronicle story about a Wesley teacher who had been wrongly suspected of
> helping students cheat on a standardized test. (Markley, 1991c)

That the updated *Prime Time Live* segment showed new HISD superintendent Frank Petruzielo embracing Thaddeus Lott at a church service
was no accident. The vocal support of African American church leaders

had been crucial to Lott's ability to survive as principal at Wesley. However, the connection went much deeper than a mere public show of solidarity. During the 1960s, nonviolent civil disobedience had become a cornerstone of the church-based African American civil rights movement. Leaders like the Rev. Martin Luther King had appealed to "the court of public opinion" to provide a voice to the otherwise voiceless. Thaddeus Lott, who had for years served as organist at his own church, had similarly relied on "the court of public opinion" to vindicate him when he came under attack for his work at Wesley. The groundswell of support for Lott that had followed news reports of the accusations leveled at his school by HISD officials had its roots in the same social dynamics that had created the old church-centered civil rights alliance.

As Comer (1997) noted, church membership has traditionally played an important role in Black social networks, offering a framework for framing social justice demands. Orlando Patterson (1997) observed, "Christianity is nothing if not a profoundly universalist religion. Its definitive break with Judaism, under the leadership of Paul—'the apostle to the Gentiles'—was on precisely this issue. In Christ, said Paul, 'there is neither Jew nor Greek, there is neither slave nor free, there is neither male nor female' " (p. 199). Scholars might point out (as Patterson did also) that "This is, of course, all very naive sociologically" (p. 199). Certainly there exist any number of sects and cults that have not allowed mere scriptural texts to divert them from attempting to "prove" that their members are more worthy, more deserving, than their neighbors. But, as Patterson also insisted, "Religion is about what ought to be" (p. 199). As a sociologist, he was keenly aware that what is and what ought to be are separate epistemological realms. A vision of what should, and could, be can have great motivating value. "For the majority of lower-class, poorly educated Afro-Americans, the Christian creed has been the only escape from the twin grip of racist biological determinism and liberal environmental determinism" (Patterson, 1997, p. 105).

What Patterson pointed out is that to explain one's own situation only in terms of outside influences is to reduce oneself to the level of an object. In the case of a victim of injustice, this not only demeans the victim by attributing all agency to the victimizer but, in assuming and legitimizing a wholly determinist social and moral universe, it explains away the injustice of the victimizer. All too often, the end result of subscribing to a deterministic view of the world is a resigned acceptance of the unacceptable. Whereas, despite the failings routinely pointed out by sociologists, Christianity provides a moral framework for critiquing the existing social system and for affirming the essential humanity of even the most disadvantaged.

At its best, Christianity offered comfort, solace, and dignity to Afro-Americans. . . .it also eventually provided the organizational framework and leadership for the triumphant civil rights movement (Patterson, p. 198).

So what does all this have to do with the public schools? Like religion, education is a universal activity of human societies. The form it takes may vary radically. But there is nothing inherently "Black" or "White" about either religion or schooling. What can be learned from the example of the Black church is how effectively Black Americans have been able to adapt forms of worship and religious organization, originally developed in Europe, to the needs of their own community. This was made possible by the organization of community-oriented churches by African-Americans, who focused on meeting the needs of their own community. This created a very different set of incentives than exist in a large bureaucracies, where individuals rise through the system by effectively aligning themselves with the priorities of those above them.

In contrast, public school bureaucracies in large urban areas have traditionally tended to discourage innovation at the school site and to encourage delivering a uniform curriculum in all neighborhood schools. Inner city residents have traditionally been perceived to be passive victims of oppression, unable to act effectively on their own behalf. When a "maverick" principal like Thaddeus Lott is able to create a "break the mold" school and to garner widespread community support, the reaction from the school district is too often a defensive one, an impulse to fend off a threat to the bureaucratic *status quo*. The long-term result has been predictable. As Yale law professor Harlon L. Dalton has observed, "Despite vast changes in our society, we often slide into familiar patterns. Those in control tend to remain in control. But their continued dominance comes at a price: a siege mentality and fear of revolt. Those at the bottom remain at the bottom, seething, and more than occasionally directing their anger outward" (1995, p. 100).

Generalizing from a single case is always risky. Yet it is worth noting that twice in its history Wesley has been a school known for academic excellence. The first era of excellence was before school desegregation in the South, when Wesley was part of a separate Black school system under Black control. At the time, work in the schools was one of the primary career opportunities available to educated African Americans. Black teachers and principals were looked on with respect in their own community. With integration, three things happened:

1. The Black community lost control of its own schools, many times resulting in a breakdown of communication between home and school.
2. Career opportunities for African Americans expanded, so that a lower percentage of Black college graduates went into teaching.

3. As more successful Blacks moved away, children living in inner-city neighborhoods were left without role models who made traditional forms of success seem attainable.

By the time that Thaddeus Lott took over as principal, Wesley had become a demoralized inner-city school, where the average sixth grader read at a second-grade level. Under the leadership of Dr. Lott, who had grown up in the old segregated Black school system, Wesley Elementary School became a very different place, with its students scoring as well on standardized tests as children in affluent suburban districts. However, the school's record of achievement was once again put at risk as the result of another initiative undertaken in the name of reform. Arguments both for and against the more radical formulations of whole language have already been discussed at length. But, in the present context, such arguments are beside the point. There can be little argument about the fact that school integration, as a reform, was both justified and long since overdue. Yet the manner in which school desegregation was carried out still had devastating consequences in many African American communities.

Whenever significant reform is attempted, one prediction that can be made with confidence is that there will be unintended results. If there is an effective feedback loop built into the system, needed corrections can be made in mid course, strengthening the overall reform effort. But when communication is weak or faulty, a real danger exists that the reform may be sidetracked, or that detrimental effects may outweigh the beneficial effects of reform. Moreover, such has been the history of race relations in the United States that effective communication between Black and White Americans has, over and over again, proved to be especially problematic. When White school district administrators mandate a reform to be carried out within schools that serve a predominantly Black student population, communication can be especially difficult. On the one hand, Whites tend to play down the racial issues involved. As Dalton (1995) noted:

> Dealing with race takes a considerable psychic toll, especially on those who are most attuned to the felt grievances of people of color. To recognize other people's pain and to contemplate that one might have contributed to or benefited from it is not easy. It is no wonder that genuinely decent White people sometimes try to make race disappear. (p. 126)

Yet this very reluctance to discuss the racial dimension of controversies like that which flared up around Wesley Elementary has tended to raise suspicion in the Black community. None of this is inevitable. However, it does make effective top-down reform difficult to carry out in large urban school districts with diverse populations. There is, of course, no guarantee that piecemeal reforms such as creating charter schools will work, either. But they do offer advantages. As the history of Wesley Elementary School suggests, there exist within the Black community resources that could significantly strengthen present school reform efforts. Neighborhood-based charter schools extend the promise of tapping such community resources.

One factor that must be faced is that, in contrast to the era before desegregation, African Americans no longer share the same geographic space, shop in the same stores, attend the same churches and schools. By 1990, 32% of Blacks in metropolitan areas lived in the suburbs (Dent, 1992). Yet there persists an impulse to experience a sense of kinship and connectedness, to gather together with others of similar background, with whom a frank and open dialogue can be carried on relatively easily. There has recently been much public discussion of the need for ways in which affluent African Americans who now reside in the suburbs can have an impact on the education and life chances of school children in the inner city. Charter schools open up such a possibility, that of joining with others who share a similar vision, in creating an autonomous public school.

In such charter schools, as in the neighborhood Black church, the possibility of new kinds of interactions might be opened up. As Dalton (1995) pointed out, there are reasons why even successful Blacks may find Black-dominated settings energizing:

> Being together in the same place and time does not necessarily mean that people are interacting on terms of true equality. More often than not, integration occurs exclusively on White people's terms. It consists of people of color being allowed to participate in a culture, an undertaking, or an environment from which they previously were, or felt, excluded. At best they are the new kids on the block, dependent on Whites for guidance. . . . Even when Whites and people of color are peers, there is often a significant difference in their comfort level, sense of security, and sense of belonging. Frequently the new kids feel out of their element, especially if they are having to perform on unfamiliar terrain or in a language in which they feel less than comfortable. (pp. 224–225)

Both eras of Wesley Elementary School's academic success took place under Black leadership. Parents, students, and school administrators felt themselves to be part of the same community. This made possible a level of "straight talk" and decisive action, in terms of addressing academic and disciplinary challenges, that was not possible during the era of the school's decline following desegregation. The charter school movement might allow other schools to use similar means to encourage effective action. Just as, in the arena of higher education, traditionally Black colleges have continued to have an important mission, even in an era of racial integration,

Black-led charter schools may turn out to play an important part in opening pathways to academic success for those who might otherwise have found themselves shut out.

FOLLOWING IN THE FOOTSTEPS OF HOUSTON'S MOST FAMOUS PRINCIPAL

Wesley Elementary School is currently in the process of confronting the challenges that any school faces when a charismatic leader passes the baton to someone else. Dr. Lott has now become director of a special charter school district, with responsibility for four schools. For several years after Dr. Lott ceased to be at Wesley full-time, veteran Wesley teacher and former assistant principal Wilma Rimes acted as site administrator, allowing the school to continue much as before. However, in the fall of 1999 Mrs. Rimes resigned as Wesley's principal, in order to assist Dr. Lott in his reform initiatives at other school sites. A number of veteran Wesley teachers have also taken positions elsewhere, with several working as teacher-trainers at other schools. This left Wesley's new, considerably younger, principal with the challenge of recruiting and training new teachers, while also building a new leadership team.

For Wesley Elementary, now under new leadership, as well as for the other schools in the charter school district, a new era is now beginning. In a sense the entire history of Wesley Elementary, as it has been described in this chapter, can be seen as the "prehistory" of a new organizational epoch. The challenges that Wesley and its sister charter schools now face are similar to those inherent in the creation of a new setting. The final result cannot yet be discerned. Thaddeus Lott, for one, is well aware of the challenges ahead. Thus it seems fitting to give him the final word on whether other schools, and other school administrators, will be able to replicate his record of success at Wesley Elementary:

> A lot of people ask, "Can this program be replicated?" The thing that bugs me is when somebody answers: "Well, I guess it could be replicated, but you know Thaddeus. . . . It takes somebody like him!" Hey, other people can do this! It can be replicated! I do have a zeal for children, and I do have a passion for it. But there are other people who have passion for helping. It's not like, "If he's not doing it, then, hey, nothing will happen." That's wrong! It can be replicated. But you've got to want it.

EPILOGUE

Over the last 42 years, the Houston Livestock Show and Rodeo (which draws nearly two million visitors annually) has contributed more than $68 million to educational causes—mostly in the form of college scholarships.

In 1993, rodeo officials decided to expand their efforts by reaching out to the 135,000 students in the Houston Independent School District who were unable to read at grade level. The Rodeo Institute for Teacher Excellence (RITE) would train teachers in specialized reading and classroom management skills. In May 1997, an innovative 3-year pilot program was begun, patterned on teaching methods used at Wesley Elementary School and supported by a $4.5 million funding commitment from the Rodeo.

Working with the Houston Independent School District, RITE serves teachers in HISD elementary schools with identified "at-risk" populations. After a week-long summer institute, participants are teamed with teacher/trainers for a year-long program of follow-up and support. Each teacher trainer visits participants' classrooms, offering advice, assistance, and reinforcement of acquired skills. Monthly meetings offer an opportunity for participants and the teacher/trainer to discuss problems, share experiences, and report progress. Students in these classrooms are tested at the beginning and end of the school year to measure their learning. In 1997, the program began with 75 teachers. By fall 2000, the RITE program was in 256 classrooms on 20 elementary school campuses, serving 5,643 Houston children.

Now under the leadership of Mrs. Wilma Rimes, the RITE program has received an additional $4.5 million from the Houston Livestock Show and Rodeo, providing funding for another 3 years. Given the program's rapid expansion, some variation in the degree and effectiveness of implementation is to be expected. However, an evaluation study carried out by researchers at the University of Houston showed that children who began the program in kindergarten achieved test scores that surpassed national norms. Those students who began the RITE program as first graders showed slightly greater performance gains than children in comparison classrooms and maintained those performance levels in second grade.

REFERENCES

Allen, R. V. (1976). *Language experiences in communication*. Boston: Houghton-Mifflin.
Bateman, B. (1991). Teaching word recognition to slow learning children. *Reading, Writing and Learning Disabilities, 7*, 1–16.
Becker, W. C., & Gersten, R. (1982). A follow-up of Follow Through: The later effects of the Direct Instruction model on children in fifth and sixth grades, *American Educational Research Journal, 19*, 75–92.
Bereiter, C., & Englemann, S. (1966). *Teaching disadvantaged children in the preschool*. Englewood Cliffs, NJ: Prentice Hall.
Bereiter, C., & Kurland, M. (1981). A constructive look at Follow Through results. *Interchange, 12*, 1–22.
Bergeron, B. S. (1990). What does the term "whole language" mean? Constructing a definition from the literature. *Journal of Reading Behavior, 22*, 301–329.

Broyles, W. Jr. (1980, February). Behind the lines, *Texas Monthly*, pp. 5, 6, 16.

Brunner, M. S. (1993). *Retarding America: The imprisonment of potential*. Portland, OR: Halcyon House.

Chall, J. S. (1991). *American reading instruction: Science, art, and ideology, all language and the creation of literacy*. Baltimore, MD: Orton Dyslexia Society.

Colvin, R. L. (1999, June 12). School segregation is growing, report finds. *Los Angeles Times*, pp. A1, A31.

Comer, J. P. (1997). *Waiting for a miracle: Why schools can't solve our problems—And how we can*. New York: Dutton.

Dalton, H. L. (1995). *Racial healing: Confronting the fear between blacks and whites*. New York: Doubleday.

Dudley-Marling, C., & Murphy, S. (1998). Editor's pages. *Language Arts, 76*, 8–9.

Edelsky, C. (1992). A talk with Carol Edelsky about politics and literacy. *Language Arts, 69*, 324–329.

Feldman, C. (1998, December 20). Roland moves on. *Houston Chronicle*, Lifestyle Section, p. 1.

Frazier, E. F. (1957). *Black bourgeoisie*. Glencoe, IL: Free Press.

Gagne, E. E. (1977). Educating delinquents: A review of research, *Journal of Special Education, 2*. Cited in M. S. Brunner (1993). *Retarding America: The imprisonment of potential*. Portland, OR: Halcyon House.

Gersten, R., & Dimino, J. (1993). Visions and revisions: a special education perspective on the Whole Language controversy. *Remedial and Special Education, 14*, 5–13.

Gersten, R., Keating, T., & Becker, W. (1988). The continued impact of the Direct Instruction model: Longitudinal studies of Follow Through students. *Education and Treatment of Children, 11*, 318–327.

Goodman, K. S. (1996). *Ken Goodman on reading: A common sense look at the nature of language and the science of reading*. Portsmouth, NH: Heinemann.

Greene, A. D. (1988, November 3). City does badly on TEAMS: HISD gets scores on state's skills test. *Houston Chronicle*, p. 1A.

Henry, M. K. (1993). The role of decoding in reading research and instruction. *Reading and Writing: An Interdisciplinary Journal, 5*, 105–112.

House, E. R., Glass, G. V., McLean, L. D., & Waler, D. F. (1978). No simple answer: Critique of the Follow Through evaluation. *Harvard Educational Review, 48*, 128–160.

Huizinga, et al. (1991). *Program of research on the causes and correlates of delinquency; urban delinquency and substance abuse*. Washington, DC: U.S. Department of Justice. Cited in M. S. Brunner (1993). *Retarding America: The imprisonment of potential*. Portland, OR: Halcyon House.

Lieberman, P., & Colvin, R. L. (2000, April 3). Can TV teach reading to kids 4 to 7? Tune in and see. *Los Angeles Times*, pp. A1, A12.

Lyon, G. R. (1998). Why reading is not a natural process. *Educational Leadership, 55*(6), 14–18.

Markley, M. (1990, November 10). HISD Board asking only one question of Raymond: Do you share our vision? *Houston Chronicle*, p. 1A.

Markley, M. (1991a, April 15). Teacher's humiliation called part of pattern. *Houston Chronicle*, p. 1A.

Markley, M. (1991b, October 27). Sounds of change: 8 Schools test return to phonetics. *Houston Chronicle*, p. 1C.

Markley, M. (1991c, November 30). Principal Lott's story has upbeat postscript. *Houston Chronicle*, p. 15B.

Mosse, H. L. (1982). *The complete handbook of children's reading disorders*. New York: Human Sciences Press.

National Commission on Excellence in Education. (1983). *A nation at risk: The imperative for educational reform*. Washington, DC: United States Government Printing Office.

Patterson, O. (1997). *The ordeal of integration: Progress and resentment in America's "racial" crisis.* Counterpoint Press.

Raspberry, W. (1998, March 31). Direct instruction sounds awful, but works. *Houston Chronicle*, p. 18A.

Rose, M. (1997, May/June). An instructional program that's worth stealing. *American Teacher, 18*(8), 10–12.

Schweinhart, L. J., Weikart, D. P., & Larner, W. B. (1986). Consequences of three pre-school curriculum models through age 15. *Early Childhood Research Quarterly, 1,* 15–45.

Serwer, B. L. (1969). Linguisitic support for a method of teaching beginning reading to Black children. *Reading Research Quarterly, 4,* 449–467.

Stahl, S. A. (1990). Riding the pendulum: A rejoinder to Schickedanz, and McGee & Lomax. *Review of Educational Research, 60,* 141–151.

Stahl, S. A. (1999). Why innovations come and go (and mostly go): The case of whole language. *Educational Researcher, 28*(8), 13–22.

Stahl, S. A., & Kuhn, M. R. (1995). Does Whole Language or instruction matchedto learning styles help children learn to read?, *School Psychology Review, 24,* 393–404.

Stanovich, K. E. (1986). *How to think straight about psychology.* Glenview, IL: Scott, Foresman.

Stauffer, R. G. (1970). *The language experience approach to the teaching of reading.* New York: Harper and Row.

Tannen, D. (1998). *The argument culture: Moving from debate to dialogue.* New York: Random House.

Theis, D. (1991, October 3). *Houston Press,* pp. 32, 33.

Tyack, D. (1974). *The one best system: A history of American urban education.* Cambridge, MA: Harvard University Press.

Vellutino, F. R. (1991). Introduction to three studies on reading acquisition: Convergent findings on theoretical foundations of code-oriented versus whole-language approaches to reading instruction. *Journal of Educational Psychology, 83,* 437–443.

Walker, E. S. (1996). Can institutions care? Evidence from segregated schooling of African American children. In M. J. Shujaa (Ed.), *Beyond segregation: The politics of quality in African American schooling.* Thousand Oaks, CA: Corwin Press.

Yates, G. C. R. (1988). Classroom research into effective teaching. *Australian Journal of Remedial Education, 20,* 4–9.

Chapter 6

Understanding the Complexities of Success in the Making of a New Setting: Case Study of the University of Houston Charter School of Technology

Barbara Korth
Indiana University

Sarason suggested that, at least tacitly, each new charter school that is developed poses a critique of traditional schooling. That critique gains validity if the new setting not only runs counter to existing schooling endeavors in its intentions and practices, but also succeeds at the attempt. Sarason (1972, 1998) argued that many attempts at creating new settings fail to live up to their original goals or vision. He pointed out that new settings would stand a better chance of succeeding if they (a) had expectations that took into account the experiences of those who had created similar settings in the past (including what Sarason identified as a predictable set of problems) and (b) had a procedure for resolving problems and conflicts as they surfaced (which Sarason believes can be at least partially accomplished through the creation of a "constitution" for the setting). In order for school leaders to hold a set of expectations that fit the realities involved in creating new settings, the stories of those schools already being developed must be told. This chapter, as others like it in the book, represents an effort to add to the body of reports on the development of charter schools.

The University of Houston Charter School of Technology (UHCST) opened its doors to students in January 1997. Sarason suggested that external critics be brought in to examine new settings, so the university contracted with an evaluation team even prior to the first day of school operations. This chapter was generated from the findings of that ongoing longitudinal evaluation project.

In particular, this chapter describes how "success" has been conceptualized by participants as they have worked to make the new setting a stable reality. It is hoped that this description will answer Sarason's call for "concepts that mirror the realities" entailed in constructing a new setting. Although several concepts could have become the focus of this chapter, it is fitting that the concept of success be described here because success is what creators of new settings hope to achieve. The concept *success*, as it is understood here, is derived of the experiences of participants in their work to establish a charter school. Thus, the concept necessarily references cultural ideologies and practices within the school.

The major points of the chapter can be summed up in two statements. The first is that success is conceptualized through complex constructs and is therefore not sufficiently captured through vague mission statements or broad goals as articulated by the lone perspectives of school organizers. As Catharine Perry (chap. 4, this volume) learned through her case study, success is not a mere matter of an institution remaining open and operationally functional. The second point is that once one is aware of the specific complexities involved in how success might be conceived and manifested, one can develop a path for reaching success and for doing so in a way that does not prohibit future growth and change.

THE UNFOLDING OF EXPECTATION
AND THE MEASURE OF SUCCESS

This chapter describes how people involved in the development of one specific charter school conceived of success to date—what they thought constituted a successful school. The University of Houston Charter School of Technology, presently in its fourth year of operation, was established financially through private startup funds obtained by a large public university. On the political level, the school was the first in the state to be granted a charter through a university. The school was informally and loosely aligned with (not formally coordinated with) a child development center run by the same university, housed in the same building, that employed the same philosophy (constructivism). The University of Houston Charter School's commitment to Piagetian constructivist philosophy has been its most important orienting characteristic.

During the planning stage (late fall 1996), organizers of the University of Houston Charter School of Technology decided to fund annual, thorough, external, qualitative evaluation studies of the school. Money was allocated to this qualitative evaluation project during every year of operation thus far, and the project was accomplished through a contract with the Houston Institute of Cultural Studies. Although institute representatives were involved in the planning of data collection prior to opening the school doors, the bulk of the evaluation work (performed through the institute) began on the day children arrived at the new school. This longitudinal evaluation project has documented the development of this new setting through more than 300 hours of classroom observations; participation in faculty meetings and school-wide activities; hundreds of hours of intensive interviews with parents, teachers, and administrators; and the collection of artifacts such as newsletters and reports to parents. Although it would not be possible to provide readers with a full report of this extensive case evaluation, this chapter is at least able to describe for school leaders the complexities embedded in how the school might be considered either a success or a failure or some measure of both. In other words, how would people involved with UHCST know whether or not it was succeeding? By what process and criteria would they be able to count UHCST a success or not?

Each year the evaluation study has reported the school a success, and yet this success is tempered by the presence of a modicum of conflict, struggles over priorities, challenges involving the bureaucracy, unmet needs, shifts in staff, and so forth. It is important for readers to know this because, as reported here, being able to recognize the successes was not always an easy matter: Success is not an all-or-nothing pronouncement. By detailing what criteria were used to label UHCST a success, it is possible to identify what specifically constituted the "success" of the school. These criteria are drawn from the actual experiences of the school and represent a rich view of success that organizers of new schools might find useful. Analysis of the qualitative data suggested that "success" was an evolving, multivoiced, and logically diverse concept.

After further introducing the readers to the University of Houston's Charter School, the chapter examines the nature of the concept of success employed by those people involved with UHCST. The concept *success* is understood through three substantially distinct categories. To fully grasp the manner in which school folks thought of success, one needs to see it as (a) evolving, (b) multivoiced, and (c) logically diverse. The final section of the chapter addresses the implications for coordination entailed in success as it developed within this one particular setting, leaving readers with a rich understanding of success and various strategies for the tracking and coordinating the notions of success as they emerge naturalistically.

WELCOME TO THE UNIVERSITY OF HOUSTON CHARTER SCHOOL OF TECHNOLOGY

As mentioned earlier, the UHCST is a public school committed to constructivist principles of education. Simply put, constructivist education emphasizes "learning and conceptualizing by doing." Following the developmental theories of Piaget, Kohlberg, Devries, and others, the UHCST aims to maximize opportunities for student choice, student-initiated projects, and student interactions within a rich and stimulating environment. Teachers act as resources, guides, and facilitators to nurture spontaneous learning activities in a student-centered classroom.

Proponents use the term *constructivism* because they believe that humans construct reality, concepts, worldviews, and so on through interactions with the environment. Staff members at the school believe that children develop cognitively, morally, and socially through their interactions with the physical and social environment. The charter school aimed both to embody constructivism and also to serve as an exemplar of constructivism for other educators (Peterman, 1996). Thus, the UHCST's most salient feature has been its commitment to constructivism. This does not mean that constructivism was similarly interpreted and practiced by everyone within the school, but that the philosophy provided points of dialogue, a set of standards for critique, and motivating force.

On entering a K–1 classroom for the first time, a visitor would immediately notice activity. Students are engaged and busy: They might have been interacting with each other while also manipulating blocks or puzzles or playing a game like "Sorry." The teachers would not be immediately visible because they are typically engaged with students in very informal ways, sitting on the floor, for example. The rooms might seem noisy because the multitude of separate student interactions would not be individually discernable unless one was involved in them. The physical environments are colorful and stimulating. Student creations are displayed prominently throughout the classrooms, including rules, poems, ideas, pictures, stories, and games. The student population is diverse: Ethnicity, size, and other differences are visible in a positive way. A visitor might also notice a warm atmosphere of community in the classrooms.

Students appear cooperative, interactive, and self-directing. Some youngsters might be on the rug building with blocks. A mixed-gender group could be spotted in the home center developing a play for future performance. Another group of children might be engaged in a game with one of the teachers. A couple of kids would be interacting on the computers. Others might be doing some artwork while another pair of students snuggles up together on the carpet to read books and look at pictures. The level of spontaneity, creative exploration, curiosity, and idea sharing is high. The children are expressive and happy. The teachers laugh and play with the children. A high degree of mutual respect and appreciation can be recognized. The teachers' "work" during this time seems so natural that only an astute visitor might notice the use of questioning to encourage higher order thinking, the quality of individualized attention to students, the high level of awareness, and the deliberate planning that the teachers employ. There is no front to the classroom, no teacher's desk, and no rows of students' desks. The visitor would see no signs of workbooks, standardized texts, or worksheets.

The UHCST has experienced incremental, planned growth. The number of classes has steadily increased and with it, staff, physical needs, and instructional opportunities. These increases were projected in the school's Strategic Plan. The UHCST started with one mixed-age kindergarten–first grade class in January 1997. There were 1 principal, 1 lead teacher, 1 assistant teacher (all three of whom had many years of experience in constructivist education programs), 21 children (all pulled at midyear from classrooms around the city), and an emerging parents' association. In the second year of operation the school doubled its size and boasted two classes, two lead teachers, two assistant teachers, twice as many students, an administrative assistant, and the same principal. In the third year of operation, the school again doubled—the original class of students moving up and new classes of students being added at the kindergarten–first grade level. In its fourth year, the school was comprised of 5 classes, 5 lead teachers, 5 assistant teachers, 2 administrative assistants, 1 principal, and 101 students and some special programs instructors (e.g., people to teach physical education and music). Of the 101 students, 7 were Asian, 31 were African American, 27 were Hispanic, and 36 were White.

Thus far only two of the teaching staff have left the school and only a handful of children have left. Even though organizers planned the systematic growth of the school, there have been crises related to its growth. For example, at the beginning of the third year, a new class was added at the last minute (because of demand for placements). This meant finding space on the university campus (because the school proper still lacked its own designated building), hiring new teachers, and increasing administrative responsibilities. By all staff and parent accounts, this time was one of enormous stress for the school community. The principal had to teach the new class for several weeks. The administrative assistant quit. The coordination of staff became a bit more formalized.

Until its fourth year, the school was housed in various rooms in existing university buildings. With the exception of one class, during the third year of operation, the building used for classes and offices was part of the College of Technology. There was an outside open-air, science lab space (built for the school by architectural graduate students enrolled in a design course) and a grassy area outside the same building, both of which UHCST used on a daily basis. By the fourth year (1999–2000), a portable building was rented and placed adjacent to the College of Technology. Two classrooms were housed in this portable building so that the school was able to serve five classes of students, kindergarten through fourth grade, mostly in mixed-aged classes.

The staff met formally once a week; once in a while they would have lunch together on a Friday. The teachers and principal saw one another most days of the week, but the principal's visibility in any one class diminished as the school grew. The principal used e-mail to interact during hectic times of the day/week. Teachers greeted the parents on a daily basis, the most direct and informal mechanism for staying in close communicative touch with the parents. It was not uncommon for the principal to see the parents too.

The UHCST classrooms are active places where parents, principal, and others are welcome. The child-centered environments were naturalistic, interesting, and developmentally sensitive, with children and teachers cooperatively developing them. These environments represented one part of the critique UHCST manifested against traditional public schooling.

SUCCESS UHCST STYLE

Knowing that the groups of people who start up a new school are hoping for success, we might expect the creators of the new setting to have a vision or a plan that would establish some criteria for success. Often such criteria for success are articulated in vague and broad terms, terms that do not facilitate the kind of specificity required in establishing that one's school is succeeding. For example, if a school had a goal like "Strive for knowledge and truth in all you do" (see Korach, chap. 3, this volume), it would be very difficult to know when the school has succeeded.

The broad mission statement of the UHCST, as articulated in its Strategic Plan, is "to provide a student-centered curriculum for the 21st century that enhances the intellectual development, technological literacy, and leadership ability of students" (p. 4). This mission statement is immediately buttressed with the articulation of seven advantages that graduates of the school are expected to experience. These seven advantages are:

1. Be successful students who enjoy school.
2. Be technologically competent in academic and varied practical areas.
3. Be fully developed physically, socially, and intellectually.
4. Be confident problem-solvers who are willing to "figure it out."
5. Be actively, willingly literate in reading, writing, quantifying, and computer technology.
6. Be experienced and confident in cooperative effort and communication.

7. Be on the threshold of mature rationality, combining the beginning stage of hypothetical logic with long-practiced respect for the exchange of reasons. (Peterman, 1996, p. 4)

Although these statements are certainly more specific, they are not all equally easy to pin down in terms of how people at the school might know that they are succeeding with them.

In addition to the mission statement and its seven qualifiers, school organizers (primarily constructivist consultant Dr. Barbara Peterman) included a list of five goals for the Charter School. These five goals, as stated in the Strategic Plan, were:

1. To establish a commitment to learning on the part of the students, parents, and educators through constructivist educational practice.
2. To develop the problem-solving and knowledge-building abilities of the students toward the goal of mature judgment and scientific methodology in dealing with their environments.
3. To design and implement an educational program that applies the principles of human development and scientific technology as a motivational curricular base.
4. To offer research opportunities that University of Houston (UH) faculty and graduate students can use for testing and analyzing pedagogical theory and practice.
5. To serve our students and the community as one of the Houston schools exemplifying a clearly defined model of effective appropriate practice. (Peterman, 1996, pp. 4–5)

Plans for external assessment of school practices, as well as assessment of student learning and development, were also articulated. Assessment was meant to determine the extent to which UH was succeeding and the manner through which such success was being obtained. Assessment would also reveal any limitations to success. However, none of these prearticulated "guides" for success would prove sufficient for understanding the success (or the lack thereof) experienced by the school once it became operational.

For UHCST, *success* entailed these characteristic constructs: Success was evolving, success was multivoiced, and success was logically diverse or multirelational. Each of these domains is next described as they were experienced by those involved in the development of the UH Charter School. The domains represent ways in which the people active at UHCST understood success as it related to the school specifically. These domains were informed by the goals and mission of the school, but were also broader. That is, this view of success includes the ideas of success that were articulated as part of the original vision, but this view is neither limited to that plan nor is it as vague.

Success as an Evolving Construct

Success was not conceived as a static phenomenon. Rather, *success* was understood in evolutionary terms: How successes were recognized (counted) and classified continually changed over time. Participants' expectations changed over time. Through this long-term evaluation project it has been possible to note shifts in what was touted as either success or the lack thereof. The shifts were evidenced through the following forms: successive approximations (toward an overall goal), emergent–cumulative developments, and problem-solving responses.

Successive approximations were steady, empirically recognizable increments toward larger or overall goals. These approximations were somewhat predictable and were, to some extent, planned. For example, when organizers designed the development of the school, they decided to start with one class. This one class would progress through the grade levels, and new classes would be added at the base (K–1 level). In this way the school would experience steady, incremental growth toward the overall goal of serving kindergarten through fifth-grade students. According to the Strategic Plan (Peterman, 1996), enrollment goals were established as shown in Table 6.1.

At the time of this writing, the charter school was in Phase 4 as articulated in Table 6.1 (*Strategic Plan*, 1996, p. 11). No PreK was ever implemented, and there were shifts in this plan, some of which are discussed in what follows.

Another example of the way success evolved through successive approximations was evidenced in how participants viewed the charter school not having its own building. For the first year, the charter school's one class and administrative spaces were housed in the building of the College of Technology. Parents, teachers, and others involved with the school did

TABLE 6.1
Enrollment Goals

Phase	School Year	Classes	Projected Enrollment
1	Spring 1997	Prek–1	20
2	Fall 1997	Prek–1, K–2	40
3	Fall 1998	Prek–1, K–1, K–2, 1–3	80
4	Fall 1999	Prek–1, K–1, K–2, 1–3, 2–4	100
5	Fall 2000	Prek–1, K–1, K–2, 1–3, 2–4, 3–5	120

not count the lack of a school building the first year as a failure. Neverthe-less, related problems mounted so that in the third year, when the school still did not have its own building and had experienced significant frustra-tion with the architects, one of the classes was placed in another building down the street. No one liked this and it was considered a "possible fail-ure" on the part of the school if it were not to be remedied. One teacher expressed worry that the lack of a building meant that the university was-n't really committed to the school. Several parents expressed growing dis-may, saying things like, "They promised a building. Without it, I don't have any confidence that they [the university] will keep the program going through the fifth grade." The school rented a portable building at the start of the fourth year, and this was counted as a moderate success. However, if the school is not afforded its own building in the relatively near future, the lack of a building will indicate failure to advocates in a way that it did not in-dicate failure during the first year. In other words, the expectations evolved. What was not considered a failure in year 1 would become a failure over time. And the successive approximations toward appropriate and inde-pendent space—a building of one's own—carry evolving expectations.

Successive approximations were applied to some aspects of profes-sional growth and the availability of school services. Here is an example. The school does not have a cafeteria and therefore does not have any lunch options for students. These are not counted as failures, but from an evolutionary perspective, these could eventually be expected. Another ex-ample involves providing services for special needs students. This proved most challenging for the school, and the school has improved in its re-sponse to such needs. In the first year, there was one child with special needs, whose parents voluntarily provided speech support privately. These parents were both willing and able to do this. Thus, UHCST did not provide speech services in its first year. However, by the third year, not providing speech services would have been counted as a failure because more children were involved and the school was, of course, responsible for meeting these needs.

Emergent–cumulative shifts in the ways participants conceived of success were similar to those experienced as successive approximations in that they were additive and tended to build on earlier constructs. However, the emergent–cumulative shifts were more emergent, not the result of plan-ning and specified overall goals. One clear example involved parents' views of the school's "success with students." The school was opened at mid-school year (January 1997) with one K–1 mixed-age class. All of the students enrolled in that class were pulled out of another school program in the middle of the year. Interview data indicated that without exception the parents who enrolled their children at UHCST in January 1997 were dissatisfied with their children's pre-UHCST education. (This finding confirms findings that many people expect the new setting to be "better than" previous settings.) According to parents' reports, their children (without exception among this group of youngsters) hated going to school (prior to attending the charter school) and expressed negative feelings about themselves and learning. Many parents expressed something similar to this quote: "The teacher used to always tell me how bad my child was. He was so unhappy. He hated school. He hated learning. Now he is so curious. He loves to go to school. He talks all the time about things he is learning. His teachers like him."

The evaluation of that initial semester reported that parents were extremely happy with UHCST because their children were happy and seemed to enjoy school a lot. For parents, part of UHCST successfulness in the first year entailed having happy, satisfied children who "wanted" to go to school. The following comment, offered by one of the parents, was echoed by all of the parents interviewed the first year:

> Once in a while, [the child] says, "Well, I don't feel like going," but rarely. Whereas the kids walking to the other school were just larva. There was just no life and they were just dragging themselves up the steps, no smiles, no running, no . . . uh . . . You know, the Charter School, they can't wait to get in there. They're laughing and they're having fun and I think that's great.

While some parents attributed to the school a noticeable swell of curiosity exhibited by their children, the emphases and bulk of their "judgments" of the school had to do with the contentment their children seemed to be experiencing.

By the second year, these same parents (reinterviewed) extended their criteria of success to include vague notions of academic advancement. The parent just quoted said this during the second year's evaluation:

> And we should add that we understand part of the constructivist philosophy is that they learn through play. And so I will acknowledge that a lot of the playing, that there is some learning involved in that. But when the emphasis is on playing, then when we need to get him down to doing his work then his emphasis is still on playing. And we think there ought to be a balance in those areas.

Many of the parents told interviewers that their children should be learning to read and write and do arithmetic and spelling, at the very least. Some parents had more detailed articulations of academic skills that their children would likely acquire if the school were to be counted as successful. These academic notions of success were additive extensions to the idea that success entailed having happy students who wanted to go to school. The academic concerns were definitely not foregrounded in the parents' evaluations of the school the first year, as they were hardly ever mentioned except through use of the concept "curiosity."

After the second year, some parents administered academic assessment tests of various kinds (formal and informal) to their children just to gain some reassurance that their children were keeping academic pace with same-age, public school peers. Nevertheless, in every case, the parents also reported that their children were happy at the charter school and that this too was still important. One parent said that her son was very "excited and enthusiastic about school." This sentiment was expressed in various ways by every parent interviewed. These examples illustrate the emergent–cumulative evolutionary nature of success at UHCST: Children must be happy; then children must be making academic progress.

Problem solving involved deliberately making changes as direct responses to identified problems and thus also embodied the evolutionary nature of success at the UH Charter School. The staff expected to respond to problems through an ongoing process. An interesting example involved a temporary adaptation of constructivist practice in order to strengthen and support the staff. One of the teachers, after teaching a mixed-age class for one year, requested a single-grade class in an attempt to strengthen her capacity to employ developmentally appropriate teaching practices with children older than those with whom she was used to working. In response, the principal of the school established two single-grade classes even though the constructivist philosophy of the school strongly favors mixed-age classrooms and the school had intended to develop *only* multiage classes. This shift was the direct effect of employing a teacher-proposed solution to a self-identified problem—namely, inexperience with developmentally appropriate teaching practices adapted for a particular age range of student. Here success involved responding to an identified problem: a dynamic task and one completely congruent with constructivist philosophy!

To summarize, the data suggested that for UHCST, *success* meant evolution. This conceptualization did not emphasize ultimate success in the form of some final, utopian goal or idea. Even formal mission statements and goals were considered pliable and were manifested only through successive approximations, not through emergent–cumulative or problem-solving forms of evolution.

Sarason (1972, 1998) argued that new settings must establish structural mechanisms for development. These structural mechanisms must be capable of accessing the tensions produced by dynamic, evolving, changing systems. Somehow participants involved in the construction of the new setting had to be able to coordinate and negotiate the evolutionary character of success. There are practical implications to this: How would one be able to trace the shifts in a manner that would preclude losing touch with these shifts? How would one be able to evaluate the shifts as conducive to or congruent with other features of success at UHCST? UHCST has, thus far, used the annual evaluation report and data collection process as one way of systematically staying tuned in to the evolutionary specifics of success. UHCST also worked to maintain open communication among its actors. Maintaining such communication was becoming more and more problematic as the school's complexity increased. Nevertheless, the following practices were conducive to encouraging opportunities for openness: weekly staff meetings, use of technology, and Interpersonal Process Recall sessions (an interpersonal counseling process).

Because of the changing nature of the setting, some systematic process for gaining access to the views of success and their shifts over time was required. These efforts required a fundamental ethical position with respect to staying open to shifts while honoring agreed-on positions and plans. In other words, consensus was honored but its products were not sanctified. Actors had to set dependable (systematically available) means for keeping ongoing access and reflection available: means like regular meetings, ongoing evaluation, modes and procedures for reporting concerns and confronting conflict, and so on. Sarason suggested that these systematic opportunities be articulated in a constitution. Moreover, the meaningfulness of such procedures rest in their power to effect/examine change—they indicate a responsive, system, one in which there is a bounded amount of openness, forgiveness, and freedom from sanction. The teacher who identified her own need for a single-grade classroom needed to be in such a responsive context in order to generate solutions.

Success as a Multivoiced Construct

Success at UHCST was not merely a function of administrative goal setting or institutional survival. There were many voices (parents, administrators, the state of Texas, and other stakeholders) involved in the ongoing construction of this new setting. Each of the groups of voices had within it some individual variation (intragroup), and across the groups there was some perspectival variation (intergroup). Each of the many voices could be categorized as either internal or external (these boundaries were employed and defined by the actors involved with the everyday workings of the school, not by me). The findings suggested that *success* was multivoiced because no one voice accounted for all of the ways in which the school might be evaluated as either successful or not.

Internal Voices

There were several internal groups of participants whose voices regarding success were constitutive and distinguishable: principal, teaching staff, parents, and students. Each voice emphasized and brought forth a different view of success. These voices are given truncated articulation here in order to show how voices complemented, overlapped, and opposed each other. These voices are used as examples of how it is necessary to hear, or at least be aware of, all voices in order to arrive at a rich understanding what people in a setting consider constitutive of success.

The *principal's voice* was the broadest in terms of the amount of terrain covered. The notion of success embodied in her perspective included interpersonal relationships, awareness of the interests of the various participants (especially parents), safety, staff management, state and federal mandates and compliance issues, self-evaluation, and use of constructivism (among other things). The primary way that she conceived of the school's success to date was through her commitment to constructivism. Her voice brought to life the school's original and on-going vision (as articulated formally in the Strategic Plan, 1996, and as practiced within the school). Two other prominent influences over her definition of successfulness were parent satisfaction and student well-being (which is, in fact, a strong point in the Strategic Plan, but in more generalized terms than is meant here). Moreover, she did not think that the school could ultimately succeed if tensions among the staff went unspoken or unresolved. The characteristics of parent satisfaction, student well-being, and open staff relations were described by the principal as essential manifestations of constructivist schools.

Another internal voice important in the conceptualizing of success was that of the *teaching staff*. Teachers conceived of success according to the following categories: student performance, classroom environment, professional growth, collaboration with peers, and positive interactions with parents. Throughout the evaluation studies, the teachers most frequently and fluently described their work in terms of students and student activity/performance. When teachers talked about student activity/performance, they usually referred to individual student activities and the development of specific students. Teachers also conceived of success at UHCST as a matter of having a realistic, useful classroom environment full of developmentally appropriate educational opportunities. They counted as successes their incorporation of developmentally appropriate, stimulating, accessible, resourceful, manipulatable materials and pedagogy into their classrooms.

Furthermore, these educators discussed success in terms of their own ongoing professional development. Teachers talked about learning new pedagogy, developing and integrating curriculum, and trying out new materials. Moreover, teachers were able to identify mechanisms (e.g., access to professional conferences) that supported their professional growth, and they could articulate these mechanisms as part of how they conceived of the school's success.

Collaboration with peers and interacting positively with parents further contributed to how teachers conceived of their own success. Teachers counted their interactions as successful when the communication was relatively open (or free of the "need" to hide feelings, practices, or discomfort), when the communication facilitated or supported autonomy, and when the various points of view expressed were understood by all of the participants and new information was acquired as a result. When it is said that teachers counted these as successful, that is not to say that teachers evaluated themselves as successful given these characteristics. Instead, it means that these domains constituted the emergent, self-generated criteria on which each of the teachers could establish personal success or lack thereof. For example, teachers reported a few unsuccessful experiences in their collaborations with peers that were the effect of closed communication, lack of a sense of "safety" in faculty meetings, and lack of time. Thus collaboration with peers was one feature of the way teachers conceived of success and measured the extent of their own success.

Parent interviews provided access to the *voice of parents*. Analysis resulted in the construction of a set of emergent, implicit criteria indicative of how the parents, at least tacitly, determined the successfulness of the school. Parents did not count the actualization of constructivism as a success because for these parents, the school was synonymous with constructivism. In other words, they were not able to recognize that one classroom might have actualized constructivist practices more fluently or successfully than another; instead, they assumed that whatever the teachers were doing *was* constructivism. (This could change over time with more exposure to various implementations of constructivism across teachers and additional parent education.)

For parents, there were five dimensions through which they judged the success (or by implication, the failure) of UHCST: student learning, child contentment, parental involvement, quality of staff, and management and organizational structure. These dimensions, with their corresponding criteria, were "emergent" because they were derived of hermeneutic inferences involved in the meaning-making activities of the participants and were not imposed by the evaluators. Also, as noted in the previous section, these dimensions evolved over time and should not be thought of it in static terms. The dimensions are presented through a brief description of each and the articulation of sets of questions that seemed pertinent to parents' understandings of success. Those questions framed the substance of the parents' voice for each of the dimensions.

Student Learning.

- Was the child learning?
- How can I know whether the child was learning?

- How was the child performing compared to others his or her age?
- What was the child producing in the classroom?
- What activities was the child engaged in through class work?
- How can I know these activities are effective?
- Did the child learn specific things (such as math facts, spelling, and so forth)?

This domain was very important to parents, but was almost exclusively conceived of through their own experiences with traditional schooling practices. Nearly all of the questions the parents had about learning reflected a very traditional view of schooling. So although the parents had sought out a nontraditional form of schooling for their children, many of them were still conceptualizing schooling success in traditional terms. This was especially the case when parents employed criteria of "normality" about their individual child's learning (e.g., how does my child's reading compare to another child of the same age?). One parent went to the trouble of taking her child to the library in the summer to administer standardized tests and pin down the child's academic performance with reference to same-age peers. A tension between traditional outcomes of schooling and nontraditional approaches to schooling has not yet been resolved for most of the parents. Moreover, this tension indicated to evaluators a distinction between reasons for enrolling children in nontraditional schooling (child contentment) and the expectations associated with outcomes (which retained traditional schooling measurement and criteria). This is an important point for school planners.

Child Contentment.

- Was the child happy?
- Did the child want to go to school?
- Did the child feel liked by the teachers?
- Did the child have friends?
- Did the child talk positively about the school?

Student contentment was very important to the parents, but more important for the first class of children than for subsequent classes because that first class was comprised of children who were either very unhappy or unsuccessful in the classrooms in which they were previously enrolled. Nevertheless, across all groups of parents, child contentment was most often linked to reasons parents were interested in a nontraditional form of schooling, whereas the dimension of student learning was still directly tied to traditional criteria and assessment models of achievement. The tensions researchers spotted between the content of this dimension and the content of the one just discussed were being articulated in the more recent years of the school's life. Some parents expressed a belief that student contentment (some "fun") might have to be sacrificed for the sake of learning. A potential source of conflict and an existing source of misunderstanding or skepticism regarding constructivist educational approaches would have an impact on parent understanding of the success of the school.

Parental Involvement.

- Was the school open to parents? Were parents welcomed? Were they listened to?
- Was the communication positive and honest and frequent between parents and the school?
- Were there many and varied ways to be involved with the school?
- Did faculty accept parents' points of view?

Parents reported feeling very welcomed at the school. They identified regular opportunities to interact with staff, and they had many different kinds of opportunities for participating in the school activities. One parent said this: "There's an openness about the school, an accessibility that I appreciate and an opportunity for parents [to participate]. I like to know what's going on and we're kept very much informed about what's going on." Parents were, indeed, insiders in the everyday processes of the school. One can easily imagine a school site where parents are treated and thought of as outsiders.

Quality of Staff.

- Were the teachers concerned about my child?
- Did the teachers talk with me?
- Did the teachers and/or principal answer my questions?
- Was the staff accessible and friendly?
- What happened when there was a problem?
- Did I feel respected and listened to during disagreements?
- How much did the staff know about education?
- What were their credentials? (Longevity was highly valued.)
- Did the teachers have "good" personalities?

Parents of children at UHCST were pleased with the high quality of the staff. The preceding questions indicate what "quality of staff" meant for parents. This area of success probably held the greatest influence over parents' decisions to keep their children at the school. Moreover, there was an emerging sense of trust and confidence in the personal quality of the teaching and administrative staff. Parents could not have talked more positively about the teachers than they did. And this finding was very consistent across both parents and the teachers they scrutinized over the years studied to date.

Management and Organizational Structure.

- What was the size of the class?
- How were the classes organized and how were students assigned?
- How were school decisions made?
- Who could one complain to if there was a problem?
- What was the role of the university in getting things done at UHCST?
- What opportunities (both typical and special) were available for the students (e.g., after-school care, music, use of the university campus)?

Parents talked very positively about the diversity of the classrooms, mixed-age grouping, and the low student to teacher ratio. According to one unpublished spin-off study (Marsh, 1999), these views among parents were overwhelming consistent. Their views of the internal structure of the school were positive, but they viewed the university as a bureaucratic arm not exactly in sync with the school. Parents distinguished the internal organization and management of the school from external bureaucracy. There was a tendency to voice support and appreciation for the internal administration of the school while finding fault with the faceless university and state-level bureaucracies. Parents reported things like this: "The Charter School is continually hobbled by UH bureaucracy." The tension between internal voices and external ones was evidenced here. Moreover, it would be possible to imagine a time when the university officials would be considered insiders and the university bureaucracy would not hold this faceless external position.

Another internal voice constituting what it meant to be successful at UHCST was the *collective voice of the students* themselves. Observation data that indicated how students viewed themselves were reconstructed, and through this process it was possible to develop emergent "ideal" types of successful students. *Success* was reconstructed to articulate the characteristics of children who were engaged within the classroom in ways that were associated with participation, contentment, and sociointellectual involvement. The reconstructions were initially reported in the form of a narration of a typical day for successful and unsuccessful children (Korth, 1997). This analysis made it possible to list student characteristics that the children themselves at least tacitly recognized as successful within the context of their UHCST classroom. One point of concern for evaluators was that the students made sense of success by tacitly differentiating across gender. Thus, the distinctions offered next were meaningfully emergent from within the classroom cultures themselves; gender was not an a priori category. It is important to remember that this collective voice is situated and emergent—its particulars are not generalizable. Thus, the descriptions that follow only demonstrate that students develop, at least tacitly, acting notions of successfulness. These notions, whatever their specifics, are an important part of any school's success.

Most successful girls were students who displayed happiness (smiled often, walked with a bouncy step, laughed, and so on), were assertive (e.g., they articulated their points of view and talked positively about their own work), engaged in classroom routine and activities, supported fellow students (by acknowledging good work, patting or stroking others, and so on), and practiced positive conflict-resolution skills (they rarely ended up in a dispute with a peer, managing instead to resolve conflict peacefully while retaining positive social relations). Less successful girls were less content (cried more, expressed displeasure through words, did not seem happy), were less attentive during circle time and less concentrated during center time than those girls who were more successful, were frequently in disputes, were not thought of as "smart" by fellow classmates, were less integrated into the classroom routines (e.g., did not clean up centers or prepare to go outside as smoothly as others), and did not have as many self-initiated, non-conflict-oriented interactions with peers.

Most successful boys were confident (offered their ideas frequently and loudly for class/teacher consideration) and happy during almost all classroom activities. These successful boys frequently sought attention from peers and teachers (approached the teachers and peers often during center time, raised hands often during group time), were highly verbal (able to articulate theories and ideas and engage in logical–verbal disputes), and frequently took on leadership roles in the classroom. They were more often in disputes than either successful girls or less successful boys, but these disputes did not manifest as negative in the long run. The most successful boys were considered "smart" by other children in the class. Less successful boys constituted the quietest, least noticed group of students in the class. These boys did not interact as positively or willingly as other children in the classroom. They did not join already existing groups smoothly (they might, instead, jump into a group by disrupting the play that was going on). These boys, however, usually kept to themselves and often refrained from activities that might call attention to them (like raising their hands or approaching a teacher). Less successful boys were clearly less verbal, less interactive, and more often alone than more successful boys.

Given this ideal-typical kind of reconstruction, it was possible to articulate how success was, at least tacitly, conceived by students in UHCST classrooms. These notions of success contributed to the overall construction of success as a useful concept in the development of the Charter School. These forms of success probably represent tacit cultural structures shared by many of the students when interacting in the UHCST classroom. It was important to understand how the children thought of themselves as successful in the classroom because these forms of success did not surface through any of the other voices represented in the data. The gender differences were actually in opposition to views of successfulness intended by the teachers. However, the success related to verbal ability among males was a good match for the notions of success held by the teachers.

This very complex set of internal voices must be coordinated within the school in order to have a most fully integrated understanding and potential for success. Also, it is important to note that these voices do not represent entirely compatible views. Internal coordination of the views requires the integration and negotiation of various perspectives. For example, there were some inconsistencies within the parent perspective, there were some gendered views of success among students that were counter to the intentions of the teaching staff, and so on. Coordination of voices does not result in the absence of tensions and/or conflicts, but rather in opportunities to admit, understand, acknowledge, and account for them in practical ways.

External Voices

In addition to those voices raised from within the UHCST circle of immediate participants, there were voices external to that group that contributed to the conceptualization of success. Sarason (1998) claimed that "almost all leaders of new settings I have known have said that they belatedly learned that preoccupation with the internal development of the new setting blinded them to the importance of potential sources of [external] constraint" (pp. 26–27). The most powerful voices external to the UHCST included University of Houston administrators and Board of Regents, University of Houston College of Technology faculty (in whose building the charter school had been "temporarily" situated), the Texas Education Agency, the state of Texas, and various professional groups that could inform criteria for success, such as the National Association for the Education of Young Children. Moreover, the evaluation team of the Houston Institute of Cultural Studies conducting this qualitative study constituted an external voice.

Each of these external voices carried their own expectations for success. Some of these were mutually compatible and others were not. The various expectations were articulated in the form of state mandated testing, control of budget, policy implementations, waivers, recommendations and commendations, "professional" criteria on evaluation reports, and so forth. Some of the external voices were constructed through cultural practices and were open to face-to-face communication. The evaluation project was of this type. Others carried no real opportunity for communicative negotiation. State-mandated, high-stakes testing was of this type.

Data involving relevant external voices has been accruing over the last couple of years and should be reported on in future papers. Preliminary analysis indicates that the external voices and their coordination with internal voices are highly complex matters. In the first few years of the school's operation, the external voices were seldom mentioned by "internal" actors. In more recent years, this has changed, but the magnitude and effects of those changes are not yet known.

All of the forms of success articulated through external voices presented themselves as either administrative or financial statements and were coordinated within the charter school through the language of needs and interests, efficiency and effectiveness. In general, the standards of efficiency and effectiveness carried particular connotations for success, but connotations that were put into place through situated relations and practices. For example, among Texas educators, one criterion for effectiveness is student performance on state-mandated achievement tests. This criterion is imposed externally by state mandates, but can gain internal legitimation if the criterion is personally taken up by the teachers, administrators, parents, and students in the school through the priorities, goals, and other forms of explicit intentions. This would be difficult if the criteria were not congruent with other criteria for success committed to by the participants. Generally speaking, none of the educators at UHCST would voluntarily choose to employ this form of "test" as a measure of learning or as measure of "good" practice. That they did so is a mark of the power of an external voice (the state) to constrain practice in a way that does not depend on the consensus of its participants. That is, the testing policy did not require communicative assent; instead, it required compliance.

With compliance required, what was left open for communicative assent among actors were these kinds of things: how can compliance be facilitated without compromising other important constructivist educational practices, how can the test be made sense of through existing practices, how can the individual actors find merit in the practice, and so forth. The evaluation report of the second year stated, "The TAAS [Texas Assessment of Academic Skills] test and related expectations posed a major challenge for the UHCST [internal] community" (p. 32). The test represented a constraint on the school's constructivist practices: a constraint because the educators would not have freely assented to give the test to their students and had no opportunity for negotiation. A tension between externally mandated forms of success and internal ones was evidenced. With constructivism there is a deemphasis on rote learning, paper–pencil tests, and closed-response (like multiple-choice) assessments. Constructivists are interested in active, realistic knowledge acquisition that is sensitive to developmental levels of students. The TAAS test does not fit the constructivist view of knowledge, does not appropriately assess, and is (for elementary school students particularly) developmentally less appropriate than other forms of assessment.

Coordination across and among the various voices of people and positions involved with the school has been the most complex and problematic challenge for the charter school thus far. Coordination of these voices must occur on at least two levels. First, the internal voices must be coordinated with another. Second, the external voices must be coordinated with the internal voices.

The problems associated with coordinating voice internally included gaining access to the various voices, handling potential or actual conflicts, and making sure the same "language" was being used. Parents and teachers and students must have a voice. Parents, teachers, and students must simultaneously be leaders in the dialogue about success. Points of view should be respected and heard in regular ways. And no point of view should be foreclosed in an a priori way. Practically speaking, doing these things is time-consuming and requires communicative forums.

Second, external voices must be coordinated with internal voices. One of the various important points about acknowledging external voices is that somehow these external voices must be linked up with internal voices in order to affect the meaningful activity engaged in through the immediate face-to-face operations of the school. Coordination of the school's notions of success with external notions of success requires first of all that success be "communicated" in objective terms, even forms of success that are not as easily objectified, like teacher contentment. Unfortunately, the result of this can be an increasing emphasis on and prioritization of forms of success that are easily objectifiable, like number of children enrolled, scores on state mandated tests, allocation of funds, and so forth. This "reaching out" of the culture of the school to external voices was ultimately accomplished through either administrative or financial mechanisms.

Success as a Logically Diverse Construct

Success was not only constructed through a multiplicity of voices in an evolving way; success was logically diverse: constructed through various structures of logical relation. The facets included:

- Goodness-of-fit (with matching/degree-of-sameness as the core concept).
- Means–end (with needs and interests as core concepts).
- Authoritative hierarchies (with priorities, expertise, and roles as core concepts).
- Critical-reflective (with growth and optimism as core concepts).

Each of these logics implicated a different set of structural relations constitutive of success. Let's explore those logical relations a little more closely.

The facet *goodness-of-fit* was a test of match: how well and to what extent did one thing match what it was intended to match. The goodness-of-fit facet was employed in examining the success of teachers at the school, the satisfaction of students and parents, the physical environment of the classroom, and the teaching team in a given classroom. The degree of match was then one way of noting success. One could well imagine a different setting wherein the successful construction of the physical environment was a matter of reaching goals or marking off a checklist rather than being a matter of goodness-of-fit. To date, the scheme in Table 6.2 related to goodness-of-fit has been, at least tacitly, exhibited.

The *means–end* logic of success was derived from the core concepts of needs and interests and was oriented through modes of efficiency and effectiveness. This facet was predominately employed in the internalization of external voices. For example, passing state-mandated achievement tests constituted a need. Means for accomplishing this were devised. Scores on the test were used to establish success. In addition, means–end success was partially evidenced in the hiring of new faculty, at least in the sense of identifying a need, like a mathematics expertise, and using this as one way of deciding whom to hire as long as the goodness-of-fit test was passed. At the end of the day, this facet of success afforded participants the most tangible form of objectively noting successes. Teachers reported identifying a student need, devising a plan to meet the identified need, and then evaluating whether or not the need was satisfied. Comments like

TABLE 6.2
Matches Indicating Goodness-of-Fit

Domain	Goodness-of-Fit With
Teaching practices	Constructivism
Satisfaction of students and parents	Constructivism
Teaching team	As a pair: style, personality, roles
Student performance	Classroom norms, developmental expectations
School-based goals	Constructivism
Hiring new faculty	Constructivism, existing faculty

this were common: "All the children are reading [need: to have children read]. I feel good about that [means reached desired ends]." Four other kinds of needs were commonly addressed through this facet of success: material needs, instructional support needs, administrative support needs, and parental needs.

When needs and interests were identified but were coupled with limitations in the school's capacity to meet those needs and interests, an *authoritative* logic of success was evidenced through hierarchies. Hierarchies were expressed through the following core concepts: priorities, expertise, and roles. The use of priority setting, role delineation (such as principal, lead teacher), and systems of recognizing expertise facilitated the articulation of certain kinds of success. Hierarchies were used to construct success through prioritizing expectations about what should be accomplished when and in what order, in what way, through a system of hierarchically ordered experts and roles.

The principal was the main conduit for bringing the external voices into the UHCST community. This was accomplished via her role as principal. Her role as principal stood in authoritative relation to the teachers (in spite of her intentions to the contrary). This relation carried its own meaning for success. Because of the hierarchical structure, success was differentiated. In other words, the principal was considered successful or not in some ways that were different from the teachers. The principal controlled access to information (regarding such things as "less appropriate" teaching practices in any one particular class, conflicts with UH personnel, disagreements among teaching teams, etc.) that others in the school did not have. One teacher put it like this: "[She] knows things we don't, and so she has to make decisions based on the broader amount of information and experience she has. This is just her job." Another teacher said, "I have input about things that have to do with my class and I don't always agree with her [the principal], but it is her job to know what's going on." This statement suggests that the hierarchy in its unequal distribution of knowledge and its variance in role expectations were necessary for the success of the school.

The structure of expertise, as established among the staff, was oriented through the extent to which constructivism was evidenced in classroom practices, one's longevity as a constructivist educator, whom one learned constructivism from, and one's visible commitment to professional growth. This system of expertise was useful in successful problem solving and decision making. The notion of expert did not preclude the school's commitment to openness and democracy, but it did influence the way in which success was conceived by the staff. This is because certain voices were given more credence and were listened to with greater compatibility. The relationship across voices implied a certain form of success: that one should move on the hierarchy closer and closer toward the practices of "experts." That one could be an expert within the group marked the notion of success as one associated with "upward" development, the voice of standards, the voice to understand. This did not feel oppressive to staff; it felt appropriate. That is, the system of experts was respected internally and gave merit to the particular constructs of success (e.g., ways of reporting student learning) that emerged.

However, there were tensions exhibited between the authoritative nature of roles and the idealization of "equality" and "openness." This tension was one to which Sarason (1998) directed some insightful attention. Though not addressed as a part of conceptualizing success per se, Sarason did pinpoint this particular tension as the spot where reality meets with myth. According to Sarason's predictions, when enough reality intrudes on the reigning myths of staff equality and openness, a crisis is in the making. This was also how the tension presented itself at UHCST, but within the boundaries of how success was being conceived. The principal wanted to practice equality of voice and yet did take on authoritative roles necessary to administer the school successfully.

Sarason also wrote about a common practice of administrators to identify a core group with whom they can share some power, receive support, and so on. According to Sarason, this tendency to identify a core group is likely to result in conflict. The conflict is unexpected because staff assume that this core group would always get along with the principal. With the UHCST, core group patterns were continually disrupted in part through the evaluation project and in part as a function of the small size of the school. For example, disharmony among core group members was revealed and reported through the evaluation project. The principal had not yet become aware of the disharmony through the core group. Because this was reported in the evaluation and also served to explain some of the experiences that had bewildered the principal, the mythical notion of a core group was disrupted. Most specifically, in the second year of the school's operation, the teachers expressed some concern and displeasure over requests the principal made in her attempts to support parents. From the teachers' point of view, these requests were "too much" and failed to respect the "role" of teacher. From the principal's point of view, these requests were demonstrations on the part of the school to parents that UHCST staff would "go the extra mile." The principal was not aware that this differing point of view had her alone on one side, with the core group and others voicing similar dissatisfaction with the way the principal handled requests from parents. This tension between the core group and the principal involved a difference in viewpoint that was not out in the open. It was coupled with the principal's assumed authority to make job-related decisions and to make requests of the staff that did not win their assent.

The evaluation project helped to expose tensions related to the hierarchy of roles so that they could be dealt with.

Critical–reflective relations comprised a final logic for success among UHCST staff, especially teachers. The staff discussed their success in terms of their own professional development. According to one year's evaluation report (Korth, 1999), one teacher had worked through a book on guided reading and then used what she learned to improve reading opportunities in her class. Another teacher became more conscious of ways to introduce topics, developing more stimulating and developmentally appropriate modes of instruction. Teachers attended workshops. Moreover, the staff met to reflect on the evaluation documents, they engaged in a group counseling process known as Interpersonal Process Recall, and so forth. Beliefs that one should grow and that the optimism of expecting that such growth makes a difference in the outcomes and experiences of a school were influential in how success was conceived. Additionally, the specific forms of the growth contributed to goals and means–end agendas for success. The teacher who extended her strategies for engaging students in reading was successful because she extended herself and was successful because she found a way to meet a specific need.

In summary, with a logically diverse conceptualization of success, various relations must be translatable one to another and various criteria for success must be recognized according to the relation employed. In this way, measuring and assessing success is more adequately achieved and the coordination of these assessments within a dynamic system is more possible. People can recognize the relation implicit in the facets that emerge at their respective sites and use those relations to establish modes of ways to examine success. People can also describe the overarching relationships of facets to each other.

In the case of the charter school this would mean recognizing how examining success using a goodness-of-fit test is useful for evaluating the school's practices over and against constructivism. The goodness-of-fit test would yield a statement about the extent to which practices correlate with or match constructivism. However, it would be possible to examine specific constructivist-related problems using the means–end facet.

THE PROBLEM AND PROMISE OF COORDINATION

Success was a complex concept constituted of varied components ranging from highly explicit goals to tacit, barely articulated expectations and impressions. As an evolving, multivoiced, logically diverse concept, its boundaries and measures could not have been predetermined or statically fixed. The strategic plan could not have articulated the complexities entailed in the success of the new setting. In fact, the goals and alignments explicated in the strategic plan comprised only a portion of the meaning of *success*. The case study findings reported here serve (a) to articulate a concept whose complexities mirror those of the realities of new settings and (b) to reveal the demands on new settings for coordination and integration. This report illustrates a method for examining the conceptualization process involved in establishing a new setting.

Of the three domains explicated, the domain of voice carried the strongest, richest set of constructs useful toward understanding success for UHCST. Each one of the particularities of the findings is likely to be different for other settings, but the complexity might not be. Of utmost importance, both for Sarason's framework and for administrators, is the question of how to manage or coordinate or integrate the various features of success (realizing that some are incompatible) over time, across individuals, and through various logical relations.

This complex set of components contributing toward the conceptualization of success can be fruitfully applied to other settings. Any given school, especially newly forming ones, might benefit from this more complex notion of success if the complexion and extent of complexity have been adequately described. Beyond this, innovators must be able to navigate the complexity in order to fully appreciate, support, feel happy and worthy in, meet goals of, and regularly (not just ultimately) claim "success."

Any new school will be, de facto, involved in the process of increasing complexity. Sarason argued that increasing complexity can be prepared for. He posited that a constitution is able to provide a priori guidance and policy with respect to how actors work out issues that arise, with the assumption that issues will inevitably arise (this counters a popular myth that harmony and concurrence will be typical). This proposal is an acknowledgment of the pressures that increased complexity put onto a system: pressures for practical resolution of differences where reaching consensus is problematic.

In the case study reported on by Susan Korach (chap. 3, this volume), findings indicated that most of the problems experienced by the schools she studied were in the realm of governance. This aligns with the findings reported by Sarason (1994). Korach suggests, in congruence with Sarason, that constitutions (of the sort she identified in her conclusion) can clarify the mechanisms for addressing governance issues. This suggestion employs a couple of assumptions. First, constructing such a constitution assumes that there will be a need: that there will be times when governance structures are needed (everything will not be rosy). Second, such a constitution assumes that it is acceptable and okay if people do not agree, but that practical resolution might be attainable. Third, such a constitution assumes that communicative efforts at resolution and coordination will not always work or will not always be available.

It is helpful to think about the ways in which various expectations and goals associated with a school's success were and could be coordinated in the case of the UHCST. In the previous sections, there were brief descriptions of some preliminary thoughts on what it meant to coordinate ideas and expectations of success across the three domains. Coordination over time was required if the evolving nature of the concept *success* was to be meaningfully integrated into the ongoing practices of the new setting. Coordination across and among voices was necessary if the various perspectives and interests of the different participants and entities were to be integrated into a meaningful and dynamic articulation of the concept. And finally, coordination of various relations constituting facets of the concept was important to clarifying ways of noting and demonstrating the connection of the concept to empirical constructs or ways of measuring success. The subsection that follows is comprised of a brief list and description of coordination strategies and efforts tried by the UHCST or recommended by evaluators. Some of these were already mentioned and are only repeated here as way of tying the practices together.

**Strategies Useful for the Coordination of Ideas
and Expectations Related to Success**

Here are some of the mechanisms involved in the coordination of ideas and expectations related to success. The mechanisms presented are considered strategies, activities within the intentional realm of the people themselves (although it must be acknowledged that some mechanisms are coordinating effects that exceed the specific intentionality of the actors involved and can only be dealt with by first raising awareness). In this section of the report, strategies employed by those involved at UHCST are listed and briefly described. The strategies themselves are organized according to these categories: administrative, financial, or consensual.

Administrative Strategies. Administrative strategies for coordination involved using goals, mandates, policies, and plans that were formalized into a document and carried administrative legitimation through expectations for compliance. The principal and Advisory Board, at the time of this writing, were engaged in producing written policies regarding safety and crisis management. These policies were being developed through communicative efforts. They will work to coordinate the success related to safety and crisis management. This process was emergent and reflected the evolving nature of success, but would produce a document that might have to be communicatively revisited in the future. That possibility for revisitation is understood by all those involved in the formalizing process, so that the document itself has been conceived as evolutionary and fallible. This is used an example of how informal, emergent interests can be formalized, but must be retained as accessible, if the evolutionary, emergent nature of success is to benefit the schooling practices.

The charter school's *Strategic Plan*, used as a guide toward claiming success in 5 years (the length of the original charter), was the first formalized document of the new setting, and it coordinated notions of success from one year to the next. This document contained job descriptions, mission statements, goals articulated in phases, and so on. This document was no longer communicatively negotiable, although its aims could be modified by the adoption of a constitution. The document was not talked about or communicatively referenced in a regular way within the charter school community, and yet it was situated as a kind of benchmark in the background of the daily operations of the school.

Constructivist philosophy as espoused by DeVries, Piaget, Kohlberg, and local educators (such as Dr. Barbara Peterman) was enmeshed in the coordination of notions of success. This philosophy was manifest in several forms: evidenced in the Strategic Plan, employed in the evaluation process, discussed and articulated as school practices were (re)considered, and reinforced through alliances with professional organizations. Having a philosophy to reference was a fundamental mechanism for coordinating activities that were oriented toward success. This philosophy was referenced in a regular and daily way within the community and over time. The philosophy was very much a part of the intentions of the community with respect to the school's success.

A *stabilized population* (low staff turnover and student attrition) also contributed to the coordination of ideas and expectation of success over time. A stabilized population makes a shared memory possible, makes it possible to use already experienced modes of communication to keep track of shifts in views and expectations, and makes the process of change feel less threatening to participants.

Financial Strategies.   Financial coordination took the explicit form of budgets, but articulated accountability toward fiscal management and rendering services. Budgets worked through processes of allocation and prioritization. Recall that one of the ways teachers viewed themselves as successful was through professional growth. It would be possible to look at the budget to see if professional growth was being fiscally prioritized and supported in a way that honored teacher voice. The UHCST budgeted every year, so far, for the conduct of a qualitative evaluation study, which this chapter reports on. This demonstrated a commitment to the UHCST project. It seems extremely important to note that Dr. Tate, Vice Provost involved in establishing the charter school, is known to have insisted on startup funds that would make the school financially secure for its early years. For this reason, the school staff was relieved of intense financial burdens in the earliest years.

Differentiation of staff role by pay was one of the ways that success was articulated. For example, personal longevity with the school reaped financial benefits. Remember that longevity was one of the conditions employed in the way teachers conceived of success.

Searching for new money made it possible for the charter school to continually update its resources as well as its priorities and commitments toward success. New funding enables a school to keep perpetually aware of the limitation of resources and the connection between resource allocation and success. The charter school has received some federal and state grant monies for implementing various programs. For example, the charter school has received a collaborative grant to enhance reading and writing instruction. Getting new money provided the school with bonus opportunities to pursue its goals in ways that exceeded the startup funds.

Consensual Strategies.   Consensual strategies are implicitly linked to face-to-face communication, although some coordination can occur via memos, e-mail, or phone contact. These strategies are the most democratic and produce the most potential for a perpetual reformation of schooling practices and notions of success. These interactive strategies also seem the most connected to participants' comments of satisfaction with the setting and their sense of feeling good about being part of the school. The UHCST was commended in the evaluation reports for consistently addressing consensual forms of governance, conceptualizing, and professional practice. The requirements of these strategies were time, willingness, and openness on the part of actors to engage with one another, even when harmony was not to be found and the outcome was not entirely satisfying. The following consensual strategies were employed at the charter school.

The *evaluation project* served to coordinate success over time because the longitudinal data collection and report (a) communicated the extent to which the UHCST was aligned with the success it aimed to claim, (b) articulated emergent criteria for success in each given year thus exposing shifts and stability over time, and (c) provided a point of discussion regarding success. The evaluation project also served to coordinate the various voices involved in identifying success in the setting. This happened because the voices were articulated through the project.

Open and accessible interactions facilitated keeping one another aware of shifts in expectation and impressions related to success. Employing communicative practices that encourage active listening, open dialogue, and structured opportunities for interacting can accomplish this. Having safe faculty meetings and welcoming practices with parents were the two most prominent ongoing ways that UHCST folks thought open and accessible interactions were made possible. UHCST staff meetings were not always experienced as safe, so this was an area where maintaining open and accessible interactions was vulnerable. That is, staff did not always think it was okay to voice a point of view that diverged from the others. This was evidenced primarily in the expression of divergent points of view regarding relationships and interactions with parents.

An *advisory board* was an officially established group of people who worked with the principal to reflect on practices, problem-solve, and provide emotional support and practical advice for the principal. Having an advisory board produced a nonthreatening (safe) forum within which the principal could confront her own success and the success of the school. This advisory board idea might be worth extending to teachers. That is, teachers could have an advisory board or "critical friends group" within which they could safely bounce ideas around, confront teacher-related problems, coordinate efforts oriented toward success, and articulate concerns. The group should operate without UHCST administrator(s) and could at least include teachers or administrators from other schools, UH College of Education faculty, and/or graduate students.

Interpersonal Process Recall (IPR) is a counseling approach useful for learning about and dealing with the interpersonal dynamics of an organization. IPR has been widely used with families, military personnel, school faculty, and classrooms. Kagan and Kagan (1991) developed IPR over a period of years of actual experience using the process. In general, the process involves videotaping a typical interaction or group discussion, followed by participants viewing the videotape with the purpose of articulating feelings and interpretations about the interactions that had remained tacit during the interactive event itself. To facilitate this reflection, participants are invited to stop the videotape whenever they wish to talk about their feelings, perceptions, interpretive experiences, or other thoughts that came up during that particular point in the interaction. A trained facilitator encourages the exploration of issues actors themselves raise by probing in open-ended, nonconfrontive ways. The UH Charter School used videotapes of staff meetings for its IPR sessions.

IPR made it possible for the group to (a) articulate conflict, (b) examine patterns of interaction that felt unsafe, (c) express discontent and appreciation, and (d) problem-solve. This strategy is consensual because it requires the voluntary and communicative participation of actors.

Shared decision making was the consensual phase of articulating administrative policies, mandates, and practices. Shared decision making was philosophically aligned with constructivism and was considered important to the faculty and staff of UHCST. This bounded form of shared decision making was employed for decisions that really were open (e.g., the openness being bounded by such things as their inability to refuse administration of state-mandated tests), for decisions where there had been no previous record established (policies or guidelines), and for issues that emerged from the everyday life of the school. The face-to-face shared decision making almost always involved the principal, but did not always involve all of the rest of the staff. It was typical, however, for school-based decisions and general classroom concerns to be addressed through this strategy. This allowed for coordination in the development of goals and methods of assessing success. This strategy often fed the production of administrative policy or financial budget and simultaneously provided practices through which these more formalized documents were communicatively revisited as necessary: It kept the financial and administrative products pliable.

CONCLUSION

The University of Houston Charter School manifested a complex notion of success, one that was not matched by the articulation of the concept in the literature thus far. Sarason's point that there is a paucity of concepts available that are capable of expressing the complexity of new settings was found to be legitimate in this case. One implication of those complexities is this: Increasing the likelihood that the school would succeed required strategies that could work over time, across multiple points of view, through various logical relations.

By articulating the particulars entailed in how success was to be conceived at the UH Charter School, several things became possible. A more legitimate, specific view of success became clear. This helped to refine an understanding of the less-specific goals of the school as produced in the school's Strategic Plan. Increased specificity made it possible for stakeholders to note tensions, conflicts, misunderstandings, ambiguities, and impossibilities, as well as compatibilities, strengths, and exemplars. The ultimate success of the charter school as educational reform is dependent on these specific details comprising the school's successfulness. Nevertheless, articulating only the ultimate forms of success is insufficient precisely because it lacks the kind of specificity necessary to realistically coordinate its various components.

The concept as it has been developed here is entirely compatible with Sarason's work on new settings. It is possible to begin a setting with a richer, more realistic concept of success. Doing so limits the ambiguity. This kind of conceptualizing also suggests very precise structural support that can be organizationally established at the outset, for example, developing mechanisms to coordinate the various voices of stakeholders. This chapter has also indicated some limitations on the extent to which planners can be omnipotent regarding success at the outset, and yet the chapter does not negate the value of good planning. The planning should set structures into place that enable the ongoing development of the setting and that foster potential success-building. This way, the specific manner that a new school might succeed is facilitated, understood, reevaluated, and monitored.

REFERENCES

Kagan, N., & Kagan, H. (1991). Interpersonal process recall. In P. Dorwick (Ed.), *Using video in the behavioural sciences* (pp. 221–230). New York: Wiley.

Korth, B. (1997). *Qualitative Evaluation Report 1997: University of Houston Charter School of Technology.* Unpublished document produced by the Houston Institute of Cultural Studies.

Korth, B. (1999). *Qualitative Evaluation Report 1999: University of Houston Charter School of Technology.* Unpublished document produced by the Houston Institute of Cultural Studies.

Marsh, M. (1999). *Parents perceptions of a constructivist charter school.* Unpublished doctoral candidacy paper submitted to the Department of Educational Psychology at the University of Houston.

Peterman, B. (1996). *The Strategic Plan.* Unpublished document of the University of Houston Charter School of Technology.

Sarason, S. B. (1972). *The creation of settings and the future societies.* Cambridge, MA: Brookline Books.

Sarason, S. (1998). *Charter schools: Another flawed educational reform?* New York and London: Teachers College Press.

Chapter 7

Behind the Rhetoric:
The Agony, the Ecstasy
of Being First

In August 1995, the first charter school in Massachusetts opened its doors. This chapter tells the story of that school. The founders of Marblehead Community Charter Public School (MCCPS), a middle school serving fewer than 200 students, initially thought the proposed school was unlikely to cause controversy for two reasons: (a) the proposed school's relatively small size, and (b) problems with overcrowding at the existing local middle school. Yet controversy swirled around this school from the moment that award of the charter was announced. For that reason, this chapter puts more emphasis on external community influences than has been the case in the preceding chapters.

Marblehead, an affluent seacoast town north of Boston, has a highly homogeneous population, in terms of both ethnicity and socioeconomic status. Outwardly, it would seem an unlikely place for a fierce struggle over the quality of the public schools. However, at the time the charter school was proposed, the number of local children attending private schools had risen to 23%. A perception had spread among many local residents that the Marblehead public schools, once the pride of the town, had become an inferior alternative. Advocates for the public schools, on the other hand, quoted statistics that showed the town's public schools to compare favorably with those elsewhere in the state.

At the root of the debate over the Marblehead charter school were profound differences of opinion as to (a) the mission of the public schools and (b) how well the local public schools were currently being run. The inci-

175

dent that, more than any other, caused an activist group of local residents to coalesce around the idea of founding a charter school was the decision, by the Marblehead Superintendent of Schools, to move the town's fifth graders to the middle school. As one of the founders of the charter school pointed out, it all started "because of the middle school situation, where they moved the fifth grade into the middle school. The middle school was a real hot button."

The decision to move Marblehead's fifth graders from the elementary schools to the middle school was made as an efficiency move. The elementary schools had become overcrowded. Moving the fifth graders was argued to be the most cost-efficient way to deal with the situation. There was, however, strong opposition from parents, who felt that economics ought not to be the primary factor considered in such a decision. They argued that fifth graders were not developmentally ready for the social environment at the middle school. A parent whose child had spent a year at the middle school recalled:

> I remember one day I walked through the lobby [of the middle school] and there were a couple of kids necking in the lobby. I looked down at them and they looked at me, like, saying "What are you going to do about it?" So, what's a 5th grader going to think? I mean, I was uncomfortable as an adult. What's a little 5th grader going to think, watching that?

The parent group that organized the charter school not only objected to treating cost-efficiency as the most important consideration in making educational decisions; it also supported the creation of a school environment where specific values (such as hard work and respect for the feelings of others) were actively encouraged. In the eyes of these parents, the social environment at the existing middle school emphasized achieving popularity with one's peers—not academic and personal excellence. As one parent, who later sent her son to the charter school, recalled:

> The philosophy and environment [at the regular middle school] are not conducive to teaching your kids to strive to do their best. So my son was getting the message: "Act like a goon, try to fit in, try to get a lot of friends and fit right in there, do the assignment—it doesn't really matter how you do it— and you'll get through the next four years."

On the other hand, teachers and administrators at Marblehead's existing middle school saw the situation quite differently. Among the public schools in the state, Marblehead's middle school ranked well in terms of standardized test scores and other measures of achievement. Administrators and teachers felt that, in light of the constraints under which they worked, the criticisms put forth by charter school advocates were unfair.

But the validity of this argument was questioned by parents, who noted that the children arriving at the middle school came from Marblehead elementary schools—which had high achievement scores. What they wanted to know was why the "value added" by the middle school seemed to be relatively low.

A CONFLICT OF VALUES

Interpretation of the results of educational politics and policy research is facilitated by recognizing the existence of four competing public values (Mitchell, 1992). During the first quarter of the 20th century, policy formation in the public schools was intentionally defined as nonpolitical by urban reformers and education progressives (Iannaccone, 1967). Leaders of these reform movements sought to free schools from the widespread fiscal and policy abuses of nineteenth century patronage politics. Their aim—embodied in the slogan "Get politics out of the schools and get education out of politics"—was to put policy decisions in the hands of politically neutral educators. Values borrowed from industry drove policy, emphasizing *efficiency* and encouraging the professionalization and bureaucratization of education.

In the mid-1950s, following the landmark *Brown v. Board of Education* (1954, 1955) decisions, *equity* emerged as a dominant value. The Supreme Court had declared schools to be responsible for ensuring equal opportunities for all citizens. Initially, Southern governors and local educators openly resisted the Supreme Court, while in other regions community leaders conspired to influence access to housing and to gerrymander school attendance boundaries. Increasingly, schools were at the center of political controversy. Many citizens openly doubted earlier claims that fairness, efficiency, and competence would be guaranteed by relying on a professional educational bureaucracy (Mitchell, 1992).

Then, in 1983, the National Commission on Excellence published *A Nation at Risk*, describing low achievement levels in the public schools and pointing to the cost of ignoring *excellence* as a value, in terms of international economic competitiveness. The National Governors Association put education at the highest priority and shifted the initiative for educational policy toward state-level decision makers. A first wave of state-based school reforms, stimulated by pressure for more student and teacher accountability, dominated the period from 1983 to about 1986. A second wave of reform, emphasizing professionalization and teacher empowerment, was stimulated by publication of *Tomorrow's Teachers: A Report to the Holmes Group* (Holmes Group, 1986) and the Carnegie Forum on Education and the Economy report *A Nation Prepared: Teachers for the 21st Century* (1986).

178 BROUILLETTE

Through much of the 20th century, educational *choice* has taken a back seat to other values. However, as the earlier consensus on just what constitutes a good public school has come unraveled, the value of choice has increasingly been put forward as a way to let the consumer decide. As the population has grown more diverse, the early 20th-century consensus that professional educators were on their way to creating "the one best system" that will satisfy everyone has been weakened. Evidence that children with diverse sets of interests and aptitudes may in fact benefit from differing educational approaches has led to the creation of magnet and charter schools. Using the metaphor of a free marketplace of ideas, advocates of school choice focus on issues that had been little talked about through the middle years of the twentieth century.

THE MARBLEHEAD COMMUNITY CHARTER SCHOOL

According to *A National Survey and Analysis of Charter School Legislation* done by the Institute for Responsive Education (1996), the major areas of disagreement about charter schools center on funding, the contract and approval process, labor, equity, student outcomes, and the general, over-arching issue of the amount of variation from regulations that school should be allowed. The greatest issue of contention has been funding. In the current funding environment, charter schools are often seen as taking resources from the "have nots" to support an "elite" alternative. Certainly, in Marblehead, funding proved to be the most contentious issue. According to charter school legislation passed in Massachusetts, per-pupil funding would follow students transferring to the charter school. Charter school opponents argued that, given the fixed expenses involved in running a school, this weakened the financial health of existing schools.

RESEARCH DESIGN

The historical case study on which this chapter is based made use of archival materials, on-site observations, and interviews with parents, teachers, community members, and the headmaster of the school. Personal experience also played a role, as the author is a native of Marblehead and acted as an informal consultant to the charter school's founding coalition during the time that the charter proposal was being written. However, although she did serve on the school's interim board, the author at no time took a policymaking role. Her contribution was only as a resource person. Yet it cannot be denied that this study was influenced by the author's personal experience. This said, it would arguably be difficult for anyone who had not been, in some sense, involved in the process to make sense of the claims and counterclaims made in the media—and in public meetings—about this particular charter school. In an effort to create as neutral a narrative as possible, newspaper accounts are used extensively to give a sense of the character of the debate surrounding the creation of the school.

Differing understandings of the values of excellence, efficiency, equity, and choice that have been influential in shaping the public schools of the United States lay at the root of the debate over the creation of the Marblehead Community Charter Public School (MCCPS). Indeed, the insertion of the word *public* in the name of the school came in response to accusations by charter school opponents that charter schools were not "real" public schools. Insisting that "real" public schools were not limited to neighborhood schools defined by attendance areas, charter school supporters dramatized their claim by renaming the Marblehead Community Charter School, so that anyone using the school's official name would, at the same time, affirm the school's status as a public school.

Nor was this merely a bit of public posturing. Several nonparents who later became involved with the charter school saw it as a tool for reawakening voter interest in the public schools. Residents who were already paying private school tuition had been little inclined to vote for increases in school taxes. Some local residents argued that if an inviting alternative were not offered to parents who no longer saw the town's existing secondary schools as a viable alternative for their children, the perceived downward trend in the quality of those schools might soon prove to be irreversible.

The problematic nature of the new school's relationship with existing settings (which, as Sarason [1988] would have predicted, saw the new school as a threat to their own resources and prestige) was such that it was exceedingly difficult for the founders of MCCPS to put sufficient energy into the two related tasks that Sarason spoke of as central to the healthy growth of a new setting: (a) the "forging of the constitution by which the setting will be governed," and (b) sensitively handling "growth and differentiation" as new individuals with their own insights and ideas enter the setting. This meant that the internal challenges of governance and growth were given little attention until shortly before the charter school actually opened its doors.

Differing Viewpoints

As interviewing at MCCPS began, it quickly became apparent that there were two distinct narratives emerging: one narrative told by the parents who set up the school; another narrative told by the school staff. The parents focused on the struggles involved in getting the charter, the political turmoil created in town by the local school district's intense opposition to the charter school, their own motivation for getting involved, and the results of that involvement for their child(ren) and family. The staff emphasized the challenge of creating a viable school in a converted Elks hall, creating the necessary curricular materials on a very limited budget, and carrying this project to success under the direction of an inexperienced and far-from-united board of trustees. To do justice to the complex human interactions involved, it seemed most effective to tell the narratives separately, so that the differing insights offered by parents, by the head of the school, and by the teachers could be adequately explored.

THE PARENTS' VIEW

Charter schools in Massachusetts were authorized as part of the Education Reform Act of 1993. However, the charters were not authorized to begin operation until the 1995–1996 school year. In the statute, no specific grounds for approval or approval are given, except that the Secretary of Education might condition the receipt of charters on taking certain actions or maintaining certain conditions. The initial term for a charter school was to be 5 years. The program allowed a maximum of 2 charters in any city or town, except Boston and Springfield, where there was a maximum of 5 in each city; the limit for the entire state was 25. The total number of students attending charter schools in the State of Massachusetts could not be greater than 0.75% of the total number of students attending public schools. Private and parochial schools were not eligible for charter school status.

Application for a charter could be made by 2 or more certified teachers, or 10 or more parents, or a business or corporate entity. Discontent with the public schools in Marblehead had been brewing for some time. An opinion piece by Jeff Jacoby, a *Boston Globe* columnist, gives voice to a viewpoint shared by a number of charter school supporters:

> Charter schools are the pinprick of competition that the Education Reform Act of 1993 opened up. . . . They are the only real educational reform in the law. Beginning a year from September, a handful of independent, start-up public schools will be given the chance to show what education can look like when a school is more than just one small cog in a vast bureaucratic machine, governed by a stack of 300-page contracts and smothered in layers of administration.

Needless to say, there were individuals who had achieved positions of power in the Marblehead school district who perceived no need for such a "pinprick of competition." On March 27, 1994, the front-page story in the *North Shore Sunday* newspaper was entitled "Class Warfare." The subheading stated: "In Marblehead, a proposal for an alternative 'charter school' has conditional state approval. But getting community support may be something else." The article began by presenting the views of a candidate for the Marblehead School committee, a former president of the Central PTA, who was described as "not the kind of parent who is usually in the dark about major happenings in the Marblehead school system." She expressed her irritation over having been left out of the planning process for the charter school.

Opponents of the charter school mounted a furious letter-writing campaign that included a letter signed by about 70 middle school teachers. Ann Toda, spokeswoman for the Executive Office of Education, admitted that the letter campaign in opposition to the charter proposal was one reason why the Marblehead charter had received only conditional approval—even though the Marblehead charter school's educational program had been found to be "very good." To get full approval, the school needed some refinements to the educational program and to technical and legal areas of the proposal. Most importantly, the charter school needed better community support. The deadline for both the 15 approved charter schools and the 5 conditionally approved charter proposals to submit for final approval was September 1994.

Back in Marblehead, money had become the most emotional issue. Every student at the charter school was estimated to subtract an average of $5,000 in per pupil expenditures from the regular school system's budget. On the other hand, the Education Reform legislation would provide about $906,000 in "new" money to the Marblehead School system, leaving it with more state aid than it would have had without the reform legislation. However, opponents of the charter school saw the issue in terms of priority spending. In the words of a School Committee member, "If the state wants a pilot program, then the state should pay for it." The state spokeswoman, on the other hand, argued: "The money stays in the district. . . . That's part of the overall choice philosophy that if you feel schools are not providing for your child, you should not have to move out of your neighborhood to educate your child."

The chairperson of the 13-member Marblehead Community Charter School Founding Coalition was quoted in the same article. She said that she was disturbed that her group's effort to start a charter school was being viewed by some as a "behind the scenes" activity. A dedicated school activist herself, the coalition chairperson insisted that if the public did not feel adequately informed, it was because there was limited time available. The group came together and wrote the proposal only 3 weeks before the deadline. The coalition had worried that because the number of charter schools allowed in the state had been capped at 25, if the Coalition had not acted quickly, the opportunity would have been lost. The chairperson said that the 64 applications to the Secretary of Education's Office proved the correctness of her prediction that there would be intense competition to get a charter.

A Marblehead Middle School social studies teacher said that he and a majority of his colleagues took the charter school proposal as "a slap in the face," adding, "We also feel it was railroaded through. No one with an educational background was called on for input." Other opponents noted that the charter proposal, which focused on innovative approaches to curriculum development and a "learning process that will focus on the unique developmental needs of early adolescents," seemed not very different from what the existing school already claimed to be doing. The School Committee candidate quoted earlier noted: "When I read the goals and ideals, I thought they're verbatim right out of the middle school handbook."

In fact, the proposed curriculum for the Marblehead charter school incorporated a number of widely advocated reforms such as thematic/interdisciplinary instruction, a focus on academic mastery and service learning, teacher-designed curriculum, multiple means of assessment, and community partnerships. The vision was not very different from that outlined in the handbook of the existing middle school. Essentially, the debate came down to: Is the existing middle school living up to its publicly declared vision? In the *Boston Globe* opinion piece quoted earlier, Jeff Jacoby voiced perceptions that were shared by a number of charter school parents, concerning the shortcomings of the Massachusetts public schools:

> According to the state Department of Education, three-fourths of Massachusetts public school kids cannot pass statewide tests of basic competency. . . . In the Boston system, 40 percent of the budget never gets to the classroom; it is absorbed by the School Department bureaucracy. . . . In the worst urban districts, students drop out in shocking numbers—or parents transfer them, often at great sacrifice, to the suburbs or the parochial schools. . . . Like most monopolies, [the education bureaucracy] spends huge sums to lobby government officials.

After conditional approval of the charter was awarded, the chairman of Marblehead's Board of Selectmen (town council) noted that the charter school issue "is dividing the town tremendously." He observed to his colleagues on the board that Marblehead "is the only town awarded this opportunity (for a charter school) where there is this type of divisiveness." Commenting that he knew and respected individuals on both sides of the issue, he said, "I'd like to offer this board as a broker, if not to produce agreement, for a forum on the issue," adding "I've heard exaggerations on both sides—probably not intentional." A selectwoman applauded the proposal, noting, "We as a board do not have an opinion, although we as individuals do."

In June a public discussion was called by the selectmen to clear the air over the issue of the charter school. The chairperson of the charter school coalition spoke for the residents who wanted to open a charter school. She was supported by the former headmaster of a well-respected private school and by the executive director of a Boston-based research group. After making opening statements, the proponents fielded questions from teachers and local residents. *The Salem Evening News* described the polarized discussion:

> Residents taking part in a public forum on starting a charter school in town see the proposal either as a way of bringing public education out of the stranglehold of bureaucracy or as an attempt by educational leaders to establish a special school at the expense of taxpayers. (6/16/94, p. 16)

The coalition chairperson said the charter school would get parents more involved with their children's education. A selectman made a strong argument in favor of the charter proposal, noting, "When people in Marblehead talk about public education, they talk about it as being a problem." However, a middle school teacher charged that proponents of the charter school had bypassed middle school teachers when they were preparing their application. She said that although the students selected to attend the charter school would benefit from smaller classes, two-thirds of middle school students would remain in the large school with less money to educate them. She also charged that the charter school would attract the best students with the more active parents and that would hurt the remaining students. Other teachers raised questions about possible staff cuts and other reductions. Despite hopes that the forum would clear the air, tensions remained high.

Initiation/Planning

On July 15, 1994, the *Daily Evening Item* announced that the Marblehead Community Charter School organizers had chosen 10 members to serve on the charter school's interim board of trustees. These included:

- A former elementary school teacher, now director of education at Old North Church.
- The founder of an investment company.
- A former cochairman of the town's Elementary Schools Committee.
- The director of the program for senior executives, Sloane School of Management, MIT.
- A CEO and former chairman of the town's Harbors and Waters Board.
- A management consultant and editor.

- A small-business owner selling children's books.
- A former middle school teacher.
- A professor of educational administration (the author of the present case study).
- The senior internal auditor for Tufts University, also a former selectman and former cochair of the town's Elementary Schools Committee.

Task forces were created to study various areas of the charter school's final application: governance, budget, facilities, and educational program.

With only conditional state approval, the first priority was to address the issues cited by the state and submit the remaining portion of the proposal by the September deadline. A member of the interim board remembers: "I guess that everybody that was involved in it had their own personal view of the perfect school. We were going to do it all, which obviously is impossible." Feeling under siege by opponents of the charter school, who were continuing their media and letter-writing campaign, hoping to influence decision makers in Boston who would be deciding whether to approve the charter school, board members were loathe to disagree among themselves. As a result, everyone's ideas were included—with no mechanism for prioritizing the grab bag of goals when it came time to make the hard choices necessary to create a coherent curriculum, using the resources available. To use Sarason's terminology, no "constitution" for governing the setting was worked out. Thus, later on, when it became necessary to make choices, to decide "We will do this first," there would be those who felt sorely let down because their favored project did not get the nod. This created severe problems during the school's first year of operation.

However, given the fierce debate that preceded the final approval of the charter, for the moment all attention was directed toward what the charter school supporters had in common. Prominent among these commonalities was a discontent with the existing middle school. Charter school parents whose children had spent a year at the regular middle school later recalled their experiences and their reasons for seeking another alternative:

My son was labeled, I think, at the middle school as one who wasn't going to go very far. I mean, they don't rank students, but I think he was falling into that kind of a trap. He was not being excited.

I had a daughter who was supposed to have been a straight "A" student, that I knew wasn't putting in the effort. Well behaved children, if they do their homework and they're well behaved, are given, most of the time, good grades.

If everybody was the same and didn't cause any trouble, they could get through those four years of middle school, maybe not learning anything, but also not getting in trouble. Meaning we keep them down, we keep them quiet.

I think it's sad, that kids are subjected to these environments. Where most kids at this age want so badly to have a friend, to fit in, to be considered of value. And so many of them are just abused by their peers, which is kind of horrible.

Other parents had felt frustrated by what they saw as a lack of communication with teachers:

They [the staff at the middle school] want your money. They want you for fund raising. But they want you to stay out of the classroom.

I was a parent who was involved with newsletters and that sort of stuff. I was there daily. But I never got involved in the classroom because they gave you the feeling that parents weren't supposed to be in the classroom.

Some parents, however, saw the problems at the regular middle school as resulting from factors beyond the control of the middle school staff:

Most of us are products of public schools and I got a great education next door in Salem. So I know it can happen in public schools. There are great teachers at the middle school. So, to me, it basically boiled down to [social] environment.

I don't think in the middle school, because it's so big and chaotic, I don't think learning was the thing. I think the thing was trying to find a place where you belong and trying to feel accepted and popular and protect yourself as best as you could from the meanness and back biting that goes on in any middle school, but particularly in a large one like that.

It seems to me that it worked a lot better when they had the old K–8 schools, where you got to be the "big cheese" in the eighth grade, and then you went on to high school. By segregating that age, which is so tough anyway, you're creating a problem.

When you have such sheer numbers like they have at the [regular] middle school, it's very difficult. It's like with public housing, it took so long for them to realize that you can't put 1200 people in a high rise building and make it work. You have to cut it down where there is a sense of community, a cohesiveness. That's where accountability comes into play, because everyone's accountable to someone else.

Honeymoon

Once state approval of the charter came through, there began what Sarason referred to as the "honeymoon stage." Despite ongoing opposition by those in town who mounted a campaign to discourage parents from sending their children to the charter school, there was a mood of excitement among the school's supporters. Parents who chose to send their children to the charter school later described their reactions to the controversy:

> You know, with all the political pressure, and all the chaos they predicted would happen here, what I was thinking was that my daughter could fare no worse here, in a smaller, controlled environment where I felt I could have a lot of input and we could work with her.

> The political pressures on all of us who were sending our children to this school were just absolutely horrendous, as we were trying to get the information. But that's my job to get the information to make the best decision for our child.

Other parents commented on their own motivation for becoming involved with the charter school.

> I remember, back in the administration of Governor Dukakis, they were talking about their recommendations for education. We're still talking about the same issues, and my children are only children at a certain time.

> In my home—my husband and I are teachers or former teachers—the children don't have chores. They don't have other things they have to do. They have to be a good student, to get ahead. When they were in elementary school, that was pretty much in sync with everybody else's philosophy. When they went into the fifth grade [middle school] that philosophy was no longer in sync with the philosophy of the school, which was to be the same and strive for mediocrity.

Parents also spoke of what had attracted their children to the school:

> My son was the kind of student who was very quiet and would disappear into the walls. He didn't stand out or anything. He was the one who dragged us into finding out about the school, getting more information about it. "Let's really try it!" That was what we were really striving for with him, taking responsibility for his education, finding out what he really wanted.

> It was my son's idea to come here. Of course, boys don't always tell you what is on their mind. But he loves the computers.

This was also a period of "growth and differentiation" as charter school supporters reached out to additional families that might be interested in sending their children to the school. The concerns of these new stakeholders in turn modified the evolving vision for the school. As charter school advocates immersed themselves in the school reform literature, envisioning a school that would be free of bureaucratic limitations, they envisioned an environment in which all children would thrive. In some cases, charter school enthusiasts overestimated the benefits that a change of school climate might bring. A parent recalled:

> One of the founders had a son who is A.D.D. (Attention Deficit Disorder) and she told a lot of people that this was going to be the perfect environment for kids who were hyperactive, or had A.D.D. issues. So, we had significant behavioral problems, probably higher than the average classroom, because of that.

Not being educators themselves, some of the charter school founders found it difficult to differentiate between the restless boredom that may merely have been the result of a less-than-electric classroom atmosphere at a child's present school and significant individual learning or behavioral disorders. Unlike the existing middle school, the charter school did not have either the facilities or the specialized staff needed to serve children with severe behavioral problems. A number of children with mild problems did indeed do significantly better at the charter school. Many children who had been underperforming at the regular middle school put forth markedly more effort. However, parents whose children had severe emotional or behavioral problems mostly found that this school did not offer the answer they had been looking for.

Had the opening of the charter school been put off for a year, to allow for more careful planning, much of the internal turmoil that marked the school's first year might have been avoided. However, a variety of factors made it difficult to wait. Individuals close to the school observed:

> There are certain things that, it seems to me, we did wrong, [that] you hear people doing wrong all the time because they don't give themselves enough lead time. You know, they rush . . . a year seems a long time when you have this vision in your mind, of this perfect place.

> There's a problem because . . . if you are not educating any kids, you don't have any money. So, you can't hire the teachers to write the curriculum. How are you going to pay the head of school?

Moreover, the ongoing external opposition to the school made many of its supporters eager to get beyond the battle of words, to lease a building and begin to deal with something real.

Implementation

Tom Commeret was hired as head of school in the late spring. He was still working at his present school, but he was able to help get the teachers hired and to set the groundwork for opening the school. There was a surge of excitement as the new staff members began to be interviewed, but tensions rose simultaneously. Compromises were necessary. Most of the school's trustees had no experience serving on a governing board. Lack of attention to the problems associated with what Sarason refers to as "growth and differentiation" would eventually lead to frayed tempers and painful misunderstandings. Although they had hired a headmaster, some board members had trouble giving him the leeway he needed to do his job. Eventually, a workable understanding of who was to do what would have to be achieved if the school was to operate smoothly.

Nevertheless, there was a sense of momentum. The school was set to open in September. The former Elks hall had been leased as the school site. Considerable work was needed to convert the building into a school, but it was across the street from a park and had a kitchen for preparing meals. With considerable enthusiasm parents pitched in, hammering, painting, moving furniture. During the summer, the clear need to get the building ready united the charter school community. But then, just before the school was to open, a crisis loomed. Two board members began feuding. As a result, a former supporter who was influential in the community distanced himself from the school. An observer commented: "I think he just got to the point that he could not stand the emotional abuse."

The contentious atmosphere created by local opponents of the charter school was beginning to take a toll. Charter school parents recalled:

If you would watch the school meetings, the charter school would come up at almost every school meeting as the cause of budget problems.

It was just not a question that was ever debated rationally, there was so much emotion around the money issue. They will always tell you "Well, we have all these fixed costs." You know what I mean? That the buzz word "well we have fixed costs." But, they had an architect look at their building, I guess right after the charter school. The guy said to them "You know, charter school is the best thing that ever happened to you. Would you want a bunch of portable classrooms out here?"

One parent had a younger daughter and he said "I was very concerned with what she would experience at the elementary school, if I continued to be involved."

In the midst of these pressures, the members of the founding coalition—most of whom had no firsthand experience with the practical problems of running a school—also had to deal with the multitude of small decisions that had to be made in order to get the building ready and provide at least minimal curriculum materials to the teachers. Yet members of the board had never decided among themselves just what they wanted. As a board member noted:

> There were people there whose kids were totally unmotivated kids and they were looking for somebody that could flip the switch, because these kids were just dead bored in their classrooms. There were people that were looking for a parochial school environment, they wanted their kids in uniforms, they wanted them doing worksheets, they wanted it to be like a parochial school. There were people who were there because their kids had behavioral problems, they were always in trouble and I think they felt that if they switched into a different environment, maybe that would help. There were people who think their kids are geniuses and the current school that they were in, doesn't appreciate their genius and that maybe another school would appreciate how smart they really were. You know what I mean?

As a result, the actual curriculum for the school was largely worked out by the teachers, all of whom came to the school with specific ideas about what worked well in the classroom. Yet this, too gave rise to tensions, because some parents had very strong ideas about what should be done and very little experience in a management position. An onlooker noted that some board members

> made decisions [that were] not the best for all the children, for the collective good of the school. But they were trying to get decisions made to help their specific child. . . . They had no clue what their role was on the Board. Some of them came and went and never did know. They never figured it out.

In one specific case, there was a parent who did not have a college degree but had been very active in the creation of the school. She had very strong ideas about how the school should be run. Having become emotionally involved, this parent found it difficult to sit back and listen to teachers who explained that not all of her ideas could be implemented during the school's first year of operation, given the resources and personnel available. Having no practical experience with the day-to-day running of a school, she was only able to understand their reluctance in emotional terms. Thus, instead of focusing on the objective circumstances that required the school staff to focus on the most immediate priorities first, she reacted as if teachers were trying to subvert the original vision of the school. Eventually, the board as a whole found it necessary to affirm that the day-to-day decision making was the province of the headmaster; this decision caused this particular parent, in the words of a board member, to "go ballistic."

Such problems were by no means peculiar to this school. As one of the founders noted, looking back at the struggles that had accompanied the founding of the school: "The Board of Directors should have had to go to some board workshops or whatever. Finally, because our board was so dysfunctional, we hired a consultant to come in and work with us. That was funded by the State. That was because the charter schools were, almost across the board, doing the same things we were—which was they didn't know how to govern themselves. Governing a charter school, I think, is a huge issue."

Meanwhile, criticism of the charter school had continued, unabated, among those who opposed the school. The *Daily Evening Item* (Richard Fries, 8/28/95, p. 1) observed that "Exactly how many students would enroll had been subject to speculation. The [estimated number] of Marblehead students defecting to the charter school had ranged from the public school estimate of 65 to the charter school estimate of 92. The balance of the 132 students were to be made up of students from nearby communities." The same article commented, "The charter school has proven especially divisive in this affluent seaside town, which has traditionally boasted high test scores for its public school students."

Yet elsewhere, enthusiasm was high. Although students attending MCCPS who lived out of town would have to provide their own transportation, there was never any doubt that there would be enough students to fill the school. As it happened, the charter school attracted a large number of recent Russian immigrants who could not afford the high rent in a town like Marblehead but who were willing to make significant sacrifices to make sure that their children got a good education. After the school opened, one of the founders noted:

> We have an incredible group of kids that come to the school early in the morning on the [public] bus. . . . They get themselves home on the bus; they work their little butts off. You never see the parents, you know what I mean? These kids have got to be making an impact on some of these Marblehead kids, who, you know, are so sheltered and so protected. So, I think that definitely has given this school a much more interesting flavor.

A parent pointed to the sort of serendipity that was possible with a charter school:

> A woman came from Russia and she wanted to work on her English and she contacted the school because someone had told her that were Russian students in this school. She said "I would like to come in and work in the school. You don't have to pay me. I'm trying to work on my English." So, of course,

Tom said "Well, great. Come!" Now she is on the payroll and she is there full time. She has been wonderful because she was a mathematician in Russia. . . . She's been able to [act as] a go between . . . where a lot of the families don't really speak much English.

An observer commented, regarding the continuing presence of many Russian children at the school:

> You have a little Russian community, now. I am sure, as more and more people from Russia move in, the word goes out, "This is a good school. You should look at this school for your kid."

Meanwhile, however, the picture presented in the media was quite different. A supporter of the school recalled that the Marblehead school superintendent, who was very strongly opposed to the school,

> was spreading this rumor that the charter school was 'dying on the vine' and no Marblehead kids were going to go there. He made up his budget as if that were true, even though we kept letting everyone know what the real figures were. Then, when the kids at the charter school were not at the regular middle school, there was a budget shortfall. So he went to the town for more money. But the treasurer had read the accounts that told the real figures for the charter school, so there were some strong questions about "Why this shortfall?"

Crisis

Tensions peaked as the opening day of the charter school neared. For some members of the founding coalition, the accumulated stress of dealing with the ongoing media controversy, as well as with the many challenges associated with preparing to open the school, became overwhelming. Thus, the day of the opening of the school, news reports described how the former chairperson of the charter school's board of trustees (who had resigned that position the week before) tearfully cut the ribbon to officially open the school—she had announced that she planned to move out of town because of negative reaction to the school. The story in the *Daily Evening Item* (8/28/95, p. 1) explained that the former chairman:

> said she made the decision out of concern for her children. She pulled her oldest son out of the Marblehead Middle School in April because she said that he had endured repeated threats and insults due to the role played by his mother. Other board members have alleged their children have been subject to similar taunts. (Daily Evening Item, 8/28/95, p. 1)

A September 3, 1995, article by Diana Brown in the *Boston Globe* described the transformation of the old Elks hall into a school. On the second day of classes, it was possible to walk through "tidy hallways lined with coat hooks, not the file cabinets and painting supplies present one week before." Headmaster Commeret expressed relief that, with Boston television station and newspaper reporters swarming the school in recent weeks, students had not felt intimidated about coming to school. A *USA Today* article published on September 13, 1995, showed pictures of the Marblehead charter school and its students, noting:

> Parents in Marblehead, a suburb of 20,000, wielded hammers to transform an old Elks hall into a school. Such community effort makes the school unique, according to organizers. "It's not so much the programs as the whole environment," says sixth-grade teacher Marielle Palombo. . . . Not everyone in Marblehead is applauding. Many residents see the charter school as a $500,000-a-year drain. Public school board members say they've been forced to cut four public school teachers. (p. 7D)

Yet the public controversy continued. Pressures associated with opening the school caused tensions to rise among the charter school board members as well. Having endured so much stress in order to get the school open, some stakeholders found it difficult to compromise on their personal vision for the school. Their own vision became, for them, *the* vision. Other stakeholders, who happened to disagree with them, became—by definition—betrayers of that vision. This made for some acrimonious board meetings and led to considerable confusion among the professional staff. Having neglected to specify, during the planning stage, how the school would be governed, the charter school community found itself forced to hammer out a decision-making process under very difficult circumstances. Yet despite the various fallings-out among the board members, the headmaster and the teachers continued to work on curriculum and on the day-to-day challenges of running the school, gradually bringing order out of chaos.

Looking back, from a distance of several years, it seems clear that many of the problems encountered in the creation of the charter school could have been predicted. As Sarason pointed out, the creation of settings (in the earliest phases) almost always (if not always) takes place in a context containing conflicting ideas and values, limited resources, a sense of mission and superiority on the part of some, and a need to preserve tradition on the part of others, as well as a need to protect the setting from outside influences. This context almost always includes, or quickly is seen as impinging on, a large number of existing settings. Too often, those involved in the creation of a new setting fail to ask:

- What were the issues, problems, and conflicts that marked the history of the new setting?
- What reactions might be anticipated as a result of the fact that the new setting would emerge from, and become part of, an existing organization of settings that had long-standing traditions and practices at variance with the new setting (which, if successful, would establish the superiority of its mission)?

In the case of this charter school, the "prehistory" of the setting included a turbulent public debate, at both the local and state level, that focused intense media attention on this fledgling school. This created pressures that no one involved in the creation of the setting had anticipated. The founders of the school had not expected either the confrontational, angry reactions by persons allied with the existing middle school, nor the prolonged controversy surrounding the granting of the charter school. In the founders' eyes, the small size of the proposed charter school (less than 200 students), along with the crowded situation at the existing middle school, had seemed to indicate that the charter school application would draw little public attention. As one of the founders commented, "They never paid much attention to us before." (Many of these same parents had raised school reform issues previously; the school district had paid little attention.) This time, however, the response was different.

As Sarason noted, because of the implication that the new setting has a "superior" mission, the new setting competes with existing settings in the realm of ideas and values; that is, it disrupts an existing structure or pattern of relationships and causes new questions to be asked about the adequacy of the status quo. Previously this group of parents had seemed to be just a bunch of skeptical local residents given to asking difficult questions. Now the school district saw them differently, as a direct challenge to the existing system.

Aftermath

Since the spring of 1995, when the first charter schools began hiring, these grass-roots, nonunion public schools have been deluged with applications from teachers, nearly 10,000 competing for 400 jobs. . . . So far, 5,465 families have been lucky to get a seat in a charter school, where the average student/teacher ratio is 13/1. The waiting list is an eye-popping 3,600 and growing. . . .

"I think we should raise the cap," which at present limits to 25 the number of charter schools statewide, says House Speaker Tom Finneran, in the past skeptical about charters. "People are voting with their feet. We should not stand in the way of that."

This quote comes from an opinion piece published in the *Boston Globe* on January 27, 1997. Jon Keller, a political analyst for WLVI-TV's "Ten O'Clock News," argued forcefully that arguments put forward by the Massachusetts Teachers Association (MTA) against lifting the cap on the number of charter schools were disingenuous. He noted that "In the short term, with the Massachusetts Teachers Association and other charter school enemies eager to advertise every last growing pain, these schools are far more closely scrutinized than conventional public schools" and that, with charters currently teaching only 0.006% of the state's total public school population, "Unless more charters are awarded, the student pool will never be large enough for reliable conclusions to be drawn about them."

In the short term, most of the fears about charter schools had proven to be unfounded. For example, school districts had lost $3.1 million to charter schools in 1996, but had been given $1.3 billion in new funds under educational reform legislation. Fears that charter schools would prove to be elitist enclaves had thus far missed the mark, with racial and ethnic minorities accounting for 44% of the charter school enrollment. No one knew what the future might hold. However, the history of the Marblehead charter school suggests some possibilities.

From the parent point of view, after opening day the development of the school took on a life of its own. Grand visions had to be modified, both because of limited resources and as a result of compromises that inevitably must be hammered out in order to accommodate the growth and differentiation that are inevitable in organizing a new setting such as a school. Some parents left. Having put in so much hard work, they were unwilling to accept a school that offered only a part of what they wanted. Of the children who had been enrolled the opening day of the school, about one in five had left the charter school a year later.

In the next subsection of this report, we look at the perceptions of those parents who stayed. What was it about the charter school that made it preferable, in their eyes, to the alternatives available to them? Parents of the second group of graduating eighth graders were interviewed. Their children had spent 1 year at the regular middle school before the charter school opened, giving a standard of comparison. Their children had also spent 3 years at the charter school—long enough so that the initial turbulence that had accompanied the opening of the school had quieted down and the curriculum had stabilized. The goal of the interviews was to find out what differences these parents perceived the school to have made in their children's lives.

Parent Perceptions

Recalling the first year of the charter school's operation, parents noted that the first real difference they perceived was the sense of relief displayed by children who had felt lost and alone at the larger middle school. The small friendly environment of the charter school was repeatedly mentioned as an advantage:

> At the middle school, lunch is a zoo. The kids are throwing food. The place is a zoo. The language is atrocious. Here, the teachers eat with the kids. There's a staff member at almost every table. They don't talk about it, but they're part of the conversation. The kids are never allowed to get to that point of no return here. There isn't a place in the building where they're unattended. There's no dark halls that go nowhere. It's just like being in your house, having dinner with your family.

> The teachers see another dimension of the kids, and somehow that also comes back in their teaching. Secondly, it keeps the level of behavior at a more acceptable place. They just don't get many opportunities to get out of hand.

> They need so much companionship and compassion. They never ask for it. You never know . . .

Other parents were most impressed by the openness of the teachers:

> If you talk to someone, they actually respond. If you have a suggestion it seems like the people here are receptive. "Yeah, great idea!"

> When you're sharing something with the teacher, you're not telling them how to do their job. It's just: "Here's a heads up." Here we can do that.

Asked what long-term differences the charter school had made in their children's lives, parents most often spoke of a change in their child's attitude toward learning and academic achievement:

> He hated school. He didn't want to go to school. We had to argue with him practically every morning to go to school. We haven't had that at all at the charter school. . . . He's a completely different child.

> Here [at the charter school] being smart is in. It gets respect.

> Probably the top student in the graduating class is [girl's name]. I've heard my son, talking to another kid on the phone—about her—talking about how great she is, or repeating conversations he's had with this very bright girl.

> I like having my children have conversations with other children who are bright, whom they respect, and not have them saying: "Oh, so-and-so is such a nerd!"

He responded very, very well. He went from being this wallflower, background-type student to one who was raising his hand and participating in class discussions. He also, in my mind, had fabulous teachers. . . . My son was a mediocre or less than average-type student and they pulled him up to being an active student. It was extremely exciting to watch.

A number of parents pointed to the social development and sense of respect for others that have been fostered by the community atmosphere of the school:

This is the age when they just want to blend but they feel safe in being drawn out, like what they do is not going to be criticized or judged or any of that.

That's one thing the exhibitions have done, they have forced really, really shy kids to speak to strangers and to explain their work to strangers. So that's really, really positive, because there are a lot of shy children in the school.

There is a very strong value system. Take [girls name]. She had birth defects. So she's got disabilities and she's disfigured. But she is in class. She has a separate set of work which goes on at the same time.

The school's attitude toward discipline was also mentioned:

One of the things that is helpful here is that, if you get a disciplinary referral, after lunch you are responsible for helping Mr. Commeret clean the lunch room. If a parent says anything, you can say: "Well, you know what? They're helping Mr. Commeret, who is cleaning up after their lunch." So the message being sent is that nobody's above it all, or below it all. Everyone's held accountable and they are responsible for our environment. What you're doing is helping him, because he has agreed to clean the community room where all 175 people have lunch.

Curriculum issues were less frequently brought up by parents than other aspects of the school. However, a few parents spoke approvingly of the innovative aspects of the curriculum:

There are no bells. Your academic subject doesn't stop just because you're changing instructors. They'd carry on themes. For example, in community service, they were responsible for doing recycling and their teacher asked them: "What's the volume of this trash that we've now accumulated?" So, all of a sudden, they were doing math, in community service! It was exciting to see it dawn on the kids, how the things they were doing in the classroom, all of a sudden, could be applied elsewhere.

They were learning Greek myths in English. In music they were doing rhythm patterns and making up rap songs about their gods. . . . They studied the Greek mathematicians, I don't remember their names right off the top of my head, but I do remember him saying "Gee, that was a funny way of figuring out the area of a triangle." It was the method of an ancient Greek.

In PE during Greek mythology, they had some Olympic-type events that were really kind of fun because everybody got into it.

What my son liked best was when he could fool around with the computers. In eighth grade he had to do some research and come up with a demonstration. The one he liked best was the weather one, where he pulled in the Doppler Effect and the technology that could be used to enhance prediction.

A strong theme in the parent comments had to do with comparison of their experiences as parents at the charter school with the experiences reported by other parents whose children had attended the regular middle school:

I hear stories that I don't want to know. Half of those kids [my child was friends with] have now become discipline problems.

[Boy's name] is real social. He likes people. And if that's what it took to be popular, I think he would have said: "OK. If that's what it takes, that's what it takes." I could be wrong, but I'm really glad I never had to find out.

Most of them are not ready to make those choices. They shouldn't be asked to at that age.

A few parents were interviewed whose children had graduated from the charter school the year before. They were now at Marblehead High School and had not experienced the discrimination they had feared:

Some of the kids were afraid, when they went to the high school, of saying they were from the charter school. But it didn't really matter. Whether they were coming from public school, or the charter school, or from a private school, everyone was coming from somewhere else. It was a non-issue.

However, now that their child was back in the environment of a large secondary school, some parents found that the problems that had originally led them to the charter school had reappeared:

Now, at the high school, he's once again falling into that same old trap. He's once again one of many. He does well when the teacher excites him. But, over all, it's kind of discouraging. If you have a more exciting teacher, he just blossoms. If the teacher motivates him and he understands, he does very, very well.

By this time, much of the controversy that had surrounded the opening of the charter school had died down. There was a change in how parents of perspective students saw the school. A parent observed:

There were 200 people at the meeting for people interested in enrolling their children next year—the most there has ever been. In the beginning it was mostly people who were willing to try anything, who were very dissatisfied with the public schools, who were willing to take the chance to send their children to MCCPS. Others would say, "It's just an experiment. I'm not going to send my student off to a school that is just an experiment." Now people are deciding to send their children here because it is a better school.

One of the biggest questions about the charter school had always been accountability. The parents who had remained at the school insisted that their experience had caused them to view accountability qiute differently, as something that was shared, not just the responsibility of the school.

You know, they always ask: "Where's the accountability in a charter school?" But, you know, at the charter school I see accountability reaching a whole new level. Kids are held accountable. They're accountable for their behavior. They're accountable for their school work.

However, some parents did take a special satisfaction in pointing to how well MCCPS students had done on state-mandated standardized tests that had been given for the first time that year:

This was the first year with the state test. We did well on that. And, you know, it was funny. When bad news comes out about the MCCPS, people always ask me about it, because they know I am connected with the school. But when the news story came out, and the MCCPS got higher scores than the big middle school, no one from the community asked about it

Many kids at MCCPS are from Lynn and Salem, from more urban areas. So that our kids did better was even more impressive, because some kids had originally come from lower performing schools

THE ADMINISTRATOR'S VIEW

Marblehead Community Charter Public School is a middle school serving 176 students in grades 5–8. The academic program consists of project-based learning organized by school-wide global themes. Each trimester, students move from specific classroom instruction to the production of projects of increasing complexity. Each trimester culminates in a well-attended exhibition night, during which everyone's work is shared with other students, parents, and community members. (report submitted by Massachusetts Commissioner of Education)

The basic curriculum at MCCPS was set in place by Thomas Commeret, the Head of School, who had earlier worked in a private Catholic school. He explained his own reformist orientation by a bit of personal history. He started out as a French teacher. Not being a native French speaker, he had had to learn the French language. So he knew that learning French was something that English speakers could be do. Yet when he started teaching, he found that the traditional instructional methods for teaching a foreign language were effective with only a few of the students in his class. The rest just sat there and endured the class. As a result, what most of these students absorbed was not a love of French language and culture, but a bad attitude toward school. Commeret began exploring alternatives and became convinced that for teaching to be effective, students had to feel that what they were learning was worthwhile.

Important insights into the philosophy that guided the implementation of the ideas found in the Marblehead charter school's vision statement are provided by an essay written by Headmaster Commeret in the spring of 1996, at the end of the charter school's first year. He discussed insights provided by Michael Fullan in his book *Changing Forces* (1993). He noted that, when he began his tenure with MCCPS, he shared with the faculty and staff the eight basic lessons that Fullan called a "new paradigm for change." The following quotes are taken from this essay.

> *You Can't Mandate What Matters.* . . . It was with this belief that I interviewed potential candidates for teaching positions at the school. Of vital importance to my decision-making process for who would be chosen to assist in the creation of a new school was clear evidence on the part of each candidate of a critical awareness of the need for systemic change to educational practices in our public schools, a creative open-ended attitude toward taking risks, and a demonstration of effective and innovative teaching practice. Once the faculty was chosen we met together during the summer months to join our creative and professional energies to commit to a plan of action . . . time for continuing to develop a common dialogue was a non-negotiable component of our ultimate success.
>
> *Change is a Journey, Not a Blueprint.* . . . The key lies as much in the creative activity of charting a new course as it does in the desire to arrive at a planned destination. As we began our journey we were immediately confronted with the necessity to try new ideas, gather data relevant to the relative success or failure of the ideas, reflect on possible improvement, and finally modify any component of the program which needed to be changed. This process, although challenging and time intensive in our beginning months has happily become standardized practice.
>
> *Problems Are Our Friends.* . . . Teachers and administrators who embrace problems as a natural part of the change process rather than avoiding them

for fear of criticism are internally empowered to stay the course and embrace the process of change as their life's work. . . . Using a group consensus approach to dealing with scheduling issues and other programmatic problems, we creatively modified our entire integrated arts program, we created new forms of assessment, and we dealt with the myriad details of communicating effectively with a parent community with very high expectations and critical doubts surrounding unfamiliar approaches and methodologies.

Vision and Strategic Planning Come Later. . . . Fortunately for me, the ideas in the Marblehead Community Charter Public School charter were in agreement with my own beliefs and aspirations for needed changes in public school practice. (I did not participate in the writing of the charter as it had been completed before I was hired.) As fortunate was the fact that the charter, as it was written, was relatively generic in scope; it did not go into extreme detail as far as how the various ideas would be implemented. What this did was leave room for myself, the teaching staff, the students and the community to participate in the development of an effective and dynamic program. We are currently living that experience.

Individualism and Collectivism Must Have Equal Power. . . . From the outset of the charter school, the teaching faculty has participated in daily common planning blocks of time. An atmosphere of mutual respect for opinion and practice and a commitment to working things through by trying things out is standard operating procedure for our staff. They are the professionals entrusted with the day to day tasks of ensuring a rigorously academic environment and the active engagement of all students. They work collectively with me to develop global themes and the essential questions and common goals which become the cornerstone of our academic program. They then work individually and in grade-based teams to develop appropriate content rich lessons which connect to the global themes.

Neither Centralization nor Decentralization Works. . . . "What is required is a different two-way relationship of pressure, support, and continuous negotiation. It amounts to simultaneous top-down bottom-up influence" (Fullan, p. 38). Empowered teachers at the charter school create curriculum, participate in program decisions and actively and regularly communicate their professional opinions to the board of directors. This situation has resulted in a dynamic group of highly invested individuals.

Connection with the Wider Environment is Critical. Despite the overwhelming time commitment of the creation of a new school and curriculum, the teaching staff has accepted numerous opportunities to connect with the larger local and educational community. Participation in conferences, organization of education forums at the school, and the active involvement by the teaching staff in professional organizations throughout the year continues to produce a rich variety of ideas and suggestions for reflection and improvement.

Every Person is a Change Agent. "Every teacher has the responsibility to help create an organization capable of individual and collective inquiry and continuous renewal, or it will not happen" (Fullan, p. 39). Fortunately, and of critical importance to the charter school, the teachers hired to accomplish the tasks at hand were in full agreement with the concept and responsibility of active change agency of each individual in the organization.

THE TEACHERS' VIEW

For the teachers, the stages were experienced differently than for the parents. For them, initiation/planning did not begin until they were hired. The honeymoon was largely crowded into the summer as all stakeholders worked furiously to ready the building for the students in the fall. Implementation began with the opening of the doors to students. There were several crises as some board members tried to micromanage the school, openly questioning decisions made by some staff members. During the school's first semester, the governance structure was chaotic, with board members arguing among themselves. After the power struggle on the board sorted itself out, the lines of authority became clearer. A consultant was brought in who worked with the board to help members better understand their function and how they could best carry out their function as trustees, in a way that was supportive of the educational efforts of the school staff. The aftermath of this lengthy struggle was seen in the school's second year, in the development of a working consensus among teachers and parents as to the general goals and values of the school.

To put it somewhat differently, the most memorable crisis in the eyes of the parents had to do with external problems, especially competition with existing settings for resources and prestige. For staff members, the most pressing issues had to do with determining how lines of authority and communication would be established. Both parents and teachers felt the impact of growth and differentiation. Several ex-board members have since made public statements to the effect that the charter school is "not what it was meant to be." For these stakeholders, the impact of new people entering the setting was such that the school became something other than they had envisioned. To a certain extent, the parents and teachers who remained comprised a community whose members had self-selected for certain characteristics, especially having to do with the ability to negotiate amicably and reach mutually satisfying compromises regarding issues about which all parties had strong feelings.

Initiation/Planning Stage

One thing that came out strongly in the teacher interviews was the importance teachers put on collegial relationships and mutual support:

> It's about people, it really is. It's about kids, but it's about the people who make the kids what they are.

> You need people that you can count on and you can cry on each other's shoulders. I mean, that is really important.

As one of the teachers pointed out, "Everybody had their own little ideas, about having this type of program and that type of program and that type of program." During the summer, as they threw their energies into getting the school open, that had not seemed to be a problem. No one particularly wanted to argue about which ideas would be implemented first. Later, all of that changed. Teachers recalled:

> What stands out in my mind, is a bunch of parents who wanted to start a school and the only thing that they had in common, in retrospect, was that they didn't want to go to the other school. And they all had hopes and dreams, none of which were articulated very specifically. They hired us to make it happen, and they hired people who were strong willed and had strong opinions. And then they expected us to do everything that they told us to do.

Honeymoon

Tom Commeret, the head of school, was the first staff member hired. His conversations with prospective teachers laid the basis for what would become a cohesive, mutually supportive staff. As a teacher pointed out, "He hired us, so he had an idea that our philosophy would jell with his." However, the outlines of the curriculum remained vague. A teacher mentioned the advertisement she had answered when she had applied for a position at the school: "It was a terrific ad, it was exactly what I was looking for at the time. It promised everything. Imagine a school where you could do whatever you want!" Another teacher, talking about what had motivated her to apply, recalled:

> I was old enough to be a little skeptical. However, I was at a place in my career where I really was sick of doing what everybody else told me that I should be doing and knowing it wasn't working. And I really wanted it. The timing, for me, was perfect. I was moving, I was ready for a new position.

All but one of the teachers interviewed had been working in a public school prior to coming to MCCPS. As one teacher pointed out, "the one thing we all have in common is our passion for kids and for public education." The exception, a younger male teacher, described his prior experience:

> I had just started an alternative school in Lynn three years prior to that. So I was working with those students that were troubled, from the city of Lynn. And the people here know the city of Lynn is your typical post-industrial fallout city . . . , it is like a doughnut, we have a lot of nice stuff on the outside, but nothing in the actual city of downtown Lynn. So starting up that school

was very, very time consuming, very, very draining. I was actually looking to reduce my hours, but I found I had to work the same amount.

The controversy in Marblehead had the effect of creating a more diverse student body, because this left more places in the school available for students from nearby cities. Although no transportation was provided, these spaces were eagerly snapped up by parents eager to escape troubled urban schools.

Implementation

More than one teacher recalled working between 60 and 80 hours a week the first year. "It was rare that we left here before eight and nine o'clock," recalled one. Media coverage was intense, making the school staff feel as if they were under a microscope:

> This was the first school to open, the first charter school to open. We were under a microscope that had laser-like focus, not only from individuals within the community, but from the state and from those on high who were thinking that they were being judged.

> There was one strike against us because we were in Marblehead as opposed to inner-city. The [charter] schools that are in the inner-city . . . they can do anything they want.

However, the teachers felt empowered. As a teacher pointed out: "It was just the faculty with the curriculum. The parents were outside of that." Looking back, another teacher asserted that the "curriculum was probably what saved the school." Asked to briefly describe the curriculum, one teacher said: "It is actually very Montessori-based. They start with the big and move down to the small. So there is a moral thread to it." Another emphasized thematic units:

> The reason we use the global thematic unit to center goals is because kids learn better if they understand why they are doing it and if it has meaning. It matters to them.

An effort is made to furnish a meaningful context to everything the students are asked to do. Feedback is therefore not limited to letter grades. Three times each year there is a student exhibition featuring "a project, something physical, something real that is not just exhibited to each other." An evening is set aside. The school is crowded with "their parents, other educators, their friends, alumni that come back here." In the eyes of one of the teachers:

The stimulus to achieve is very motivating. The motivation, the intrinsic motivation is developed by positive feedback that comes from a community that values not only the work, but the conceptualization of the big picture, the understanding of the big picture. So a parent will walk up and ask a student not only what they did, but: How does it fit? Where does it go? And the student is reinforced when they can understand and make clear what they did, not only with the work, but conceptually, making other people understand.

Another teacher commented:

They see the reward of hard work, too. That's one thing they always say after exhibition. "It was so much work and I didn't think I could do it, and I was so proud when I did!"

Asked to compare the curriculum to that of the regular middle school, a teacher replied: "It is the way that we teach that is different from other schools. But the school sequence, the curriculum, the stuff that is taught is pretty much the same." Other teachers agreed: "It is so much about process, it's far less about the content."

Everything we teach we try to connect to the central questions of understanding goals and to the exhibition. Because we know if we connect it becomes more important and the kids learn it. If it is just something, even down to nouns, verbs, I mean everything that we teach, we try to connect. Our experience has shown us the more we connect, the better they learn and the more they want to learn.

Talking of the school's emphasis on answering the question "When are we going to use this in life?" another teacher commented:

As teachers we always kind of shy away from it, like: "You don't need to know. You will know when you grow up." I mean why not let them know, if it helps the cause, if it furthers their ability to become engaged? Then they need to know.

Crisis

Parents at the school are expected to share in their child's experience at the school and to monitor homework. They sign the homework book every night and are asked to call immediately when things aren't going well. Although parental involvement had been a major facet of the vision for the school since the beginning, when the school first opened many parents were not prepared for the extent to which they would be expected to participate in their child's education at MCCPS. As a teacher pointed out,

"When we demand that [the parents] get involved they don't always want to. It's hard work." Other teachers noted:

> They were in middle school, where parents kind of . . . because of the social atmosphere, kids want parents to stay back and parents just say "Well, I should."

> Their parents weren't involved in their education. Their parents sent them off to school. They went to school. They came back home from school. The parents said: "Did you do your homework?" They said "Yes." And it was all done.

In subsequent years, however, attitudes have changed. Teachers commented:

> We're much better now at making the parents aware of how big the commitment is. We didn't do that in the beginning and we were constantly disappointed that the parents weren't into it.

> Parents who have been here for three of four years, working parents, will turn around to other parents who will stand up in meetings and voice discontent and say "Look, this is how it is. . . ."

> They know they're getting more out of their relationship with their kids.

The first year, many of the parents who opted to send their child to MCCPS did so because the child had not been succeeding in their present school environment. In some cases, the children were troubled and needed help, yet the parents were reluctant to face this. A teacher recalled: "Especially the first year, a lot of the kids were troubled kids for one reason or other. . . . And some of them were very troubled kids." Another commented: "There were also parents who, instead of 'facing the music,' kept switching . . . it was always the school. It was never the child." Referring to these parents, a third teacher commented: "You might say they were seasoned with discontent. No matter what you gave them, it was going to go seasoned with that discontent." Although, at times, parent–teacher relationships were difficult, most of the teachers persevered. As one teacher pointed out:

> Everyone in education knows that the number one predictor of how well a student is going to do is the parent involvement, from day one. Everybody knows that and yet we keep doing other things to improve it, to improve student performance, that has nothing to do with that.

Teachers credited Headmaster Tom Commeret with enabling the school to weather the storm.

Tom was wanting people to know, right from the start, that the teachers were essentially the heart of the school. He really never allowed anything to get to them, unless it was something way beyond his control. He protected them like a father.

He was criticized, very much. But he never gave in, in his vision of what had to happen in order for the school to grow. And if it had it been a different person, this school wouldn't be growing.

A traditional administrator would've packed his bags and run the first day.

We were criticized for being such a closed group. It was scary. "Tom is your cheerleader. He should be an administrator. He should be telling you what to do and when you screw up . . ." And the people saw that as very threatening. Yet, it was the only reason why we hung in there. We needed that.

He has never really gotten the credit for that, other than the people that really watched what happened. But, he really enabled it to happen.

Looking back, the teachers credited four factors with helping them to survive the crises and controversies that marked the charter school's first year:

- The quality of the teachers recruited ("Everyone who came was one of the best in the program from where ever they came from. There were no slackers in the group").
- The esprit de corps among the teachers, nurtured by the leadership of the head of school ("If not for each other and Tom as a leader, we never would have gotten here").
- The existence within the program of support structures that promoted individual growth ("The way this place is structured organizationally now allows not only for us to continue our growth but for us to continue to experiment, continue to improve on our practice, continue to evolve").
- The ability to change policies as the school evolved ("If something is not working, we're going get together and figure out ways to change it. And we don't have to wait for the schools to okay it in the year 2005. You know, we do it the next day").

Sarason asserted that the problems associated with the formation and development of a new setting are largely a consequence of the emphasis put on one factor and the deemphasis—or ignoring—of another. The factor that is emphasized (indeed viewed as central) is the job that needs to be done: to provide some kind of service or product for others not part of the setting. The factor that is deemphasized consists of two ingredients: the professional and personal growth of its members, and the ways in which their mutuality can enhance growth. Usually, in the creation of a setting, these factors have been quite secondary to the concern with what is provided for others outside the setting. Yet the greatest source of disillusionment and disruption within a setting is usually a consequence of having ignored or deemphasized the need to nurture the personal and professional growth of members, so that they are better able to help others. Put in an alternative manner, it is of pivotal importance that members of the core group remember a simple adage: We cannot do for others, we cannot change others, until we learn how to do for and change ourselves.

What proved to be the saving factor for the Marblehead charter school was the emphasis put on growth and mutuality by the headmaster. Capable, idealistic, energetic teachers were recruited, who highly valued the opportunity for professional and personal growth. A daily opportunity for planning and sharing experiences was made part of the school schedule. Teachers could see daily evidence of how their efforts were shaping the evolving culture of the school. What was decided on one day was implemented the next. There was none of that sense of frustration that builds up when teachers are asked to attend multiple meetings at which nothing seems to get done, or when then they laboriously work out a new policy only to have it overturned by someone higher up in the administration. Thus a sense of momentum, of shared commitment and growth, was fostered. This helped teachers to maintain their enthusiasm and professionalism amid the organizational chaos and frustrations of the charter school's first year of operation.

Aftermath

Rodney Evans (1999) described middle schools as being (ideally) places characterized by the buzz and hum of activity, a barely concealed exuberance that seems ready to overflow at any moment, a collective joyful energy that carries young and old along, impish good humor and an absence of solemnity. By its second year of operation this became very much the atmosphere at Marblehead's charter school.

The school evolved a strong community atmosphere. Teachers spoke of their relationship with students:

> Students get to know the teachers even if they don't have them [for class], and so they feel more responsible, and I'm sure that works both ways. So, if it's clear that a child is suffering, for whatever reason, at least one or two adults in the building are going to pick up on it and say "Hey, what do you think?"

> There is none of this "Well, that's not my kid . . ." That happens in a lot of public schools. You know, "I'm only responsible for these 20 kids," and if an-

other kid is goofing off in the hall many teachers will just walk right by. That doesn't happen here.

I think kids feel safe. Some of the kids will say "Oh, I can't get away with anything!" But there are those who think it's pretty nice that we're right there for them.

There are very few cracks to slide through.

It's just like being in a home, where the rules are very clear cut. Generally speaking, kids won't admit it, but they are a lot more comfortable with structure.

Teachers noted the strong emphasis on communication and on values:

Parents know that I'll call them and tell them what's up, and the kids know that.

The strong sense of community makes it easier to talk about issues that tend to be avoided in other public schools.

In a lot of public schools there is almost a culture where you don't talk about values with kids. But we do that every morning.

We talk about things everybody values like truth and honesty and working hard.

It's not an after thought, it's not like we are going: "Oh yeah, maybe we should mention it. We all need to work hard."

It's just part of their everyday existence here.

We spend a lot of time on understanding each other. We talk a lot about being there for one another, being responsible individuals within a community.

You know the kids see our relationship with each other and they see how we care about the buildings and the rooms. You know, we are there vacuuming our own room. They see that.

Faculty members described the way in which parent attitudes had changed since the first year:

You know we've matured to the degree that people are actually beginning to trust and rely and allow us to make decisions without wondering constantly if we're making the right decisions.

We spend a lot of time with our parents. Much more than a regular school teacher would.

I mean, the relationship I have with [a parent] has a lot to do with the relationship I have with your kids.

They've never had anyone take that personal an interest in them. Most teachers have 30 kids in a classroom and they don't have time to make those kinds of phone calls or conferences.

The first year, the parents attracted to the school tended to be those who felt a strong sense of discontent with the public schools their children attended. More recently, though, the parents have not so much been fleeing a situation they saw as unsatisfactory as seeking out a school of which they had heard good things. Teachers commented:

Now we're at the stage where people are beginning to trust us and the waiting lists are filling as a result of that and the type of people we are drawing are not so much the people who are initially discontent with the traditional system. They are people who are looking for other options for their children.

This year was very different from any other open house. The parents were coming up to us and saying, you know, "What are my chances? How do I get my kid in here?" They had just heard from other parents in the community. So, we don't have to sell ourselves any more.

CONCLUSIONS

Starkly different interpretations were given by charter school opponents and supporters to each of the four values (excellence, efficiency, equity, choice) that have historically influenced decision making regarding the public schools. For example, for teachers at the regular middle school, *excellence* was defined in terms of their school's ranking vis-à-vis other public middle schools in the state. In their eyes, although their school might have its problems, it was a substantially better middle school than most. Opponents of the charter school accused the parents who founded the charter school of trying to get a private school education for their children at public expense. In Marblehead, this was an especially contentious issue given that approximately one fourth of the children in town were already in private schools. Moreover, there were many families that had children in both public and private school (in some families it was traditional to send boys away for secondary school and to keep girls closer to home). On the other hand, the parents who had created the charter school judged the existing school, against a broader spectrum of schools, including Catholic and other private schools.

Charter school supporters argued that, considering the resources at its disposal and the affluent, homogeneous student population it served, Marblehead's existing public middle school was not doing an acceptable job of educating local students. As the charter school founders saw it, Marblehead's public school students compared well to their private school peers up to the end of elementary school but they learned "next to nothing" during their middle school years. From the point of view of the charter school's supporters, education was education, whatever the source of funding, just as health care was essentially the same thing, whether in a public or private setting. Why should publicly funded hospitals be expected to deliver a quality of care equal to private hospitals while public schools were judged only against other public schools?

Points of view differed just as vividly in regard to efficiency. Opponents of the charter school saw it as an inappropriate and therefore inefficient use of state funds, arguing that the transfer of students to the charter school drained away funds from the existing public schools. Fixed costs ate up much the school district's budget. When a student left the existing middle school and went to the charter school, bringing along the per-pupil funding that accompanied him or her, there was not a corresponding drop in the school district's expenses. State mandates (such as those regarding the education of students with special needs) and existing contractual obligations (such as those negotiated with the teachers' union) limited the school district's ability to adjust to drops in funding. Charter school advocates took a different view, arguing that the money spent on the existing middle school was of little value if students were not learning. They also pointed out that the public schools already possessed the facilities (buildings, playing fields, computer and science labs, etc.) that the charter school had to finance out of per-pupil funding. This meant that the charter school was operating on a far leaner budget than the existing middle school. They questioned whether there might be a fair amount of "fat" in the school district budget in terms of nonteaching administrative personnel.

Viewpoints regarding the meaning of *equity* were also strikingly different. In the eyes of opponents, the charter school constituted an attempt by a group of elitists to fashion a special educational environment for their own children at public expense. They argued that the charter school had put the children at the existing middle school at a disadvantage, forcing their school to get by on less funding. Since the charter school did not have the same accountability obligations as the regular middle school it had, in effect, been given special privileges not available to the regular middle school. Supporters of the charter school, in contrast, argued that *equity* did not mean forcing children whose families could not afford to put them in private school to accept an inferior education. Equity meant making sure that all children got an equal chance in life. Moreover, there had been a time when public schools in Marblehead had delivered a superior education; why was it unreasonable to demand that they do so now?

Predictably, *choice* was the value regarding which these two groups differed most of all. Opponents of the charter school argued that public education was a government function, like police protection or the repair of city streets. Voters chose the school board members, who then made decisions in their name. They also felt it was best to leave education in the hands of professionals, as parents were ill-equipped to make the best educational choices for their children, or to make decisions that would serve the best interests of all children served by the public schools. Charter school supporters, however, saw education not merely as a government service, to be distributed more or less efficiently, but as a highly personal matter, intimately bound up with individual growth and development. They argued that within a democratic society educational choice had value in and of itself, a value that was intimately bound up with principals of individual freedom. Parents knew their child best and were the ones most strongly motivated to serve as the child's advocate when things were not going well at school. Moreover, for that advocacy to be meaningful, alternatives had to be available for children who were not succeeding in their present school environment.

A SUMMARY OF ASSERTIONS MADE BY CHARTER SCHOOL SUPPORTERS AND OPPONENTS

This section summarizes the radically differing points of view taken by charter school opponents and supporters regarding the values of excellence, efficiency, equity, and choice. In each category, one or two typical comments are quoted. Where existing media accounts addressed the difference in question, these are also quoted.

- **Excellence**

  Residents taking part in a public forum on starting a charter school in town see the proposal either as a way of bringing public education out of the stranglehold of bureaucracy or as an attempt by educational leaders to establish a special school at the expense of taxpayers. (*The Salem Evening News*, 6/16/94, p. 16)

  Charter School Opponents. Marblehead's public schools rank well among the public middle schools in the state in terms of student achievement. Although the middle school may have some problems, it is a better middle school than most. The founders of the charter school were just trying to set up a private school with public money. In effect, they sought excellence in education for only a few students, while leaving the remainder with fewer resources than before.

While the students selected to attend the charter school would benefit from smaller classes, two-thirds of middle school students would remain in the large school with less money to educate them. (Teacher at regular middle school)

Charter School Supporters.   U.S. public schools do not compare favorably to those in other industrialized countries, or with private schools in the United States, in regard to student achievement. The existing middle school has a high level of per-pupil funding and a homogeneous and well-prepared pool of students. Why should it not be expected to get better results?

When people in Marblehead talk about public education, they talk about it as being a problem. (Member, Marblehead Board of Selectmen)

- **Efficiency**

Charter School Opponents.   Regular public schools are required to spend a large percentage of their budget in a manner mandated by the state, or by teacher contract commitments, and by fixed facilities maintenance expenses. This limits the options open to them and makes cost efficiency a high priority. The loss of funding that results when students opt to go to the charter school limits options still further, making meaningful reform more difficult.

[Marblehead] Public school board members say that they've been forced to cut four public school teachers [due to loss of students to charter school]. (*USA Today*, September 13, 1995, p. 7D)

Charter School Supporters.   The existing middle school already has a building and playing fields. These facilities do not have to be financed out of per-pupil revenues—as they must be in the case of the charter school. The charter school operates on a leaner budget, which suggests that there is a fair amount of "fat" in the form of administrator and other salaries in the school district budget.

They started out with a building, with all sorts of facilities. We had nothing. (Charter School Parent)

- **Equity**

Charter School Opponents.   The charter school is elitist in that it serves only those children whose parents take the time to investigate options and apply for the school. Moreover, the charter school does not have the same accountability obligations as the regular middle school and thus, in effect, enjoys special privileges not given to staff and parents at the regular middle school.

> The charter school would attract the best students with the more active parents and that would hurt the remaining students. (Teacher at regular middle school)

Charter School Supporters. All Marblehead students can enter the charter school lottery and thus have equal opportunity to attend. Moreover, no claim is made that this is the best program for all students. What the charter school does do is challenge the conception that "public" must mean inferior, that a public school education cannot be as good as any education offered anywhere.

> The regular middle school is overcrowded. They just would have to add on if our kids were all there. So, in a sense we have helped. (MCCPS parent)

• **Choice**

> Parents in Marblehead, a suburb of 20,000, wielded hammers to transform an old Elks hall into a school. Such community effort makes the school unique, according to organizers. 'It's not so much the programs as the whole environment,' says sixth-grade teacher. . . . Not everyone in Marblehead is applauding. Many residents see the charter school as a $500,000-a-year drain. (*USA Today*, September 13, 1995, p. 7D)

Charter School Opponents. Voters choose school board members who make decisions, in their name, regarding what is best for all the town's students. Parents are ill-equipped to make the best educational choices for their children, or to decide what is best for all children in town. Education is best left in the hands of professionals.

> We also feel [the charter school proposal] was railroaded through. No one with an educational background was called on for input. (Marblehead Middle School social studies teacher)

Charter School Supporters. If only one choice is provided, inevitably some children will not be well served. Parents know their child best and are the ones most strongly motivated to serve as that child's advocate when things are not going well. Why should parents who want to be actively involved in their child's schooling not be allowed that option through a charter school?

That's part of the overall choice philosophy that if you feel schools are not providing for your child, you should not have to move out of your neighborhood to educate your child. (Spokeswoman for MA Executive Office of Education)

IMPLICATIONS

On the charter school's opening day, a group of local history buffs showed up in Revolutionary War uniforms and lifted their muskets aloft to fire a salute. The symbolism was by no means accidental. As the revolutionary imagery implied, the charter school coalition saw themselves as having mounted a revolution—against state mandates, teachers' unions, local "educrats," and others intent on telling Marbleheaders how their public schools "ought" to be run. In their eyes, control of the local public schools had passed out of the hands of parents, into the hands of bureaucrats and special interest groups. By reminding onlookers of their town's role in the American Revolution, they were implicitly announcing that Marblehead was once again at the forefront of those resisting antidemocratic forces.

Among the specific changes that MCCPS parents said they would like to see in all contemporary public schools were:

- Maintain close communication between teacher and parent, at least through eighth grade.
- Create a school culture where achievement and hard work are respected, not just popularity.
- Use assessments requiring articulate verbal and written expression, reduce use of few multiple-choice tests.
- Insist that children treat adults, each other and their physical environment with respect.
- Make sure students can use what they learn, that it is not just inert "school knowledge."
- Return to K–8 elementary schools, so children would not experience "teen culture" until later.

That these goals were not entirely "out of sync" with the views of other local residents was implied by the lengthening waiting list for the charter school. Moreover, quite aside from the debate over the charter school, there were indications of continued discontent and upheavals at the regular middle school. For example in the April 25, 1999, edition of *The Boston Sunday Globe*, the Marblehead school district advertised its 1999–2000 vacancies. Although this is a district where there tends to be little turnover (only seven teaching positions were advertised in the entire school district), that year there were six middle school openings.

The depth of disillusionment felt by some parents with their existing public school options is attested to by the determination shown by the parents who set up MCCPS. Politically diverse, the parents who created this school did not share a single ideological or religious orientation. They received no financial gain from their efforts. Nor were they escaping a threatening urban environment. Many were long-time local residents who had always been active in local affairs. A number of the MCCPS parents had formerly been among those stalwart volunteers who never failed to show up for meetings or to provide help to classroom teachers when their children were in elementary school.

Although it would be a mistake to overgeneralize, some patterns were discernible. Many of the charter school's supporters were "Townies" who had grown up in Marblehead and gone to school in town. Some were wealthy, but many were not. Some MCCPS students were the children of plumbers or electricians. Their families could not easily afford private school tuition, yet they wanted something for their children that the local public schools no longer seemed to provide. Whereas many outspoken opponents of the charter school had moved to Marblehead more recently, perhaps in part because the town was reputed to have a good public school system. These people saw the establishment of—and conflict over—the charter school not only as a disruption of the public school system but also as a "black eye" for Marblehead's public schools, whose reputation was important to them.

Arguably, much about the situation in Marblehead was unique. Yet the conflict in this town may also be a harbinger of a changed relationship between parents and public schools. In earlier generations, school teachers often were among the best educated people in a given town. Since the 1960s, however, the percentage of Americans holding college degrees has risen dramatically. In many affluent suburbs like Marblehead, whatever educational advantage might once have been held by school personnel has long since disappeared. So has much of the deference with which school teachers and administrators were once treated. Parents interviewed for this study described the decision-making process vis-à-vis choosing a school for their children in much the way they might have described choosing an HMO (health maintenance organization) to take care of their family's health needs. They saw teachers and physicians as providing a valuable service, but they also felt that the consumer had a right to "vote with her feet" if the care provided did not seem to be adequate.

The politics surrounding the creation of the Marblehood charter school were local. Even now, few MCCPS parents speak of the founding of the charter school in ideological terms. Most talk of getting a charter from the state as an option that became attractive when they realized that their concerns were unlikely to be addressed by the school committee and superintendent. Had different decisions been made by school district officials, it is unlikely that this charter school would have come into existence. The charter school families decided to secede from the existing middle school because they had become convinced that it would not provide a healthy environment for their children.

What did these parents value in terms of providing a "healthy environment"? In many respects, what they ended up creating differed little in essential characteristics from the Catholic schools studied by Anthony Bryk and his colleagues (Bryk, Lee, & Holland, 1993): a relatively narrow curriculum that all students were expected to master, small school size, decentralized governance, broad roles for staff members that reflected a commitment to the transformative potential of education, and a conception of the school as a voluntary community. This allowed faculty to serve in multiple roles as classroom teacher, coach, counselor, and adult role model. As Bryk and his colleagues saw it, having the chance to interact with teachers in a variety of situations enabled students to "encounter a full person, not just a subject-matter specialist, a guidance specialist, a discipline specialist, or some other technical expert," so that the exchange between students and staff was "personal rather than bureaucratic" (p. 141).

Given that the headmaster at MCCPS had formerly been an administrator at a Catholic preparatory school, such a result is perhaps not surprising. Yet the majority of the children attending the school came from families that were Protestant, agnostic, Jewish, or Russian Orthodox. The school culture at MCCPS could not be said to be the result of the explicitly religious values. However, such an approach has advantages that cross lines of religion, ethnicity, even social class. For example, in analyzing community organizations that were both highly valued by at-risk young people and effective in helping them to move toward adult lives that seemed promising, Heath and McLaughlin (1994) found that successful youth organizations saw young people "as a resource to be developed rather than a problem to be managed," conveying interest in "the whole person, not just a single issue or component such as ethnicity, pregnancy, substance abuse, or school success" (p. 217).

Academic standards at MCCPS are demanding, yet students from economically disadvantaged backgrounds who attend the school have been able, with faculty help, to handle these demands and to achieve on the same level as their peers. Time has been set aside for teachers to meet daily to work on a curriculum that emphasizes helping students to understand the basis for theories and theorems. Teachers have been given a strong voice in the governance of the school. Although arbitrary demands made by the school's founders created problems and conflicts during the first year the school was in operation, a culture has slowly evolved at MCCPS that recognizes the professionalism of teachers and that treats parents with respect. There is no tracking at MCCPS. The small size of the school makes it possible for teachers to individualize the program so that the needs of all students are served.

Clearly, each charter school is unique. Much depends on the individual parents, teachers, and administrators who become involved with each school. At MCCPS, the financial strains and emotional stress involved in opening a new school were considerable for all involved. Startup funding provided by the state was woefully inadequate. However, the educational background and the dedication of many MCCPS parents were such that it was often possible to patch "holes" in financing and/or curriculum by calling on parents, who offered equipment, resources, and expertise. Had the school been located elsewhere, or had another headmaster been appointed, events might have taken a different turn. Even so, the history of this school does raise questions about several common assertions about charter schools. Far from "creaming" away the most successful students, in its first years of operation MCCPS tended to attract those students that were not succeeding at the regular middle school. Due to the influx of students from less affluent cities nearby, the student population was markedly more diverse than at the regular middle school—even though lack of funding meant that transportation was left entirely to parents.

EPILOGUE

> At the September 28th Board of Education meeting, I will recommend renewal of two public school charters: Cape Cod Lighthouse Charter School; and Marblehead Community Charter Public School. (David P. Driscoll, Massachusetts Commissioner of Education)

On September 15, 1999, the Massachusetts Commissioner of Education sent a memo to members of the state Board of Education, along with briefing materials for the board meeting, at which he would recommend renewal of two public school charters. Attached were Summaries of Review of the applications for renewal. At the September 28th meeting the Massachusetts Board of Education voted unanimously in favor of renewal. The somewhat dry language of the commissioner's report and ensuing board discussion gave little hint of the storm of controversy that had accompanied the founding of Marblehead Community Charter Public School (MCCPS) 4 years before.

The Commissioner's report noted that the MCCPS student-to-teacher ratio during the 1998–1999 academic year was 11:1. Student enrollment had been at capacity and stable. For the past year the ratio of applicants to available seats was more than 3:1. Regarding the long struggle to solidify the school's innovative curriculum, the report said only:

> The school's staff appears to be highly skilled and well guided by the school's principal. The faculty demonstrate a uniform and enthusiastic commitment to the school's central goals as well as close attention to each child's development. The faculty built the school from scratch, and, despite the exhaustion inherent in that task, have experienced remarkably little attrition.

No other school in this study experienced such staff solidarity, amidst so much external controversy.

REFERENCES

Bryk, A. S., Lee, V. E., & Holland, P. B. (1993). *Catholic schools and the common good.* Cambrige, MA: Harvard University Press.

Carnegie Forum on Education and the Economy. (1986). *A nation prepared: Teachers for the 21st century.* New York: Author.

Evans, R. (1999). *The pedagogic principal.* Edmonton, Alberta, Canada: Qual Institute Press.

Fullan, M. (1993). *Changing forces: Probing the depths of educational reform.* Falmer Press.

Heath, S. B., & McLaughlin, M. W. (1994). Casting the self: Frames for identity and dilemmas for policy. In S. B. Heath & M. W. McLaughlin (Eds.), *Identity & inner city youth: Beyond ethnicity and gender.* San Francisco: Jossey-Bass.

Holmes Group. (1986). *Tomorrow's teachers: A Report to the Holmes Group.* East Lansing, MI: Author.

Iannaccone, L. (1967). *Politics in education.* New York: Center for Applied Research in Education.

Institute for Responsive Education. (1996). *A national survey and analysis of charter school legislation.*

Mitchell, D. E. (1992). Governance of schools. In M. C. Alkin (Ed.), *Encyclopedia of educational research* (pp. 549–557). New York: Macmillan.

National Commission on Excellence in Education. (1983). *A nation at risk: The imperative for educational reform.* Washington, DC: U.S. Government Printing Office.

Sarason, S. B. (1988). *The creation of settings and the future societies.* Cambridge, MA: Brookline Books.

Chapter 8

Building a Theoretical Framework:
Commonalities and Contrasts

In an ideal world, the founders of charter schools would have a relatively simple task. Freed from bureaucratic restraints, charter schools would be able to pursue the educational vision their founders believed to be most effective for the children they served. All of each charter school's constituents would have actively chosen to be there. (None would have signed up simply because they disliked the other options available to them.) In an ideal world, all charter schools would have adequate startup funds; all schools would be able to find facilities well suited to their purposes; staff members would not find their energies drained by ongoing political struggles outside the school. However, as is clear in earlier chapters, none of the schools described in this book existed in an ideal world.

This chapter focuses on patterns that emerged among the challenges faced by the seven schools. Some problems were all but ubiquitous. For example, the unified vision that the founders of most schools thought they shared tended to break down when decision making got down to specifics. Parents serving on governing boards had to learn to look beyond what they wanted for their own child; if the school was to be successful, board members had to adopt policies that would enable all children at the school to thrive. Teachers found the burden of taking over functions that at their previous schools had been handled by administrators was, in the beginning, somewhat overwhelming. Almost everyone who had been involved in starting a charter school expressed surprise at how much work was involved, how many regulatory hurdles had to be jumped, how many people felt entitled to have input into the process.

Creating a climate and culture consistent with the school's philosophy and vision was a challenge for all schools. As noted in connection with the Model School (chap. 4), there was a tendency to believe that, because the founders had agreed that a particular goal was important, that goal would somehow take care of itself. But in a situation where everything that the school did had to be created from scratch, there was also a tendency to fall back on what was familiar. Even though dissatisfaction with the "same old thing" had been an important part of the motivation for starting a charter school, at some point a feeling akin to "innovation fatigue" began to set in. As discussed later in this section, help from a friendly external critic often proved to be of great value in helping charter schools to regain their bearings, remove roadblocks, and move forward. Despite the struggles, many stakeholders spoke of the opportunity to participate in the creation of a new school as a source of tremendous personal satisfaction and growth.

STARK DIFFERENCES IN ORGANIZATIONAL DYNAMICS

Overall, the problems encountered by charter school founders closely resembled those predicted by Sarason's theoretical framework (summarized in chap. 1). However, some challenges proved more problematic for one kind of school than for others. Grouping the schools according to type (parent-founded, educator-founded, institutional sponsor) highlights the differences. For example, parent-initiated charter schools had different organizational dynamics than schools created by professional educators. Schools that had come into being through the sponsorship of an existing public agency (a school district or a city government) were strongly influenced by the institutional cultures of their sponsors.

The Model School and Opportunity Preparatory School

When this research project began, the clearest contrast was expected to be between the six charter schools and the K–8 Model School (chap. 4) that had been set up as a collaborative venture between an elite private university and a large urban school district. The Model School, created during the same time period as the charter schools, had been included to provide a comparison between the charter schools and a well-financed, district-controlled reform effort. When the data were analyzed, however, it became clear that the bureaucratic constraints that had shaped the early history of the Model School were similar in their effect to the restraints that had shaped the early history of Opportunity Preparatory School (OPS, chap. 3).

Both schools were, essentially, subordinate units within a politically run bureaucracy.

At both schools, teachers' efforts to build an independent school culture proved no match for organizational pressures originating outside the school itself. There had been critical periods during each setting's early history when a unique vision for that school might have been solidified. Teachers expressed a desire to actively address challenges involving curriculum and governance structure. However, the required leadership was lacking. Teachers were "left hanging" by decision makers elsewhere. In the end, no action was taken because no one at the site had the required authority. Both schools were initially headed by an established administrator who had expressed great enthusiasm for the program, yet who continued to have significant duties elsewhere. These duties made it impossible for either school's appointed leader to spend much time with teachers during the crucial planning period prior to opening the school.

In the case of the Model School a well-respected district-level administrator was to have acted as the school's full-time principal. However, a political crisis elsewhere in the school district called this administrator away during much of the summer prior to the opening of the Model School. As a result, teachers hired to staff the new school ended up spending much of this critical period marking time, attending "canned" staff development workshops provided by the school district. Without the presence of the site administrator, no one had the authority to begin the important processes of (a) hammering out a "constitution" for the new school and (b) initiating discussion of pivotal curriculum implementation issues. Confidence and enthusiasm among the teachers wavered.

As opening day approached, there was great uncertainty about how the innovative programs described in the school's vision statement would be implemented. Many of the teachers had never taught in multiage classrooms. They had signed on because they were willing to try, but there had been an assumption that they would receive extensive training in multiage grouping before the school opened. None of this happened. With the principal away, the decision-making role fell to school district administrators who had not been active in planning the school. They proceeded as they would have when opening any other school. Teachers had been promised a strong voice in governance, yet no structure for site-level governance had been set up. As an innovative site within a custodial system, the Model School found itself continually swimming upstream. Whenever circumstances precluded staff members from putting maximum effort into fighting the current, they began to be swept downstream.

Over and over, the same phenomenon could be observed. When teachers were not given adequate training in the innovative practices the school had been set up to implement, they fell back on the teaching methods they had used at their former schools. This tendency was intensified by the controversies that marked the school's first year. Feeling besieged from the outside (as a result of the controversies described in chap. 4), teachers were hesitant to take risks. They retreated to doing what felt safe. The social justice concerns that had been much discussed during initial planning sessions got far less attention after the school opened. For example, although the original vision statement called for a bilingual school, allowing the Black and Anglo students who made up the majority of the student body to become fluent in Spanish, after the school opened the bilingual curriculum was never expanded beyond grades K–2.

What could not be set aside was the need to serve the diverse student population that had been recruited (through separate lotteries that ensured that 50% of the students at the school would be drawn from across the district—with half of these students being African American and the other half Latino—while 50% of the Model School's student population would be drawn from the affluent neighborhood near the university). When funding for the school was first approved, it was to have been a neighborhood elementary school, serving the community near the university. Later, school district officials bowed to criticism that too much money was being spent in a few White enclaves within the district and decided to double the size of the Model School, so that it would serve children from throughout the district, in grades K–8.

The major crisis of the school's first year took place at the middle school level. Teachers had been recruited from what were considered to be the "best" middle schools in the district. Accustomed to teaching affluent students, from elementary schools that were able to provide children with a strong academic foundation, the Model School's middle-level teachers understood their role to be that of upholding high academic standards. However, many of the middle-level students who came to the Model School as a result of the district-wide lottery were from low-performing elementary schools, where academic expectations had been quite different. As a result, at the end of the first semester many of the minority students who had been recruited from across this urban district were found to be failing subjects like math.

The resulting controversy embroiled the Model School in charges of racism. Many minority students in Grades 7–8 eventually decided to leave the school. Meanwhile, the school district focused its efforts on placating important constituent groups; the university distanced itself. Teachers at the Model School hunkered down and concentrated on bringing along the children in the lower grades, so that by the time these children reached middle school, they would be able to meet the school's academic standards. This had a profound effect on the culture at the school. Instead of developing an innovative model for teaching diverse populations, the Model School grew into a fairly traditional institution whose benefits were enjoyed primarily by those students who "won the lottery" and gained entrance.

At Opportunity Preparatory School the initial dream had been to create a college preparatory school for at-risk students. However, the noninvolvement of the city employee who had been the primary force behind opening the school crippled efforts to adapt the curriculum to the perceived needs of these students during the school's first year of operation. At this school, the titular principal was not just absent for a few months; he had many other duties and took the attitude that, having set out the blueprint for the school, he ought to be able to step back and let the teachers run it. But, lacking his participation, there was no one with the authority to flesh out the original vision, creating a school culture with well-understood rules and disciplinary procedures. There was an assumption that those whom the school was intended to benefit would recognize that they had been offered an important opportunity, and that they would respond—on their own—in the manner required for the school to succeed. Often this did not happen.

The problems faced by these two schools did not differ significantly from those faced by some other charter schools studied. However, in the other schools there were no layers of administrative structure to insulate administrators from the conflicts and challenges that arose almost immediately. In contrast, at the Model School and (especially) at OPS much of the decision-making power lay in the hands of persons who, at pivotal periods in their schools' history, had little day-to-day contact with events at the school site. As a result, both schools were deprived of one of the greatest advantages pointed out by stakeholders at the other charter schools: the ability to respond to emerging challenges in a timely manner, without having to bother with bureaucratic procedure.

OPS students split their time between computer-aided instruction that helped them catch up on basic academic skills and Paideia seminars that were intended to prepare them for future college work. However, a majority of the OPS students had little interest in college. The OPS students simply wanted to have a diploma in their hands; they had little interest in preparing for, or participating in, the seminars. Yet the founder of the school, who had little contact with the students, held firmly to his original dream of a college preparatory program for at-risk students. As a result, teachers found themselves floundering in a vacuum, unable either to change the mandated curriculum or to make it work for the students who were actually attending the school. Morale withered and dissension grew.

At the Model School, the problems were not so readily apparent. Nationally recognized experts had been brought in as consultants during a 3½-year planning period. On the surface, this would seem to have been a carefully designed school. However, the planning activities had been financed by grant funds raised through the university. Proceeding according to its own institutional culture, the university had held a series of stimulating seminars, to which all individuals involved in planning the Model School were invited. Visits by renowned educators excited a great deal of interest; committees of stakeholders were formed to explore various possibilities. Yet there was no mechanism in place (a) to coordinate the efforts of these committees or (b) to decide which of the disparate innovations discussed by the committees would become part of the curriculum.

As the planning period drew to a close, the stakeholder committees delivered suggestions on subjects ranging from curriculum to school governance. These suggestions were sewn together into an expansive vision statement that included something for everyone. No attempt was made to decide which of the many innovations listed should be given the highest priority. Moreover, the teachers for the school were not hired until the spring before the school opened (after the planning process was completed). Many teachers never saw the planning document. Some never knew that it existed. Nor had the school district had ever actually committed to following up on the suggestions that came out of the planning process.

Both the university president and the school district superintendent who had set the planning process in motion had, since that time, accepted positions elsewhere. With their original sponsors out of the picture, no one connected with the Model School project wanted to "make waves." All of the problems that Sarason described in connection with the "honeymoon" period were therefore present in especially acute form. No one wanted to disturb the good feelings that had been aroused by the discussion of intriguing new ideas by asking hard questions about what would happen when the school actually opened. So the project went forward, virtually on "autopilot," with backers worried that any attempt to address predictable problems might cause tensions that would result in the project being shelved.

Had those charged with the creation of this school actively made use of a theoretical framework of the sort suggested by Sarason, many problems might have been avoided. The benefit of theory, in this case, would have been to give decision makers a ready rationale for bringing up issues they might otherwise have been reluctant to mention. Sarason (1988) pointed out that project directors involved in the creation of a new setting routinely fail to ask two pivotal questions:

- What were the issues, problems, and conflicts that marked the prehistory of the new setting?
- What reactions might be anticipated as a result of the fact that the new setting will emerge from, and become part of, an existing organization of settings that had long-standing traditions and practices at vari-

ance with the new setting (which, if successful, would establish the superiority of its mission)?

At the Model School, volatile emotions were aroused when preadolescent children from inner-city schools were brought into a school where half the students came from upper-middle-class homes. In addition, a keen sense of resentment was expressed by school-district employees at other schools as they watched extra resources, procured through university contacts, being poured into this particular school. Had advance planning made it possible to prepare stakeholders to cope with these challenges, their impact might not have been so traumatic. Programs might have been put in place to address these challenges. Without such programs or preparation, natural self-protective instincts kicked in, setting off a chain reaction. Many aspects of the school's innovative vision were abandoned as the staff sought safety through sticking to practices that were safe, familiar, and noncontroversial.

Of the seven schools studied, the Model School and the Opportunity Preparatory School ended up furthest from their initial visions. This is not to say that these programs were failures. By traditional academic standards the Model School offers an excellent educational program. Yet the dream of creating an innovative program whose influence would extend beyond the school's immediate stakeholders has been all but abandoned. Similarly, Opportunity Preparatory School has come to resemble many other last-chance programs for at-risk students. Both schools are now under the direction of new leaders. Both have adapted in ways that were largely dictated by the requirements of the school district and the city council that had administrative authority over these two schools.

The Core Academy and Marblehead Community Charter Public School

The two parent-initiated charter schools—the Core Academy (chap. 3), located in Colorado, and Marblehead Community Charter Public School (chap. 7) in Massachusetts—encountered strikingly similar challenges. In both cases, the founding coalition was made up of parents brought together primarily by a shared discontent with the educational options currently available to their children. Both schools were located in affluent suburban areas where the neighborhood schools would be considered "good" relative to the national average. However, as the charter school parents were quick to point out, the U.S. national average does not compare well with achievement levels in other industrialized nations.

An article entitled "America's Education Choice" in the April 1, 2000, issue of a British news magazine, *The Economist*, summarized statistics similar to those that had set off alarm bells for many charter school parents:

At fourth grade (ten years old), American children score better in reading
and science than most pupils in 20 other rich countries, and are about average in mathematics. At eighth grade, they are still slightly better than average in maths and science but fall behind in reading. By 12th grade, they are
behind 95% of the children in other countries. The longer children stay in
American schools, the worse they seem to get.

The same article points out that the growing educational disparity cannot
be traced to differences in spending. The United States spends almost 6%
of its national income on primary and secondary education, more than
any Organization for Economic Cooperation and Development (OECD)
country except Denmark and Canada. Some inner-city schools get less
money than suburban ones—but others get more. Although providing sufficient funding is important, the crisis lies in the delivery system:

> Almost three-quarters of ten-year-olds in the poorest public schools have not
> yet begun to read or write; the illiteracy rate among 17-year-olds is one in
> seven. Poor education lies behind the looming problem of inequality, be-
> tween the new economy's winners and losers.

The charter school parents were determined to procure for their children an education that would enable them to compete with students anywhere. The problem they faced was that there existed significant disagreement among the founders, themselves, as to exactly what the educational
excellence they collectively sought would look like in practice. This lack of
consensus led to a very turbulent "shakeout" period. Sarason pointed out
that when people do not anticipate, and discuss in advance, how predictable challenges affecting them all will be handled, uncomfortable issues
too often end up being faced and "resolved" in the worst of all situations:
when feelings are high and smoldering controversy is present.

These challenges became evident in the early history of both these
schools. Most noticeable, however, were problems related to creating an
effective working relationship between the original core group (which
consisted of parents) and the teachers who were hired to make the parents' vision for the school a reality. Many of the parents had never before
served on the board of a nonprofit organization. Nor had they supervised
employees. Nor did they have a firsthand knowledge of what it takes to
guide a class of 20 through a rigorous academic curriculum (while also
supporting the children's emotional growth and social development).
However, the parents had invested an enormous amount of time and energy in getting the school started; they very much wanted the school to
come into being just as they had envisioned it.

Sarason noted that whenever he has asked people to choose between
the opportunity to become leader of an existing setting or to create a new

one, the choice invariably seemed to be the latter. People felt that creating a setting allowed one to mold it to one's purposes, unhindered by any existing tradition or practice. Although this answer always refers to socially acceptable, impersonal practices, underpinning this answer is a vision of the leader in the role of the artist, someone who chooses one's *own* material, fashions and refashions it, and ends up with the concrete embodiment of one's *own* ideas and efforts. Moreover, when people explain their preference for creating a new setting they seem unaware that they are describing the relationship between the leader and the setting as analogous to that between the artist and the artist's materials: The setting is passive, malleable, at the service of the leader.

As Sarason pointed out, there is, at this point, nothing inherently "wrong" in the leader's way of thinking; there is no setting; the leader is alone with his or her thoughts. What is fateful for the leader and the projected setting is how the leader's attitude changes as the setting is created and the leader must confront real people, along with the need to accept some compromises between what he or she wants and what others want. The fact that what others will want for themselves will always be somewhat different (and may frequently be quite different) from the leader's own vision presents the leader with deeply personal issues. The leader does not question the obligation to be consistent with his or her values and goals. But to what extent, if any, should the leader accept limits in order to help others in the realization of their goals?

At each of the parent-initiated schools, one or more very enthusiastic parents had spearheaded the organizing effort. These enthusiastic parents had communicated their vision of the school to other parents in such a way that setting up a charter school had seemed merely a matter of selecting teachers, imparting to them the vision for the school, and watching as everything and everyone fell into place—precisely according to plan. Moreover, in their eagerness to win support, these enthusiastic parents had emphasized somewhat different aspects of the planned school when they were speaking to different groups of potential supporters. In addition, two sources of all-but-inevitable disappointment had been present from the beginning:

1. Lack of recognition that the teachers who would be hired would inevitably have a powerful impact on the character of the school.
2. Lack of any mutually understood way of making decisions as to which of the innovations to be introduced at the planned school would be given highest priority.

Such challenges were made more explosive by the fact that some members of these parent-led boards had become so identified with the new setting that each obstacle was viewed not as a problem requiring compromise but as a moral battle in which good was pitted against the forces of disillusionment and evil. These board members had created an imaginative vista in which the happiness of everyone involved with the setting would stem from willingly—and completely—identifying with these board members' vision for the school. As Sarason noted, this way of thinking is, psychologically, quite similar to the way parents tend to fantasize the future of their firstborn: He or she will be an independent and unique individual—possessing strivings and characteristics that are completely in accord with what is in the minds of the parents.

The teachers, for their part, saw things from quite a different perspective. During the hiring process, the charter school's prospects had been described in glowing terms. The opportunities for professional growth had been emphasized, along with an a sense of how much the school staff would contribute to making the school a reality. Those who did the hiring were aware that there was more turbulence behind the scenes than they were letting on. However, they felt that such difficulties would somehow be surmounted. In addition, they were convinced that if a capable administrator and talented teachers could be attracted to the setting, the difficulties would be minimized. Thus a situation evolved in which, because of the desire of those doing the hiring to attracts good staff (and the staff members' desire to be attracted in ways fulfilling to their own ambitions), an "understanding" was arrived at that did not include any explicit discussion of personal or professional ambitions.

All through the hiring process a kind of dance took place, such that the discussion did not explicitly and directly deal with possible conflicts of ambition. The new setting was, for the parents who founded it, a deeply personal affair. Arguably, a number of influential board members were motivated by a fantasy of the new setting that was populated by only one set of "real" people, the members of the founding coalition. All other actors were their creation—their actions in accord with the founders' needs and ambitions. Sarason pointed out that often the leaders of new settings use naval language in talking about the hiring process, subtly communicating the expectation that if others choose to "come aboard" it is because there is a captain who decides directions. What the leader is not aware of is that such attitudes tend to produce a ubiquitous organizational problem: "faulty communication."

In contrast to the Model School and the Opportunity Preparatory School, where organizational pressures external to the setting became the greatest obstacle to the attainment of the setting's original goals, at the two parent-led schools the greatest obstacles turned out to be internal: (a) growth and differentiation and (b) the forging of a "constitution" by which the setting will be governed. Among the most important challenges in the creation of any setting is the anticipation of problems—and the ways they will be handled. At both of these schools, failure to think in constitutional terms maximized ambiguities, leading over time to informal, individual kinds of resolutions, among them attempts by individual board members to actively intervene in the day-to-day running of the school.

At both sites, the stabilization of the school as a viable setting was directly connected with solving governance problems that had bedeviled these schools from their early days. Both settings could have benefited from access to a theoretical framework that warned of common pitfalls that arise in the process of creating a setting. Such a theoretical framework might have provided a "early warning system," (a) alerting the parents who founded these schools to dangers of which they would not otherwise have been aware, and (b) suggesting how problems that presented themselves might be effectively dealt with, as well as what interpersonal dynamics might have given rise to these problems. Had stakeholders been able to think of the challenges they faced in constitutional terms, they might have been able to avoid personalizing predictable problems. This, in turn, might have enabled stakeholders to avoid destructive interpersonal tensions as they struggled to deal with conflicts and misunderstandings.

The histories these two schools would seem to support Sarason's argument that the creation of a setting is a set of internal and external problems that are fairly predictable. Among these predictable challenges are the following:

- History is always a variable.
- People represent different values, interests, and ambitions.
- The uses and allocation of power are best not left solely to the ambiguities of motivation.
- The individual and general welfare are not always perceived as synonymous; conflict is neither bad nor avoidable, but ignoring it is calamitous.
- Checks and balances are necessities, not luxuries.
- Growth is a double-edged sword—the problem is how to manage it consistent with first principles.

Facing these predictable needs, problems, and issues may take some of the joy out of the honeymoon period. Yet they are the realities around which the constitution of a new setting has to be forged. If they are addressed effectively, through hammering out a mutually agreeable "constitution" for the setting, steps taken to cope with these early problems can increase the likelihood that a viable setting will eventually be created.

Passages Charter School, Wesley Elementary, UH Charter School

The last three charter schools were initiated by educators and were based on successful existing programs. Passages Charter School (chap. 3) serves students from kindergarten to 12th grade, offering a highly individualized curriculum based upon that of a successful "open school" in the same school district. Wesley Elementary (chap. 5) had a lengthy "prehistory" as a successful neighborhood school. In the 1990s, Wesley Elementary became a charter school, part of a special charter school district organized under the leadership of Dr. Thaddeus Lott, who had been Wesley's principal since 1975. The University of Houston Charter School of Technology (chap. 6) was created in cooperation with a large public university as an extension of a successful preschool program that had been established to provide a living demonstration of constructivist education.

The programs offered by these schools could not have been more different. Wesley Elementary used a highly structured direct instruction curriculum, while the UH charter school emphasized spontaneous teacher–child interactions in the classroom. Passages Charter School used a highly individualized, experiential approach built on the philosophical principals associated with progressive education; at Passages, each student had a personal learning plan created by the student, advisor, and parent. There were also sharp differences in the demographic characteristics of the schools. Passages was located in a middle-class suburban area, in sharp contrast to the central-city neighborhoods where Wesley and the UH charter school were located. Yet similar organizational challenges shaped the development of each of these schools.

The demands on staff members at each school were high. As one teacher at Passages Charter School commented, explaining her decision to resign: "This school has dealt with too many stressors. The stress of the first year, the stress of an inadequate facility. . . . It's just not worth it anymore." Staff members were asked to throw a tremendous amount of effort into the school. How long they could sustain this level of effort was open to question. At Wesley Elementary School, whose 20-year history as a high-achieving school made it possible to study the results of such energy demands over time, only a small cadre of teacher-leaders had remained at the school year after year, whereas large numbers of young teachers had stayed only 2 or 3 years. After a stint at Wesley, where they honed their teaching skills, many opted to "throttle back," moving to an "easier" school as they began thinking of starting their own families.

As Sarason observed, during the planning of a new setting, the factor that is emphasized (indeed viewed as central) is the job that needs to be done. Attention is focused on providing an important service. The factor that is too often ignored or deemphasized is the professional and personal growth of the setting's members. Yet the greatest source of disillusionment and disruption within a setting, later on, tends to arise as a consequence of having ignored or deemphasized such motivational factors. When a setting becomes so focused on its relationship to the outside world that it loses sight of what it can (or must) do for its own members, staff burn-out becomes an immediate threat. Unfortunately, the culture of public education affords little opportunity to recognize and head off this problem.

All of these schools performed functions that others needed and valued. In the beginning, this alone had tremendous "reward value," particularly because it also served as the basis for justifying the charter schools' existence. A more subtle factor was also at work: In the early stages of each teacher's involvement, the process of helping others tended to be accompanied by a personal sense of growth. Teaching at these innovative schools was not experienced as a routine, without personal challenge or intellectual excitement. Over time, the sense of challenge and change diminished; teachers' work became more routinized. Teachers were still working very hard, but they were getting less in the way of stimulation, excitement, a sense of personal growth. Sarason noted that the widespread assumption that teachers can create and maintain those conditions that make school stimulating for children *without those same conditions existing for teachers* has no warrant in the history of the human race.

Here we touch on a deep-seated problem, endemic within public schools in the United States. For education is not just the learning of useful skills and facts, but also the opportunity to draw from the collective cultural inheritance passed down to us from earlier generations, and to learn from our contemporaries in every part of the world. There is much in what educators do that could be the source of excitement and inspiration. However, the way public schooling has been structured all too often cancels out these aspects of the profession, instead emphasizing rules, routines, and paperwork.

If we are to experience a renaissance in the field of public education, a way will have to be found to make more room for the life of the mind. Despite the difficulties they have faced, charter schools offer a promising venue for exploring ways this might be done. For these are schools that were born out of enthusiasm and hope, founded by people who believe that the future need not be a repetition of the past. What is lacking at many of these schools is someone with the experience to help staff members recognize problems before they begin to undermine the effectiveness of the school.

TAKING A BROADER PERSPECTIVE

Given the differences in viewpoint and opinion that exist within many charter schools, how could such schools be expected to diagnose their own problems in time to head off trouble? Sarason (1988) suggested the appointment of an external critic, who would accept the task of understanding and responding to the purposes and values of the setting, the consistency between words and actions, and the sources of actual and potential problems. This external critic would be an outsider, independent, knowledgeable about, and sympathetic to the purposes of the setting. The external critic has no responsibility except to observe, study, and report. The critic does not wait for problems to be brought to him or her, but seeks them out. In justifying the need for such a critic, Sarason quoted Gardner's (1995) analysis:

> I have collected a great many examples of organizations or institutions that have fallen on evil days because of their failure to renew themselves. And I want to place before you two curious facts that I draw from those examples. First, I haven't yet encountered an organization or institution that wanted to go to seed or wanted to fall behind in the parade. Second, in every case of organizational decline that I know anything about, there were ample warning signals long before trouble struck. And I don't mean warning signals that only a Monday-morning quarterback could discern, I mean that before trouble struck there were observers who had correctly diagnosed the difficulties to come.
>
> . . . When organizations are not meeting the challenge of change, it is as a rule not because they can't *solve* their problems but because they won't *see* their problems; not because they don't *know* their faults, but because *they rationalize them as virtues or necessities.*

The use of mediators to settle trade disputes might provide a model for how this could be done. To be effective, a mediator must be acceptable to all involved. Similarly, the external critic who advises a charter school must be trusted and respected by stakeholders at the school. Charter school participants in this study often spoke of the important role that outside advisers—some paid for by the state—had played in their schools' success. As the charter school movement expands, one way state government could help to promote the healthy development of charter schools would be to invite charter schools to identify an external critic, who was also acceptable to the state, to visit the school regularly, providing advice and assistance. A list of previously approved candidates (representing a range of curricular specialties and political viewpoints) could be provided, with schools also given the option of nominating an external critic who was not on the list but whose expertise was deemed especially useful to that school.

We have long framed the debate over charter schools in terms of whether or not such schools ought to be given "freedom from" certain restraints. Providing funding for an external critic would help to give schools the "freedom to" succeed. For most founders of charter schools are strongly motivated to learn from mistakes, to change, to grow, to provide an example for others. Yet the very intensity of stakeholder involvement often makes it difficult for those at the site to stand back and objectively assess both what is happening and what needs to be done if the school is to remain true to the vision of the founders. This is where an external critic could provide an invaluable service.

OF VOUCHERS, POLITICS, AND PUBLIC PERCEPTIONS

> Thirty-six states and the District of Columbia allow citizens to start charter schools; more than 2000 are now open, focusing on everything from African history to entrepreneurship. (Lord, 2000, p. 72)

In chapters 3 to 7, we looked at the challenges faced by individual charter schools. Then the first part of this chapter focused on problems that have plagued specific types of charter schools. The last part looks at challenges faced by the charter school movement as a whole. Repeatedly, those interviewed for this project expressed frustration at the tendency, among those outside the charter school movement, to uncritically group together a wide assortment of disparate school reform proposals, as if all were but differing versions of the same thing. Reform ideas often grouped together in this manner range from "privatization" (the use of private contractors to perform school district functions, ranging from serving lunch in the cafeteria to the managing of entire schools), to magnet and charter schools, to school tuition vouchers. The reform initiatives about which there appears to be the most confusion are charter schools and voucher programs. For that reason, it may be useful to clarify the differences between charters and vouchers.

Research on Voucher Programs

There are, as yet, only two, relatively small, publicly funded voucher programs in operation (one in Milwaukee that, in 2000, enrolled approximately 8,000 students and one in Cleveland that enrolled about 4,300). The Milwaukee program awarded its first vouchers to 341 low-income K–12 students in 1990 (the year before the first charter school legislation was passed). As pointed out in the *Policy Research Brief* published by the National School Boards Association:

> Participation is limited to Milwaukee residents in grades K–12 with family incomes below 175 percent of the federal poverty level, including K–3 students previously enrolled in private schools. The total number of vouchers cannot exceed 15 percent of the total enrollment of the Milwaukee Public Schools (MPS). When families choose to send their children to schools that have been oversubscribed at a particular grade level, voucher students are selected by lottery. (Drury, 2000, p. 1)

Several analysts have examined the data collected in conjunction with a mandated evaluation of the Milwaukee voucher program. John Witte, the program's official evaluator, compared the achievement of voucher students with that of a representative sample of students from the Milwaukee Public Schools and concluded that there was no consistent pattern of differences in achievement. In a later analysis, Jay Greene, Paul Peterson, and Jiangtao Du compared voucher students' achievement with that of unsuccessful voucher program applicants (students rejected in the school lotteries) who returned to the public schools. They argued that because these students had been "randomly" rejected (according to program rules) they provided the ideal control group (Drury, 2000).

Although Greene, Peterson, and Du found little evidence of greater test-score gains for voucher students during the first 2 years of the program, they reported a significant achievement advantage in years 3 and 4. By the fourth year, they estimated that the math achievement of voucher students exceeded that of unsuccessful applicants by a substantial margin (nearly 11 percentile points), with a smaller advantage in reading (nearly 6 percentile points). This finding was important because math is considered an especially good measure of school quality in that—unlike reading and writing, which are strongly influenced by language use within the home environment—most children have learned most of their math skills at school. Moreover, the math scores of these charter school students seemed to close the stubborn gap between standardized test scores of Anglo and African American students that had been the focus of extensive debate after publication of *The Bell Curve* (Hernstein & Murray, 1996).

However, in another study, which used a broad range of analytical strategies and included both the MPS and unsuccessful-applicant comparison groups, Cecilia Rouse found no advantage in reading for students admitted to or participating in the voucher program. She reported a small math advantage for the voucher students of approximately 1 or 2 percentile points per year. What is striking about these results is that they are all based on the same data, examined in different ways. Results of evaluations of the

Cleveland voucher program (which imposes no income cap on eligibility, but is designed to give vouchers to the lowest income families first) are similarly mixed. Moreover, even if the results of such studies were more conclusive, they would still tell us only about the performance of a relatively small number of students on standardized tests that are, themselves, often criticized for measuring only a narrow spectrum of academic skills.

Given that vouchers remain a relatively untested and, as yet, little implemented idea, the frequency with which mention of "charters" is immediately followed with a discussion of "vouchers," both in the media and in the research literature becomes, in itself, intriguing. Repeatedly, one hears charter schools characterized as a "step toward" vouchers, even though charter schools have in recent years been the major competitor to voucher proposals in the arena of school choice. Part of the reason may be the media's tendency to simplify any issue in such a manner that it becomes a two-sided debate, in this case pitting voucher advocates against the defenders of the status quo. This narrowing of a complex discussion into a competition between two opposing camps—a phenomenon that Deborah Tannen describes in some detail in her book *The Argument Culture*—was already discussed in chapter 5, in reference to the "phonics wars."

As with the reading debate (where the media, at times, seemed determined to depict reading instruction, not as a decision involving many varied options, but as an "either/or" proposition), so it has been with the issue of school choice. The long-term effect may be to make the strategy (long popular among critics of expanded parental choice) of lumping charter schools and tuition vouchers together into a self-fulfilling prophesy. In previous generations, public school teachers were often among the best educated people in town. These days, however, professional educators often find themselves facing a highly educated parent population, which insists on having more voice in decisions about their children's education. If a climate is created where tuition vouchers are seen as the only practical alternative to the status quo, voters who are not content with the education their children are receiving could easily perceive vouchers to be the only practical alternative.

A Changing Social Landscape: Tensions Along the Fault Lines

The complexity of the situation is multiplied by recent political trends. During the 2000 presidential campaign two intriguing opinion pieces, one by David Friedman and one by Gregg Easterbrook, appeared in the same Sunday edition of the *Los Angeles Times*. Both described political pressures that have helped to shape the school reform debate (but have been largely ignored within the field of educational research). In one, Friedman (2000a) argued that stark regional conflicts now shape U.S. politics. He pointed out that the political base of Democratic presidential candidate Al Gore was drawn almost exclusively from the nation's slowest growing, most urbanized states, including New York, New Jersey, and California. In contrast, Republican presidential candidate George W. Bush drew his strongest support from fast-growing states like Texas, Georgia, and Arizona. Friedman noted that slow-growth states supported Gore because a strong government role helped to soften economic hardship and to mediate between haves and have-nots, whereas fast-growth states supported Bush because regulation limited opportunity for those who are not already "haves."

In terms of social stratification, the struggle had become one of "both ends against the middle." Regulations in place in slow-growth states limited the options open to those families and businesses that depended on reasonable costs of living and did not benefit from targeted government assistance. Despite rhetoric about regulation helping the poor (supposedly at the expense of the wealthy), those who already possessed wealth tended to benefit from increased regulation. This was "because, over time, high-end development pursued by the wealthy or well-connected—such as big-ticket stadium projects and large, urban, mixed-use projects backed by influential investors and corporations—stood the best chance of navigating the growing maze of bureaucratic and interest-group constraints" (Friedman, 2000a, p. M6). Thus, the privileged in places like New York and San Francisco were willing to pay higher taxes and live with a more intrusive government as long as that government kept the peace and their assets appreciated in value.

Politicians in highly regulated areas have also developed a complex system of transfer payments to "targeted" recipients chosen by government. These range from high-tech companies courted and subsidized by urban governments to a spectrum of social programs aimed at pleasing ethnic-advocacy groups. As a result, urban economies in slow-growth states are characterized by a burgeoning group of super-rich (along with the high-end amenities they desired), a large public bureaucracy, and targeted intervention to ameliorate potential social conflicts. Contributing to achievement of a fairly stable political compromise in slow growth areas is the fact that so many disaffected middle-class voters and manufacturing enterprises had given up and left. Instead of fighting against the political tide in slow-growth states, these people and businesses had flooded into boom towns like Dallas, Raleigh–Durham, Denver, and Phoenix. This exodus had helped to create the stark differences in outlook that had come to characterize fast- and slow-growth states.

Parallels between these political dynamics and attitudes toward the charter school movement are easily drawn. Fast-growth states have been among the most enthusiastic supporters of charter schools. Five of the charter schools examined in this book were located in Texas and Colorado, both fast-growth states during the 1990s. These are also places where there has traditionally been a strong emphasis on family, providing a ready audience for the argument of charter school supporters that no one knows an individual child better—or has that child's interests more at heart—than that child's family. On the other hand, the sharpest controversy to surround any of the charter schools we investigated took place in Massachusetts, a highly urbanized state where greater regulation has gone hand in hand with greater reliance on the helping professions to judge what is best for children.

Wesley Elementary in Houston, Texas, demonstrates the complexity of attitudes toward the charter school issue. Although parents at Wesley Elementary School were aware, on a daily basis, of the stark urban realities faced by inner-city residents, they still insisted on the centrality of a sense of community, of "looking after one's own," even in difficult circumstances. Having been on the "receiving end" of a plethora of school district and other governmental initiatives (whose observable effects had frequently been quite different than initially promised), stakeholders at Wesley were convinced that leaving educational decisions in the hands of school district officials was no cure-all. As they saw it, the charter school movement at least gave them a chance to exercise a degree of control over the kind of education their children would receive.

The Widening Social Class Divide

Just as government regulations can influence the ability of individuals (and of social groups) to better their own situations, the manner in which financial and cultural capital are passed from generation to generation can have far-reaching effects upon the social and political dynamics of a nation. There are interesting similarities between the increasing social stratification in the United States and long-standing social patterns in Europe. As Gregg Easterbrook (2000) pointed out in a *Los Angeles Times* opinion piece, almost everyone in the traditional European elite received his or her financial position through inheritance; for although most European nations have enacted estate taxes in the postwar era, these are easily evaded.

Europe's "idle rich" have performed no productive labors and created no wealth. Those who have to work for a living resent this sort of privilege fiercely, which helps to explain Europe's sharp class hostilities. By contrast, in the United States most wealth has been earned. As Easterbrook noted, almost all American millionaires and billionaires are self-made:

> The rich may be obnoxious, they may have terrible taste in rugs and art, but their position in life is earned through effort. . . . It is the absence of an idle rich, as much as anything else, that explains "American exceptionalism"— the fact that although Europe is rife with bitter class tensions, America is not. Lack of large amounts of inherited wealth also explains U.S. economic vibrancy: if you want to become rich, you've got to be productive. (Easterbrook, 2000, p. M2)

Easterbrook himself noted that American exceptionalism has been on the decline: "In 1976, the richest 1% of society held 21.8% of wealth. By 1983, it held 33.8%; today, it holds 38% of all wealth" (p. M2). But he also argued that such changes are not inexorable. In the coming two decades, many in the top 1% will die, causing the economic deck to be reshuffled (assuming the estate tax redistributes some of this accumulation). On the other hand, if the estate tax is repealed, the rate of wealth concentration will continue to accelerate, creating a more stratified society. A similar observation might be made regarding school reform.

The manner in which public schools are presently run has had the effect of rationing access to cultural capital in such a manner that the amount a family pays for housing is strongly correlated with the quality of the public schools available to that family's children. Nor does the stratification stop there. The private schools attended by many children from wealthy families expend considerable effort to neutralize those influences that undermine mental exertion, thus creating an environment that supports hard work. In contrast, the culture at most American public high schools is not set up to "push" students academically. (See chap. 9.) Viewed from a broader perspective, the effect can be to create a two-tier system where only the most highly motivated of public school students will achieve on the same level as a majority of private school graduates.

Resisting the "Sorting Mechanism" of the Public Schools

> For the last twenty years the communiqués from the nation's classrooms have resembled the casualty reports from a lost war. . . .
>
> The expressions of alarm I take to be a matter of pious ritual, like a murmuring of prayers or the beating of ornamental gongs. If as a nation we wished to improve the performance of the schools, I assume we could do so. Certainly we possess the necessary resources. We are an energetic people, rich in money and intelligence, capable of making high-performance automobiles and venture-capital funds, and if our intentions were anything other

than ceremonial, I don't doubt we could bring the schools to the standard of efficiency required of a well-run amusement park. (Lapham, 2000, p. 7)

This quote (from an essay by Lewis Lapham, editor of *Harper's Magazine*) aptly expresses the attitude of many charter school supporters interviewed in connection with this study. Many were veterans of previous, unsuccessful school reform initiatives. They described their slowly growing conviction that if the public school system were capable of reforming itself (without relying on measures such as creating charter schools), it would have done so by now. These individuals saw charter schools as providing a way of opening up an otherwise closed system, letting in fresh energy and initiative.

Not all charter schools are successful, by any means. Yet those that are successful raise intriguing questions about what *might* be. A school like Wesley Elementary offers a far more hopeful future to children who might otherwise been written off as inherently "at risk." The Marblehead Community Charter Public School challenges the hardening socioeconomic barriers within American society in a very different way. By offering a more rigorous academic option to public school children, MCCPS enabled public school students to receive an education that would allow them to compete on an equal basis with their peers at private preparatory schools. Whether charter schools will succeed in introducing a new level of academic rigor into the public school system as a whole remains to be seen. Yet the best charter schools stand as a reminder of what public schools *could* do.

Many unionized teachers and public school administrators continue to see charter schools in a different way. The storm of protest that broke when the Marblehead charter school was approved was, in large part, led by public employees. Not all school administrators or teacher union officials feel this way; Wesley Elementary school found one of its most vocal supporters in the head of the local teachers union. However, in Marblehead, an affluent town where more and more students were leaving the public system to attend private academies, public school teachers feared that the charter school would constitute an additional layer in an increasingly stratified educational system, with the neighborhood schools where they taught destined always to constitute the lowest layer.

In contrast, charter school supporters saw themselves fighting to prevent a situation from evolving in which not only was the public school system seen as a "lesser" option, but public school graduates were seen as somehow "lesser" as well. They noted, for example, the tendency to speak of students as the "products" of one kind of school or another (as opposed to individuals with unique characteristics). Other observers noted that the assumption that "public" means "lesser" was by no means limited to education. For example, we talk of that which unites us as that which we hold "in common." Yet when we use the word "common" as a descriptor, the implication is often that the thing described is somehow lacking in worth.

To understand the source of such attitudes, one need only take a walk in a run-down city park noting the battle-scarred benches and the trash tossed into once-beautiful fountains. As a nation, we have long struggled with the dilemma of how to take care of that which belongs to "everyone." The water in our streams and the air we breathe tend to get only that level of protection that the most careless among us are willing to voluntarily extend. Charter school supporters would argue that a similar problem has long plagued the public school system, which is steadily crumbling under a flood of unfunded mandates, intrusive regulations, and demands that schools be all things to all people. They point out that the charter school movement allows groups of stakeholders to feel a sense of ownership toward their school; teachers, parents, and students become invested in a deeper and more meaningful way.

Looking Forward to Chapter 9

For most of the nation's history the protection of individual rights has been a central theme in American culture. Beginning with the Constitutional guarantees contained in the Bill of Rights and extending through such liberal classics as John Rawls's *A Theory of Justice* (1999), a just society has been envisioned as providing a neutral framework of rights within which individuals would be able to pursue their own conception of the good. There has been a deep resistance to allowing government to have a free hand in shaping the character of the citizenry. In recent years, however, state governments have exerted more and more control over what each child learns (and the environment in which the child learns it). This has raised sensitive questions.

Despite the emphasis on individual rights, for most of the nation's history the individual was not seen as standing alone but as enmeshed in, and supported by, extended family, friendship networks, community, religion, profession, and so on. Following World War II these personal support systems were increasingly undermined by an ever more transient social structure. This gave rise to a new question: How can we best protect our democratic institutions, given the growing power imbalance between the unsupported, atomized individual and the modern bureaucratic state? For educators, the question was more specific: How do we safeguard the interests of children and families, within a compulsory education system so huge that individual human beings can, all too easily, come to be treated like mere numbers? Chapter 9 looks at tensions triggered by the existing power imbalance and explores how drawing on the resources of civil society could assist the public schools in meeting this challenge.

REFERENCES

Drury, D. W. (2000, Summer). *Vouchers and student achievement: A review of the evidence. Policy Research Brief*. Alexandria, VA: National School Boards Association.

Easterbrook, G. (2000, September 17). What makes America exceptional. *Los Angeles Times*, pp. M2, M3.

Friedman, D. (2000a, September 17). The politics of growth: The widening divide between fast- and slow-growing states is shaping presidential preference. *Los Angeles Times*, pp. M1, M6.

Gardner, J. W. (1995). *Self-renewal: The individual and the innovative society*. New York: W. W. Norton.

Herrnstein, R. J., & Murray, C. (1996). *The bell curve: Intelligence and class in American life*. New York: Free Press.

Lapham, L. H. (2000, August). School bells. *Harper's Magazine*, pp. 7–9.

Lord, M. (2000, October 9). Unhappy? Do it yourself. *U.S. News and World Report*, pp. 72–73.

Rawls, J. (1972). *A theory of justice*. Cambridge, MA: Belknap Press.

Sarason, S. B. (1988). *The creation of settings and the future societies*. Cambridge, MA: Brookline Books.

Chapter 9

Beyond Economics and Politics: Charter Schools as Mediating Institutions

> *If circumspection and caution are part of wisdom when we work only upon in-*
> *animate matter, surely they become a part of duty, too, when the subject of our*
> *demolition and construction is not brick and timber but sentient human beings.*
> *(Edmund Burke,* Reflections on the Revolution in France, *1790)*

In the preceding chapters we have looked at a diverse group of charter schools, paying close attention to the dynamics involved in creating a setting. This chapter is broader in scope, focusing on the influence of the burgeoning charter school movement, both in strengthening parent voice and in bringing the administrative structure of U.S. public schools more in line with the system of checks and balances that characterizes our political system as a whole. First we review the historical and organizational factors that have shaped public education. After this, we examine the special challenges faced by the most vulnerable segments of the school-age population. Next we explore external political developments that have had an impact on the charter school movement. Finally, we will investigate how drawing on the resources of civil society could help the public schools to effectively address questions of academic quality as well as tensions created by the power imbalance that has grown up between a bureaucratized public school system and the families it serves.

A CENTURY OF UNINTENDED CONSEQUENCES

During the years when they are attending school, young people are also gaining a sense of their own place in the world (and of the possibilities that

243

may be open to them). When we ignore this, we lose sight of the larger role schools play in preparing students to fulfill their role as citizens of a democratic society. Chapter 2 examined historical, political, and cultural factors that had worked to undercut academic achievement. Before going further, it is useful to quickly review some of the factors that have led to widespread criticism of the public schools. In the 20th century, public schooling in the United States has been shaped by the following developments:

- Local control of schools in the United States has increasingly been superseded by a centralized bureaucratic model of schooling that was first introduced in the United States in the late 19th century, at a time when admiration for the German educational system and the hierarchical organizational model favored by large businesses was high.
- Borrowing from the German model, high school education in the United States has fragmented into "vocational," "general," and "college preparatory" tracks, with traditional liberal arts courses offered only to students in the college preparatory track.
- Schools and school districts began sorting students into categories through use of standardized testing and other measures; as a result, the options open to many students were narrowed; children from low-income families were less likely to be assigned to a college preparatory track.
- As a result of repeated lawsuits challenging school regulations and disciplinary actions, relations between students and school staff became increasingly compartmentalized and formal; the doctrine of *in loco parentis* was increasingly abandoned.
- Policymakers focused their attention on curriculum, school facilities, and other systemic concerns; little emphasis was put on creating a school culture that empowered students to make healthy choices, as such choices required value judgments that were seen as infringing on territory that rightly belonged to home and family.
- As they progressed through school, many students reacted to the combined effect of compulsory schooling and impersonal "group processing" by adopting a "draftee mentality," viewing school as a collection of "hoops to be jumped through"; resistance to the demands of school came to be seen by many as an admirable assertion of individuality.
- Lacking the sort of "hammer" other nations had in their school-leaving tests, U.S. teachers found it difficult to motivate students; teachers struggled with the student resistance created by a system whose basic dynamic was one of compulsion (rather than choice), yet

that lacked the kind of built-in consequences that might motivate higher levels of effort.

- In many cases this resulted in the negotiation of informal "classroom treaties" whereby teachers did not ask too much of students, in return for which students were reasonably cooperative in class, a settlement that allowed all involved to "get by" without having to work too hard or experience undue unpleasantness.

The Struggle Over Accountability

In recent years, there have been widespread efforts to enforce accountability by mandating standardized tests that have significant consequences for schools (such as mandating penalties for schools that do not score well). Such remedies have had disappointing results, for the following reasons:

- Unlike students in those nations where high-stakes tests have marked effects on a student's future educational or employment prospects, U.S. students are less affected by standardized test results; schools (whose aggregate test scores often are published in newspapers) are under more performance pressure than are individual students.

- Under pressure to raise test scores, schools have often taken advantage of the fact that the mandated tests are of the machine-scored, multiple-choice variety; schools can pump up test scores through repetitive drills that focus on likely test questions, through teaching test-taking techniques, and/or reclassifying students expected to do poorly on the examination so as to excuse these students from taking the test.

- Raising test scores through repetitive drill means dedicating less time to meaningful teaching of academic content; as a result, students are actually deprived of opportunity to learn as a result of state efforts to boost standardized test scores.

- The current accountability-by-multiple-choice-test approach has resulted in a political version of the "classroom treaty": An illusion of academic achievement and accountability is presented, yet whenever a new standardized test is introduced (for which drills have not yet been developed) student test scores tend to be disconcertingly low.

If meaningful school reform is to take place in the United States, that reform must build on the principles of individual freedom built into the nation's constitutional form of government, inviting rather than attempting to compel the cooperation of students and their families. How might this be done?

Changing the Organizational Dynamics

Charter school legislation has attempted to switch the emphasis of school reform initiatives from developing rules to delivering results. Arguments suggesting that charter schools may serve as a valuable tool for achieving that goal might be summarized as follows:

- Different children have differing skills, aptitudes, and affinities, and thus may thrive in different environments; honoring human diversity by offering a choice of educational environments avoids privileging some students over others throughout their school years.
- Schools are not only places where children learn important facts and skills; they are also small communities, places where children live out a large portion of their childhood, learning to collaborate with others and see themselves as part of a larger world; breaking down large schools into smaller schools or schools-within-schools creates a more humane environment for young people, allowing children to know those around them and to be known by them, so no child is just a face in the crowd.
- Through allowing families to choose a more rigorous and demanding educational program, charter schools avoid the conflicts inherent in attempting to make such a program compulsory, while also creating a sense of community and purpose.
- Allowing teachers to participate in creating charter schools increases the likelihood that they (a) will be teaching curricula they are enthusiastic about and (b) will communicate that enthusiasm to students, allowing for creation of learning communities where achievement is admired and past success translates into future motivation.
- Charter schools may help to combat problems of teacher burn-out and keep highly motivated teachers in the profession by allowing them to set up charter schools that are, in essence, a variety of a group practice, much as physicians might set up a clinic where they can implement a shared vision of excellence.
- Living within a community where learning is respected and enthusiastically pursued can be much more motivating for young people than the kind of external pressures created by state-mandated high-stakes tests.

COMMUNITY PARTICIPATION
IN THE DECISION-MAKING PROCESS

Charter schools are not the first reform that has attempted to counteract the stifling effect of the increasing bureaucratization of the public schools. During the 1980s, advocates of site-based decision making argued in favor of establishing school site councils—made up of parents, teachers, school administrators, and community members—that would take over some of the decisions traditionally made at the school district level. The goal was not just to give the community a larger voice but also to provide young people with a model of democracy in action. The assumption was that, when children watched the adults in their lives struggle with issues that had a visible effect on the child's school or community, the democratic process became more than just an abstract ideal; grass-roots democracy became a matter of personal experience.

Children who watch their parents take part in making school-wide decisions are given an opportunity to see that participation matters. They see how the environment in which they spend their time is affected by specific policies, which their parents or guardians helped to set in place. In contrast, children who grow up in an environment where rules and regulations are routinely handed down by unseen bureaucrats may receive a message of powerlessness. Young people whose world is one in which regulations are always handed down by "higher ups" are given no sense of how they might make their voices heard on issues that they care about. Feelings of personal efficacy may suffer, and feelings of frustration may give rise both to resentment and to an urge to resist decisions in which students had no voice.

Unfortunately, site-based decision making often did not work out as planned. School site councils were advisory bodies whose influence depended on the school principal. When a principal did not feel comfortable with a collaborative management style, the principal might give little weight to parent input, even when shared decision making had been mandated by the school district (Brouillette, 1997b). In a study of six schools in a district with a long tradition of "shared governance" and substantial experience in the implementation of school site councils, Malen and Ogawa (1988) found that, although the program included specific training provisions intended to support a redistribution of decision-making authority, the councils did little to alter the relationships typically found in schools.

> On councils composed of principals, teachers, and parents, professional-patron influence relationships are not substantially altered primarily because principals and, at times principals and teachers control council meet-

ings. . . . Since professionals can set the agenda, manage the meeting time, disperse information, and shift politically contentious issues to more private arenas, they essentially control decision processes and ultimately control decision outcomes. Parents are reluctant to challenge this dynamic. As a result, the traditional pattern where administrators make policy, teachers instruct, and parents support is maintained. (Malen, Ogawa, & Krantz, 1990, p. 53)

Even where the shared decision-making process worked well at a school site, uncertainties remained about how decisions made by school site councils might be altered as a result of politically motivated decisions made by the district's elected school board (Brouillette, 1996, 1997a). However strong the consensus behind suggestions advanced by a particular school site council, legal authority always remained in the hands of the school board. When highly politicized issues arose, school board members were free to overrule consensus-based decisions made by school site councils. This tended to make parents and teachers at each school site hesitant to commit the time and energy necessary to make collaborative decision making successful.

At the heart of the debate over site-based councils there simmered unresolved tensions between the ideal of participatory democracy, represented by a collaborative decision-making process involving parents and teachers at the school site, and the ideal of representative democracy, exemplified by the statutory authority of state legislatures and local school boards (Brouillette, 1996, 1997a, 1997c). Advocates of school site autonomy pointed to a need to actively involve those closest to the problem in the decision-making process; in contrast, advocates of forceful state intervention voiced doubts about the democratic character of site-based decision making, pointing to differences in power that could keep some groups from being heard. This raised questions about whether elected school boards and/or state legislators were more effective than school site councils in safeguarding the interests of individual children and families.

Limitations of the School Board

Norman Kerr (1964) pointed out that under some conditions, which may not be uncommon, the chief contribution of school boards to the continuance of our educational system is their legitimization of school policies, rather than their representation of the community. He identified a number of influences that act on school board members so as to deflect their behavior from formally prescribed goals, and even from school board candidates' own goals for the system. One of these is the absence of visible constituencies, which support their candidacy, ensure their election, and watch the behavior of their representatives after election. This lack of a watchful constituency permits new board members considerable freedom in adjusting to the expectations of school administrators and older board members.

Another factor influencing the behavior of new school board members is the relative unfamiliarity of most candidates both with school board activities and with the programs of their school district. The greater familiarity of older board members with technical matters and past board policies makes the newcomer hesitant to speak up. Even after the initial induction period is over, there is still a great deal to learn about state laws, financial practices, the school program, and school board policies. In some respects the learning process serves as an induction into a new culture, the norms of which the school board member is less and less inclined to overstep. The combined effect of these forces can act to free board members from community restraints and expose them more to the values of the school district administration. In this way the function of a school board can be largely transformed from that of making educational decisions on behalf of the community to that of explaining and justifying the needs of the system to the community.

Interest-Group Politics

The U.S. Constitution embodies a Madisonian solution for dealing with tyranny of the majority that emphasizes decentralization through a system of representation, separation of powers, federalism, bicameralism, judicial supremacy, and the Bill of Rights. Theodore Lowi (1974) argued that the original Western liberal approach to government was that, as long as there were multitudes of interests with no possibility of any interest becoming a permanent majority, the free interaction of these interests would provide a public good. In the 20th century, however, the thinking of liberal policymakers has undergone a drastic transformation, in the direction of accommodating group interests. Lowi questioned the point of view that the group is simply a way of looking at the individual and asked whether individuals are represented accurately or their concerns are heavily distorted.

Putting these issues in historical perspective, Lowi (1979) asserted that, in the latter part of the 19th century and the early years of the 20th century, it was possible to make a fairly precise distinction between "liberal" and "conservative." In general, liberals favored the use of government to bring about social change, usually in the direction of greater equality. Conservatives were opposed to the use of government for such purposes, either because they found the existing order satisfactory or because they felt that change should occur slowly and gradually through natural social processes. In Lowi's view, that old distinction has broken down. "The old dialogue has passed into the graveyard of consensus. Yet it persists. Old habits die hard. Its persistence despite its irrelevance means that the liberal-conservative debate has become almost purely ritualistic" (p. 57).

In effect, Lowi argued that the liberal–conservative conflict has been shifted to when government intervention should occur, in what form, and on whose behalf. Cigler and Loomis (1995) pointed out that the factors that promote the rise and influence of special-interest groups include the spread of affluence and education; advanced communication technologies and, in the 1960s and early 1970s, the emergence of "causes" ranging from civil rights, to environmental issues, to consumer protection. In addition, postindustrial changes have altered patterns of conflict, giving rise to an "intensely emotional setting in which groups rise or fall in status" and creating expectations of entitlement among emerging groups and the disadvantaged.

Both political scientist Theodore Lowi and economist Mancur Olson (1982) found the significant increase in the number and type of special-interest groups to be particularly troubling because of the costs they pose for society. These costs include the tendency of these groups both to resist needed societal change and to require ever-increasing governmental resources. Special-interest groups are also likely to become governmentally institutionalized because they provide valuable administrative support and stability to a government that is decentralized. The impact of interest-group politics has become an important issue for those who study school reform because, in recent years, single-issue special-interest groups have had a growing role in determining educational policy.

Backstage at the State Legislature

In a study of decision making at the state level, Baxt and Brouillette (1999) found that state legislatures may be ill equipped to act as guarantors of equity and quality in the field of education. Amid the pressure and bustle of a legislative session, during which part-time citizen-legislators were called upon to vote on 5,000 widely varied bills, there was no chance for the careful study of individual bills or prolonged debate on the merits of specific policies. In the case of the specific policy change that was the focus of the study, passage of the key legislation was a result not of carefully reasoned arguments presented by a broad spectrum of knowledgeable stakeholders but of persistent effort by well-financed, single-issue lobbyists who were able to get the ear of key legislators at that point in time when new policy was being hammered out. Their influence went all but unnoticed in the heat of a legislative session when educational issues were "off the radar screen" and public interest was focused elsewhere.

The problem with applying the Madisonian argument about checks and balances to competition among interest groups in the present day is that this argument does not consider two important factors: (a) the exponential growth in the size of government and (b) the speeding up of the decision-making process in response to the increased legislative load. When government functions were limited (and decision-making processes proceeded at a relatively measured pace) there was time for all interested parties to become aware of the policy debate and to make their voices heard. There was also time for relatively extended negotiation to take place as part of the legislative process. In the present day, however, interest groups with the right connections have the ability to do an "end run" around the system of checks and balances that would, ideally, have led to a "win–win" solution that did not undermine the well being of any group.

Baxt and Brouillette (1999) pointed out that, in order to increase the likelihood of passage, the lobbyists framed their demands in such a manner as to:

1. Avoid spending new money.
2. Keep the policy statements general and "boring" so as not to draw fire (i.e., most legislators expressed little interest in the issue).
3. Use the personal approach: focus on high-profile, sympathy-grabbing examples.
4. Build the law into a larger, omnibus bill so as to keep it relatively invisible.
5. Keep supporters together and avoid division among advocates by using very general, somewhat vague language in describing policy.

Through these means, lobbyists were able to transform what might have been controversial legislation into a "stealth" bill.

The success of the Texas lobbyists might, of course, have been a result of public apathy. Few people closely follow the deliberations of their local school board, or fully understand the decision-making processes of their state legislature. But what about those instances when a particular educational issue has been decidedly *on* the political radar screen? Has the political system been more effective in addressing citizen concerns in those cases where there is widespread political support for a particular policy? In answering these questions, it is helpful to trace the history of specific issue over a significant period of time. Given the admiration that many Americans once felt for the vocational education programs of pre–World War I Germany, the subsequent history of vocational reforms undertaken in the United States provides an interesting case in point.

WHEN POLITICS INVADES THE SCHOOL HOUSE

In the early years of the 20th century, many advocates of vocational education depicted their cause as liberating the public school curriculum from its elitist academic traditions (usually expressed in terms of college entrance requirements). The public schools were favored as the site for vocational education because of organized labor's distrust of big business, which in Germany had taken a much larger role in vocational training. Kliebard (1999) noted that the heroes of the rhetorical drama described by vocationalists were the common laborers and their children, whose concerns had for so long been spurned by the public schools. "Their interests, according to the convolutions of the plot, lay in the ties between schooling and the workplace and not in intellectual pursuits or other purposes of education" (p. 230).

Unfortunately, such imagery had little to do with the evolving reality of vocational education within the public schools. "In choosing public schools as the site for industrial training, vocationalists were undertaking to accomplish a deceptively complex and difficult task. Skills that would presumably find their expression on a factory floor were taught in schools and classrooms that were both geographically and conceptually removed from the scene of action. A substantial part of the failure of vocational education in the instrumental sense stemmed from the fact that the kind of knowledge vocational teachers sought to instill cannot readily be conveyed in a school setting" (Kliebard, 1999, p. 218). Politically, the vocational education movement was phenomenally successful; practically speaking, the industrial training offered was too often outmoded, the vocational counseling offered to students inadequate.

The reasons for this are not difficult to find. Year after year, vocational teachers (like English or mathematics teachers) spent their entire day in the classroom, interacting with students. There was no time to update their skills or familiarize themselves with changes in the workplace. The classroom equipment used for training students could only be updated when funding was available. For a teacher whose subject was English literature—or geometry—outmoded textbooks and aging classroom equipment were merely frustrating. Shakespeare and/or geometric proofs could still be presented through lecture, discussion, and/or sketches on the chalkboard. This did not, however, hold true in vocational education classes. Training in out-of-date procedures, on machines that would have been considered "antiques" in the industrial world, all but negated the value of a vocational class.

As early as 1942, the release of the Menefee report cast doubt on the effectiveness of the vocational education programs offered by U.S. public schools:

By far the most comprehensive and most carefully designed evaluation up to World War Two was conducted by a staff member of the Labor Market Research Section of the WPA, Selden C. Menefee.... Designed primarily to examine the work histories of youths trained under the Smith–Hughes Act, the study was based on interviews of 3,042 youths in four cities: St. Louis, Birmingham, Denver, and Seattle. The work histories of vocationally trained youth were then compared to untrained youth in those cities, with a view to determining some of the effects of their vocational training. (Kliebard, 1999, pp. 211–212)

The findings showed no consistent advantage for trained youth over untrained youth in terms of participation in the workforce. Findings regarding average weekly earnings for trained and untrained groups were disappointing, as was the percentage of youth who had been able to make use of their training. Of 699 youth in the labor market in St. Louis, only 40% had jobs directly related to their training; another 14% had jobs that were indirectly related (Kliebard, 1999, p. 215).

The central finding of Menefee's study, *Vocational Training and Employment*, was that nonvocational education had about as much value as vocational training for the youth interviewed. Certainly this conclusion was contrary to the expectations of vocationalists—and to the hopes of the general population. Yet the results of this impressive study had remarkably little effect on public policy regarding vocational education. Why should this be?

"The public school," Dewey observed in 1916, "is the willing pack-horse of our social system; it is the true hero of the refrain: Let George do it." Schools in America take on important responsibilities, ranging from safe driving to safe sex, and their decidedly mixed record in these undertakings has not deterred lawmakers, state departments of education, and public alike from heaping new responsibilities on schools and teachers.... More often than not, these efforts are sustained not by real prospects of success but by the extraordinary faith that Americans have in the power of schools to address matters of urgent necessity. That faith can sometimes be comforting, but it also results in the substitution of symbolic action for instrumental action. (Kliebard, 1999, pp. 219–220)

As Kliebard (1999) pointed out, much of what passes for educational policy is only marginally an effort to reform curricular practices in the interest of improving the educational experiences of children and youth:

The principal effect of much of what passes for policy-making generally and educational policy-making in particular lies in its connection to the status interests of various constituent groups. Embedded in policy statements are ex-

pressions of regard and messages of status. Many policy initiatives and curricular changes are signals to certain groups that their values and vital
concerns have been officially sanctioned and, at least nominally, are being
addressed. (p. 229)

Because the members of these groups are seldom in a position to accurately assess the adequacy with which their concerns are being addressed,
perceptions often count for more than real results. What makes the history
of vocational education of interest in the context of the present discussion
is that it demonstrates the power of partisan rhetoric to sidetrack rational
discussion, even in regard to problems of national importance, and despite widespread informal recognition that the program or policy being
discussed has not been successful.

   Also of interest is the gradual migration of vocational programs to the
postsecondary level. Community colleges have gradually shifted away
from serving primarily as feeders for 4-year colleges and universities as
the number of college-aged young people has declined and 4-year institutions have moved to enroll a broader range of students (Copa & Copa,
1992). The 1987 Postsecondary Student Aid Study conservatively estimated that vocational enrollment comprises 35% of the total undergradu-
ate enrollment in postsecondary education and 77% of the enrollment in
less than baccalaureate institutions. As a result, the position of vocational
programs within the K–12 public schools has become ever more marginal.
As Swanson (1982) pointed out:

   It is not unfair to say, in summary, that American education is design-poor
   and that it suffers from a condition in which there is an abundance of super-
   ordinates preoccupied with fine-tuning and a dearth of leaders. Meanwhile,
   vocational education and training appears to have a residual claim on, or assignment to, marginality with respect to both students and resources. (p. 24)

   Whether the "default" solution of moving vocational training into the
community colleges worked out for the best can certainly be debated. Students must now pay for training that they might have received free of
charge had more effective vocational programs been instituted in the
K–12 schools. Putting off vocational training might not be a bad trade-off
in those cases where students receive, in exchange, a mastery of basic skills
in the areas of communication, computation, problem solving, and interpersonal relations. Unfortunately, too many do not. For those students
who end up simply dropping out of school with few marketable skills, the
end result of the fiery rhetoric that once animated the vocational education movement has been ironic, indeed.

Facing Up to Unintended Results

> First we should realize that the overwhelming majority of American children—perhaps 90 percent—are not learning very much in school. Middle-class parents are happy with the education their children get because the kids go on to colleges. They don't realize that most of these youngsters would not be admitted to a university in any other industrialized country. These kids are getting their junior and senior high school educations in college. (Shanker, 1991, p. A10)

These words are taken from an opinion piece published in the July 15, 1991, issue of the *Wall Street Journal*. Written by the late Albert Shanker, long-time president of the American Federation of Teachers, this essay offered a forceful indictment of the state of American public education. Implicitly, Shanker highlighted the differing impact that inadequate public schools have on the affluent and the poor. Middle-class families can afford to allow their children to "cruise" through high school, then buy the education they need at the postsecondary level. However, for those who must struggle just to provide life's necessities for their families, the long-term effects of inadequate public schools can be devastating.

When the Declaration of Independence speaks of "life, liberty, and the pursuit of happiness," there is no stipulation that the pursuit of wealth must come first. But in a society where only those with money can afford to live in communities with excellent public schools—or to pay for private schooling if the public schools nearby do not provide a high-quality education for their children—the life chances of children are closely tied to the income level of their parents. Far from offering a high-quality education to all students, public schools in low-income areas may not even provide a safe and healthy physical environment. The sad and ironic truth is that students attending under-funded rural or inner-city schools often lack even those protections against slum conditions that tenants have enjoyed since the early 20th century. Gary Blasi, a professor at the University of California, Los Angeles (UCLA), School of Law, described problems he found in California:

> Thousands of California children go to schools with conditions for which we really only have one word: slums . . . Where there are standards for schools, no one ever bothers to find out whether they are routinely violated. We regularly inspect workplaces, restaurants and apartment houses. No one inspects public schools. In 1989, the Legislature empowered local building departments to inspect schools for violations of slum-housing standards. Reports of these inspections were to be sent to the state architect, who has yet to receive a single such inspection report. The reason is that the state gave local build-

ing officials the right to inspect, but neither the duty to do so nor any money to hire more inspectors. So local officials do not inspect schools. No one does. (Blasi, 2000)

The patchwork of laws and regulations that govern public schools, combined with the division of responsibility among many levels of the educational bureaucracy, make it exceedingly difficult to determine who is accountable when things go wrong. The problem has been compounded by rapid social change. As recently as the 1960s (when President Lyndon Johnson declared his war on poverty), half of those Americans classified as "poor" lived in rural counties, particularly in the South. Now only 22% live in the countryside, while 43% live in city centers (*The Economist*, May 20, 2000, p. 28), in neighborhoods that the affluent seldom visit. Without some mechanism for reaching out to children trapped in inadequate public schools, children who grow up in such neighborhoods cannot be said to have an equal chance to know true liberty or to pursue lasting happiness.

Who Should Have Power to Decide?

A century ago, most Americans lived on farms or in small towns. However, as the 20th century dawned, U.S. cities were burgeoning in size. Buildings shot upward, creating a vertical urban landscape. Technology was transforming human expectations. Telephone and telegraph wires made it possible to communicate with people far away. Railroads and automobiles made long-distance travel routine. Everything seemed to be getting bigger, faster, more confused. Cities struggled to provide services to ever more people. Public schools did the same. Capacity to serve increased numbers of people came to be seen, itself, as an important indicator of progress. Efficiency was emphasized, delivery of services centralized. Only as the 20th century drew to a close did questions begin to be raised concerning the cost of elevating efficiency above all competing concerns.

The changes have been so dramatic that it is easy to forget that before World War II few people had automobiles; the large suburban belts that now surround American cities did not exist. The natural human tendency is to adjust in small increments; this makes it easy to lose sight of the total extent of change over time. As a result, we sometimes find ourselves thinking in terms of how things once were (as opposed to how they are now). For example, the public school is often spoken of as a place where people of all social classes come together, rubbing shoulders in the classroom in a way that they may never do again. This romanticized image is left over from the small-town America of another era, when one high school served a whole town. These days most Americans live in urban and suburban neighborhoods that are highly segregated according to socioeconomic class. Although the image of the public school "melting pot" lives on, most students now go to school with classmates whose families are of similar background and income level.

Charter schools represent an experiment in breaking with the custom of making place of residence a proxy for choice of public school. No coercion is involved. Charter school laws allow teachers who share the same vision of what a school should be to band together in a manner reminiscent of the way physicians form clinics. Just as parents decide whether to take a child to visit a general practitioner or a specialist, charter school parents make a decision about where they want to enroll their child in school. As with medical care, there is always the chance that a parent will not make an informed choice. However, an argument can easily be made that if society is willing to rely on parental judgment in the field of medicine, then it becomes difficult to assert that parents lack the competence to choose a school for their child. Faith in the ability of ordinary people to order their own affairs has long been a basic tenet of the American democratic tradition. As Thomas Jefferson once insisted:

> I know no safe depository of the ultimate powers of the society but the people themselves; and if we think them not enlightened enough to exercise their control with a wholesome discretion, the remedy is not to take it from them, but to inform their discretion by education. (Jefferson, 1899, vol. 10, p. 161)

Debate over who should hold the ultimate powers of society goes back at least two millennia. The Roman satirist Juvenal put the question succinctly: "Who is to guard the guards themselves?" As British historian Lord Acton famously observed, "Power tends to corrupt and absolute power corrupts absolutely" (Creighton, 1904). Acton's words have been much quoted, usually in reference to abuse of political power. Yet as Garry Wills points out in his book *Papal Sin* (2001), the Catholic Acton was referring not to political leaders but to popes. Few powers are, after all, so great as the power to decide what others should be taught to believe. Moreover, it is this same power—the ability to determine what others should be taught to accept as true—that lies at the heart of current debates over who should control the public school curriculum.

CHARTER SCHOOLS AS MEDIATING INSTITUTIONS

> Government and the market are similar to two legs of a three-legged stool. Without the third leg of civil society, the stool is not stable and cannot provide support for a vital America. (former senator Bill Bradley, 1995)

For much of the nation's early history, the exercise of government power was viewed with considerable wariness. This sense of caution can be seen clearly in the nation's founding documents, especially in the careful system of checks and balances built into the U.S. Constitution (e.g., in division of the federal government into legislative, administrative, and judicial branches). There also existed a more informal system of checks and balances, which also had a tripartite character. The government, in the election of which each voter (ideally) had an equal voice, formed one part of this informal system. A second part was made up of the nation's economic institutions, where the laws of supply and demand held sway. The third part consisted of civil society, which brought citizens together in voluntary associations to carry out common tasks and to pursue common interests. As Alexis de Tocqueville (1990) pointed out in *Democracy in America* (the first portion of which appeared in 1835):

> The Americans make associations to give entertainments, to form seminaries, to build inns, to construct churches, to diffuse books, to send missionaries to the antipodes; in this manner they found hospitals, prisons, or schools. (Vol. 2, p. 106)

Tocqueville argued that voluntary associations, composed of individuals who had banded together in defense of mutual interests, were of pivotal importance in preserving the health of American democracy. He was convinced that, despite their many advantages, democratic governments had a weakness that could potentially undermine the very freedoms such governments had been set up to secure. "In aristocratic nations the body of the nobles and the wealthy are in themselves natural associations which check the abuses of power" (1990, Vol. 1, p. 195). In democratic nations other means of dealing with possible abuse of power had to be found. For, even though the citizens of a democracy were independent, most were unable, by themselves, to wield more than a minimal share of political power. Only by joining with others could the individual in a democracy effectively stand up for his or her interests.

When people formed voluntary associations to carry out a task, their ability to direct their own affairs grew stronger. Tocqueville predicted that these sorts of voluntary associations would, in future, become ever more important. He saw a time drawing near when individuals would be less and less able to produce—of themselves alone—the necessities of life. Without voluntary associations, the tasks of the government would perpetually increase. The danger was that, the more government "stands in the place of associations, the more will individuals, losing the notion of combining together, require its assistance" (1990, Vol. 1, p. 108). Tocqueville warned that:

A government can no more be competent to keep alive and to renew the circulation of opinions and feelings amongst a great people than to manage all the speculations of productive industry. No sooner does a government attempt to go beyond its political sphere and enter upon this new track than it exercises, even unintentionally, an insupportable tyranny; for a government can only dictate strict rules, the opinions which it favors are rigidly enforced, and it is never easy to discriminate between its advice and its commands. (Vol. 1, p. 109)

The importance of social relationships that exist largely outside the political or the economic sphere has been highlighted in recent years by the struggle of the nations of Eastern Europe to rejuvenate civil society following the collapse of authoritarian regimes. After the euphoria that accompanied the success of popular movements like Solidarity in Poland has come the arduous task of nurturing self-governing citizens capable of (and personally responsible for) making the political, economic, and personal decisions that will shape their lives and those of their children. Similar efforts at democratization are currently underway in many parts of the world.

Realizing the importance of helping democratizing nations to develop a robust civil society, the United States, the European Union, as well as individual European countries have funded assistance programs. Programs to foster civil society receive about a third of the more than $600 million the United States spends annually to promote democracy worldwide (Ottaway, 1990). In addition many foundations, such as George Soros's Open Society Institute, the Ford Foundation, German party foundations such as the Friedriech Ebert Stiftung, and the British Westminster Foundation have their own assistance programs. Yet, even as efforts have been made to support the growth of a vibrant civil society in developing democracies, doubts have been raised about the health of civil society in the United States.

As noted by Robert Putman in *Bowling Alone: The Collapse and Revival of American Community* (2000), fewer Americans now participate in voluntary associations. Economic pressure has played a part in this decline. With more women working outside the home, there are fewer volunteers available to lead Cub Scout troops, serve as room mothers, work with the League of Women Voters. The export of blue-collar jobs has undermined urban neighborhoods. William Julius Wilson explains: "Neighborhoods plagued by high levels of joblessness are more likely to experience low levels of social organization; the two go hand in hand. High rates of joblessness trigger other neighborhood problems that undermine social organization, ranging from crime, gang violence and drug trafficking to family breakups. And as these controls weaken, the social processes that regulate behavior change" (1996, p. 28).

Do such systemic problems make solutions that draw upon the resources of civil society irrelevant? After all, how can the Girl Scouts or membership in a bowling league to turn such a situation around? Such questions that are routinely asked by critics who see discussion of civil society as irrelevant to addressing the nation's "real" problems. But those who would urge us to act, and act quickly, making use of direct government intervention to address social problems tend to pay little attention to the bitterly ironic results that such intervention has had in the past. For example, government intervention has succeeded in gentrifying many troubled urban neighborhoods. But, all too often, this has been accomplished in such a manner that the original inhabitants are forced out.

The role of voluntary associations, whether they take the form of neighborhood associations, labor unions, or environmental protection groups, is to provide citizens with a way to exercise a kind of agency that is not available to them otherwise. Arguably the mediating role of voluntary associations is nowhere more important than among the most vulnerable segments of the population. One has only to study the history of urban child welfare services, such as arranging for foster care, to find daunting evidence that government agencies are ill-suited to safeguard the welfare of those who are unable to organize and lobby on their own behalf.

What makes organizations like charter schools effective is their mediating role. They enable citizens to come together to pursue collective solutions to shared problems. Government support is provided, but in such a manner that stakeholders still maintain a sense of agency. The effect of this empowerment is often most noticeable in the most demoralized neighborhoods. Few issues so energize parents and community members as concern with the welfare of children. The children benefit from community involvement. So do adult stakeholders, who may have had little prior experience with participatory democracy. Speaking of the New England town meeting, Tocqueville (1990) described the benefits of such grassroots involvement:

> The native of New England is attached to his own township because it is independent and free; his co-operation in its affairs ensures his attachment to its interests; the well-being it affords him secures his affection; and its welfare is the aim of his ambition and of his future exertions. He takes a part in every occurrence in the place; he practices the art of government in the small sphere within his reach; he accustoms himself to those forms without which liberty can only advance by revolutions; he imbibes their spirit; he acquires a taste for order, comprehends the balance of powers, and collects clear practical notions on the nature of his duties and the extent of his rights. (Vol. 1, p. 68)

Of course it is important not to exaggerate the virtues of either charter schools or town meetings. These are not the only organizational structures that might achieve the same result. What should be noted, however, is the capacity of grassroots organizations such as these to unleash energies that increase the vitality of the democratic process. What the charter school movement offers is the opportunity, for those who choose to participate, to make a commitment to a specific school community. As in other human relationships, there is some risk involved. Not all charter schools work out as the participants had hoped, any more than do all friendships or marriages. Yet there seems to be something about commitment, about being at the center of someone else's universe, that engages the vital energies of human beings in a special way. A different set of expectations is created, opening up a new range of possibilities.

The charter school movement may not be *the* answer to what ails the public schools. Yet it suggests the direction in which an answer might be found. Through the charter school movement new ideas, new energies, new perspectives have been brought into the nation's public schools. Those who recognize an educational need have been empowered to offer a remedy. School reform has become an effort in which all can take part. By allowing a wider range of citizens to make their own characteristic contributions to the improvement of their community's public schools, charter schools have pointed the way toward making education, once again, a community-wide concern.

REFERENCES

Baxt, V., & Brouillette, L. (1999, March). The state, the lobbyists, and special education policies in schools: A case study of decision making in Texas. *Journal of School Leadership*, 125–159.

Blasi, G. (2000, May 19). If you've seen slums, you know a lot about our schools. *Los Angeles Times*, p. B13.

Bradley, B. (1995). America's challenge: Revitalizing our national community. *National Civic Review, 84*(2).

Brouillette, L. (1996). *A geology of school reform: The successive restructurings of a school district*. New York: SUNY Press.

Brouillette, L. (1997a, Spring/Summer). Who is in charge here?: Juggling school board and consensus-based priorities as a school district implements shared decision making. *Planning and Changing*, 74–87.

Brouillette, L. (1997b, September). Who defines democratic leadership?: Three high school principals respond to site-based reforms. *Journal of School Leadership*, 569–591.

Brouillette, L. (1997c, December). Revisiting an innovative high school: What happens when the principal leaves? *Educational Administration Quarterly*, 546–575.

Burke, E. (1790). *Reflections on the revolution in France, and on the proceedings in certain societies in London relative to that event in a letter intended to have been sent to a gentleman in Paris*. London: J. Dodsley.

Cigler, A. J., & Loomis, B. A. (1995). *Interest group politics* (4th ed.). Washington, DC: CQ Press (A division of Congressional Quarterly, Inc.).

Copa, G. H., & Copa, P. M. (1992). Vocational education. In M. C. Alkin (Ed.), *Encyclopedia of educational research* (6th ed., pp. 1500–1509). New York: Macmillan.

Creighton, L. (1904). Letter from Lord Acton to Bishop Mandell Creighton, 3 April 1887. *Life and Letters of Mandell Creighton* (Vol. 1, chap. 13). London: Longmans, Green.

The Economist. (2000, May 20). Out of sight, out of mind. *355*(8171), 27–31.

Jefferson, T. (1899). Letter to William Charles Jarvis, 28 September 1820. In P. L. Ford (Ed.), *Writings of Thomas Jefferson*. New York: Knickerbocker Press.

Kerr, N. D. (1964). The school board as an agency of legitimation. *Sociology of Education, 38,*

Kliebard, H. (1999). *Schooled to work: Vocationalism and the American curriculum, 1876–1946.*

Lowi, T. J. (1974, May). Interest groups and the consent to govern: Getting the people out, for what? *Annals of the American Academy of Political and Social Science, 413,* 86–100.

Lowi, T. J. (1979). *The end of liberalism* (2d ed.). New York: Norton.

Malen, B., & Ogawa, R. T. (1988). Professional-patron influence on site-based governance councils: A confounding case study. *Educational Evaluation and Policy Analysis, 10,* 251–170.

Malen, B., Ogawa, R., & Krantz, J. (1990). Site-based management: Unfulfilled promises. *School Administrator, 30*(32), 53–59.

National Commission on Civic Renewal. (1998). *A nation of spectators: How civic disengagement weakens America and what we can do about it,* p. 12. College Park, MD: Author.

Olson, M. (1982). *The rise and decline of nations: Economic growth, stagflation, and social rigidities.* New Haven, CT: Yale University Press.

Ottaway, M. (2001, June 29). Strengthening civil society in other countries. *The Chronicle of Higher Education,* p. B14.

Putnam, R. (2000). *Bowling alone: The collapse and revival of American community*. New York: Simon & Schuster.

Shanker, A. (1991, July 15). Give students a reason to work hard. *The Wall Street Journal,* p. A10.

Swanson, G. I. (1982). Vocational education matters in the United States. In H. F. Silberman (Ed.), *Education and work,* 81st Yearbook of the National Society for the Study of Education. Chicago: University of Chicago Press.

Tocqueville, A. de. (1990). *Democracy in America,* 2 volumes. New York: Random House. (Original work published 1835, 1840)

Willis, G. (2001). *Papal sin.* New York: Doubleday.

Wilson, W. J. (1996, August 18). When work disappears. *New York Times Magazine.*

Author Index

Subject Index